T0248142

Praise for A *Measure of Intelligence*

"Has there ever been a measurement device more widely abused than the IQ test? In this compelling, nuanced, and (it has to be said) fiercely intelligent book, Pepper Stetler takes us through the dialectic of raising a child with an intellectual disability—worrying whether one is doing too much or not enough, knowing that the quantitative measurement of intelligence is absurd yet acknowledging that it is necessary for obtaining the support services your child needs. *A Measure of Intelligence* carries on the noble and necessary project begun by Stephen Jay Gould's *The Mismeasure of Man.*"

—MICHAEL BÉRUBÉ, author of
Life as Jamie Knows It: An Exceptional Child Grows Up

"This book is not just about the concept of intelligence and the use of IQ tests. It is a riveting and well-researched account of a parent's search for understanding and embarking on a journey to a new way of thinking. The paradigm shift discussed in the book moves us from the past into a future that provides a fuller and more positive picture of humanity, and one that provides space to be oneself. Reading this book will force you to rethink assumptions and historical practices."

—ROBERT L. SCHALOCK, PHD, Professor Emeritus of Psychology at
Hastings College, former President and Fellow of the American
Association on Intellectual and Developmental Disabilities

"This remarkable book fuses memoir, investigation, and social critique. With searing clarity, Stetler chronicles the origins and the developments of intelligence testing, and at the same time, with grace and warmth, she reconsiders her own ideas of intelligence and worth. In the end, Stetler offers us a chance to examine with nuance and care how we think about the intellectual capacities of the people we love. This is an important and illuminating contribution to disability studies."

—DAISY HERNÁNDEZ, PEN/Jean Stein Book Award winner
and author of *The Kissing Bug: A True Story of a Family,
an Insect, and a Nation's Neglect of a Deadly Disease*

"This book is amazing! Masterfully weaving research of all kinds with personal experience and insight, Pepper Stetler tracks the origins and history of the IQ test and its impact on our world. But *A Measure of Intelligence* is about so much more than a test. It›s a profound, well-researched, wise reckoning with our values and how we might reshape them to prioritize what matters most: community, belonging, and the inherent worth of every human person. And those are values that can liberate us all."

—HEATHER LANIER, Author of *Raising a Rare Girl*

"Intelligence testing has been a hotly contested subject since its earliest days. Pepper Stetler has joined the debate with extraordinary insight and empathy as she recounts society's attempt to reduce her beloved daughter to a number— and how she fought back. This is a fresh and enlightening take—and a very compelling read."

—ADAM COHEN, National Book Award finalist,
and author of *Imbeciles: The Supreme Court, American
Eugenics, and the Sterilization of Carrie Buck*

"Stetler's rigorous, accessible dismantling of our notion of intelligence is exhilarating. Told through a gripping account—personal, political, and historical—of intellectual disability and the ways it gets constructed (to our great detriment) as a moral failing, Stetler's case for inclusion, acceptance, and destigmatization is convincing, timely, and necessary."

—ANDREW LELAND, Pulitzer Prize finalist and author of
The Country of the Blind: A Memoir at the End of Sight

A Measure
of Intelligence

One Mother's Reckoning with the
IQ Test

Pepper Stetler

DIVERSION
BOOKS

NEW YORK

Diversion Books
A division of Diversion Publishing Corp.
www.diversionbooks.com

Copyright © 2024 by Pepper Stetler

All rights reserved, including the right to reproduce this book or portions thereof in
any form whatsoever. No part of this publication may be reproduced or transmitted
in any form or by any means, electronic or mechanical, including photocopying,
recording, or any other information storage and retrieval, without the written
permission of the publisher.

Diversion Books and colophon are registered trademarks
of Diversion Publishing Corp.

For more information, email info@diversionbooks.com.

First Diversion Books Edition: August 2024
Hardcover ISBN: 9781635769357
e-ISBN: 9781635769258

Design by Neuwirth & Associates

Printed in the United States of America
1 3 5 7 9 10 8 6 4 2

Diversion books are available at special discounts for bulk purchases in the US by
corporations, institutions, and other organizations.
For more information, please contact admin@diversionbooks.com.

The publisher does not have any control over and does not assume any responsibility
for author or third-party websites or their content.

Where is the wisdom we have lost in knowledge?
Where is the knowledge we have lost in information?

—T. S. ELIOT, "THE ROCK" (1934)

To Louisa, my darling girl

Contents

Author's Note: I have changed the names of several nonpublic people in this book to protect their privacy.

Introduction

I never gave the IQ test much thought until Louisa, my curious, energetic daughter with Down syndrome, took one when she was about to start kindergarten. A few weeks later, my husband, Andy, and I met with a team of educators, which included a school psychologist; her preschool teachers; speech, physical, and occupational therapists; and other school district administrators I haven't seen since. When I walked into the room, I knew this meeting would not be a typical parent-teacher conference. The signs of elementary school—cheerful colors, classroom work proudly displayed in hallways, posters reminding students about kindness and respect—were replaced with gray walls and a long conference table with a faux-wood finish. I would have rather met in a classroom, squatting in a tiny chair made for a five-year-old, but instead Andy and I sat in black swivel seats with thin vinyl cushions. This wasn't the principal's office, a place of discipline, but a space of bureaucratic discussion. We could have all been coworkers in a marketing firm, but instead we were ten adults gathered to discuss the cognitive challenges of one little girl and how she could access this elementary school world.

We touched on behavioral assessments, challenges that Louisa might face with particular daily tasks in a school setting, her love of friends and teachers, and her enthusiasm for singing and dancing. We shared a moment of gushing and great pride for what Louisa had already accomplished and for her great potential to learn. The conversation took a different tone when the school psychologist began to address her IQ score. While it was lower than average, he told us, in his experience it was high for a child with Down syndrome. I pictured a bell-shaped curve in my mind and placed an abstract dot to the left of the peak, but not too far left. Instead of discussing her love of books, eagerness to help in the classroom, and how she struggled to slow down and count a series of blocks carefully, we were now talking about a number that plotted her on an abstract graph. It was a way of understanding who Louisa was that made her seem like a stranger to me. I don't remember much about the meeting after this. My ears burned red and I was lost in a swirl of questions. What exactly is an IQ test? How do you give one to a five-year-old? What did these bureaucrats think they knew about my daughter based on this test? The IQ score seemed like a suspiciously tidy way to mark Louisa's potential. And how her potential was perceived could determine how others assessed her worth.

Before I had a chance to ask any of these questions, the school psychologist admitted that IQ didn't matter very much. The only people who would see the score were in the conference room. I glanced up at a long band of windows on the far side of the room. I could see cars pulling up to the sidewalk. Kids were tumbling out with disheveled backpacks and lunch boxes in hand, steadily filing into the school's main entrance. I agreed that this number seemed far too abstract to impact Louisa's daily education. The room seemed to breathe a sigh of relief.

It is hard to resist the seductive affirmation of the IQ test. I didn't feel comfortable associating my daughter with a number, but I admit feeling pride when the school psychologist announced that Louisa's IQ was high for a child with Down syndrome. Perhaps it was like what parents feel when they are informed that their child is gifted and belongs on the other side of the bell curve. Louisa's relatively high IQ seemed like a payoff that validated all the parenting decisions Andy and I had made up until that point—making sure she got enough sleep, minimizing screen time, and choosing only the most educational toys. The size of our children's book collection rivals our library of academic books, no small feat for a household with two art historians.

The impact of purchasing wooden toy blocks instead of battery-operated Disney characters on our daughter's IQ is debatable. Yet the socially constructed advantages of being born white in an upper-middle-class family with two educated parents are not. At least in part, I read Louisa's IQ as affirmation of my parenting decisions, and I felt a sense of relief that I was able to make what seemed like the best choices. Relieved to hear that my daughter's IQ was relatively high, it did not occur to me to wonder how the IQ test would impact my daughter's life more broadly. I failed to consider if I should have allowed the test at all.

THAT MEETING BEFORE Louisa started kindergarten was for her first Individualized Education Plan, or IEP, a legal document that defines the specific needs, goals, and accommodations to help her keep up with her peers. But before the document can be written, Louisa must be identified as in need of support. And in Louisa's case, because she has Down syndrome, which is associated with an intellectual disability, the IEP involves an IQ test. In theory, IEPs ensure different kinds of support depending on a student's needs. For Louisa, when she was five, an IEP gave her access to an in-class aide who helped her stay focused and guided her through instructions and assignments. Because she needs more time to complete her work, some of her assignments are shorter than those given to her peers. The IEP specifies that tools are available to help her visualize math problems and complete reading assignments. This document helps Louisa to do her best work and keep up with the quick pace of a classroom. It serves as an agreement between me and Andy, her teachers, and school administrators about Louisa's educational goals and how those goals will be achieved.

Intellectual disability is one of thirteen categories that qualify students for special education services under the Individuals with Disabilities in Education Act (IDEA). Forty-nine of fifty states (not Iowa) use the IQ test to determine if a child has an intellectual disability and qualifies for support services under IDEA. If I objected to the IQ test, it could threaten Louisa's access to the support she needs to learn in a classroom with her peers. It's not like Louisa's IQ would be widely known, I thought. If it qualifies her for what she needs, how harmful could IQ tests be?

So I let it go. But when Louisa was in second grade, I received a letter from her school informing me that it had been three years since her last round of cognitive testing. New testing would be given in the next few weeks. I made an appointment to talk with Brian, the school psychologist. He met me in the school's lobby and walked me back to his office. It took me a while to realize that a school psychologist is not the same as a school counselor. Rather than serving as a mental health resource for schoolchildren, the school psychologist interacts with kids in the context of cognitive and behavioral assessment. Brian is an administrator and a bureaucrat, a necessary intermediary between educational paperwork and the real needs of students like Louisa.

Brian had a round face that matched the shape of his small, wire-framed glasses. My opening attempts at small talk seemed to make him nervous, so I transitioned to the purpose of our meeting. "I'm wondering if you can tell me more about the IQ test that Louisa will take," I asked. Louisa would be given the Wechsler Intelligence Scale for Children (WISC). IDEA required that the test be repeated every three years, he told me, even though he expected her IQ score to be about the same every time. The WISC generates an IQ score, but the subtests are organized into indices of particular intellectual skills. The fifth and most recent edition of the WISC consists of sixteen subtests, and the IQ is a complex calculation of a child's score on all of them.

Brian gave me an example of a question from the subtest on similarities:

A horse and a cow are both
 a) things you ride
 b) on farms
 c) brown
 d) animals
 e) mean

He explained to me that this multiple choice question would follow a verbal conversation with Louisa about horses and cows to make sure she knew what they were. In this example, answers b and d both were reasonable to me, but I applaud the creativity it would take to come up with any of the five answers. In any case, it seemed there was a lot at stake in how Louisa decided to relate two animals. As Brian explained the test, I kept focusing on the poster of Charlie Brown on his office wall. "If you grit your teeth and show determination you always have a chance," it said. I couldn't help but take Charlie Brown's modest attempt at control seriously and hope that grit and determination might serve my daughter despite her cognitive differences.

Louisa's IEP states, "Her IQ suggests that her overall cognitive abilities are developed at a level somewhat below her typical peers. Based on this level of cognitive development it can be expected that she will have to work harder than her typical peers to progress through the general curriculum." It is important that the IEP demonstrates her need for intervention and support, but still this statement brought me some hope. It does not characterize her potential as static. Instead, it says she will have to work harder to keep up with her peers. *Fine*, I thought, *we will work harder*. Andy and I made our way through graduate school, wrote PhD dissertations, wrote books, and climbed the ranks of the brutal academic promotion and tenure system. A little like Charlie Brown, we are not deterred by hard work.

But Brian described the IQ test to me as more of a bureaucratic qualification than a meaningful assessment of Louisa's day-to-day challenges. Louisa's IQ score was "in a strange no-man's-land," he told me. She has Down syndrome, which would usually qualify her for educational services and social support. But an IQ score lower than Louisa's is also required to diagnose her with an intellectual disability, as defined by psychologists. "My fear is that the rules won't apply to Louisa's scenario," he told us. In other words, her extra chromosome would not be enough to give her the support that she needs. Perhaps a lower IQ might actually serve her better.

Not having my daughter's IQ tested might cause roadblocks, but the test, as I was beginning to learn, caused roadblocks of its own. I wondered if, in allowing her to be tested, I was exposing Louisa to a lifetime of judgment and preexisting determinations. Her IQ might be noted by any case worker, job coach, employer, or doctor that she is dependent on in the course of her life. Not to mention the more general power dynamic: my daughter's intelligence is quantified and packaged as a meaningful number, while most people have the privilege of not having their intelligence marked in such a definite way. Yet if my daughter's school record failed to show the expected evaluation, there might be questions later about her eligibility for certain services that she needs. Failing to evaluate her intelligence now might threaten the evaluation of her intelligence later. Evaluation procures further, future evaluation.

IF LOUISA HAD been born fifty years ago, it would have been much harder to ensure that she got the public education she deserved. Now IDEA ensures that every child receives a free education, although what this education looks like varies widely. I found a pamphlet for parents online, "What does the Individuals with Disabilities in Education

Act say about the IQ Test?" The pamphlet explains there is no explicit requirement in IDEA that IEPs must rely on IQ testing, but access to the educational services that Louisa needs is difficult without it. The pamphlet also suggests reasons why parents might feel uncomfortable with an IQ test in the first place. It said that IQ tests might be racially biased; African American students are almost twice as likely as white students to be classified with an intellectual disability. Students diagnosed with intellectual disabilities struggle in mainstream classrooms; they are often moved to separate learning environments. And IQ scores aren't always accurate. The errors of an inexperienced test administrator can invalidate the results.

Louisa's empathy and kindness were woven into the small college town where we live long before I talked to Brian in his office. She is a deeply social person, thriving on interaction with others in ways her more introverted, bookish parents could have never anticipated. At our local coffee shop, she chats up anyone who sits next to her. She has made friends with the ladies who work at the fish counter at the supermarket. In school she always says goodbye to her friends and teachers when it is time to go home. I thought the idea that her place among her peers and her inclusion in our community were facilitated or threatened by a test score was absurd.

The friends I told about Louisa's evaluation were surprised to hear that IQ testing was playing a role in our lives. Their faces performed the same series of reactions: brief recognition, mild bemusement, and then troubled confusion. *Is that still used?* "What do IQ tests have to do with psychology?" asked one of my friends, who was a history professor. I would soon learn that IQ tests have everything to do with psychology. At a dinner party, I told some of my psychologist friends about my daughter's IQ test. Unphased, they informed me that learning to administer an IQ test is an essential skill taught in most clinical psychology graduate programs in the country. IQ tests are highly structured and regulated tools of educational and psychiatric evaluation. In the face of IQ tests offered as clickbait on the internet, large publishing companies and professional organizations like the American Psychological Association are dedicated to protecting the professional integrity of intelligence assessment. More than a million kids in public schools have their IQ assessed every year in the United States. IQ tests like the WISC are usually reserved for kids who need IEPs or those trying to access gifted programs. But due to the predominance of standardized tests in public schools today, nearly all kids face other tests that do the same work of evaluating and predicting their potential.

Considering what I had heard so far about the bias and potential unreliability of IQ tests, I was shocked to hear that my psychologist friends took them seriously. They have a daughter who is the same age as Louisa. I was convinced she had read all the books in the Harry Potter series on her own by the age of five. Our kids played together in another room while we finished eating and I prodded them as casually as I could about how necessary IQ tests were to their work. I realized that my friends, who had mastered the skills of administering the exam and evaluating its data, never had to confront the personal, real-life outcomes that the IQ test and its culture create. Louisa's interaction with the IQ test had consequences that they, and really most people, are rarely forced to consider. I wondered whether the friendship between our daughters would outlast the convenience of a dinner party. How might their futures look dramatically different although they have been afforded similar racial and economic privileges? Would the IQ test help or hurt Louisa's chances of finding a place in the world?

Suddenly, it seemed like Andy and I faced a decision that had far-reaching consequences for Louisa. Should we let the school psychologist continue to give her an IQ test? To find an answer, I turned to literature, science, psychologists, historians, teachers, other parents, and adults with intellectual disabilities to understand how the values and priorities of IQ tests are ingrained into our world in profound but often overlooked ways. I discovered that, despite what the school psychologist told us, IQ tests matter.

WHETHER YOU HAVE taken an IQ test or not, its logic and values shape our systems of modern education and ideas of professional success with which you interact. Intelligence testing has become a primary way of measuring social and environmental difference, as well as good parental habits. It has been suggested that IQ scores correlate positively to breastfeeding, eating copious amounts of fish, and college success, but negatively to lead exposure, smog, and poverty. Hack versions serve as popular forms of online distraction, an outlet for self-gratification as ubiquitous as porn. I used to associate the IQ test with boys who dominated the Quiz Bowl team in high school, socially awkward yet redeemed by their ability to recall obscure trivia. Questioning a person's IQ has become a way to express frustration with someone who disagrees with you. Former president Trump uses it as a blunt description of a person's worth, fixating on his own, accusing his opponents of a low score, and dividing the world into clear winners and losers. Trump's insults exploit how the IQ test lingers as a simplified measure of human value, an opportunity to invoke the playground insults of "retarded," "moron," and "idiot" that the test's quest to quantify and categorize generated. Although IQ tests might seem misguided to many, they have provided our world with a statistical justification to value intelligence over morals, productivity over empathy. It was designed to make a person's worth measurable and comparable.

This is a book for anyone who has wondered what intelligence is. It is for anyone who has ever taken a standardized test in school—which is everybody—and wondered why. But it is especially for anyone who has felt as if their life has been devalued by the results of an IQ test, or who sensed that unfair decisions were made about their life or the life of someone they love based on an IQ score. The more I learned about IQ tests, the more I realized how lucky my family is. Louisa is being raised by two educated white people with enough money and time to make sure she is getting every opportunity to reach her full potential. In other words, we are in a position of privilege. My research revealed to me that those who grow up without these advantages are more vulnerable to the catastrophic outcomes—segregation, unemployment, and impoverishment—that continue to be based on the results of IQ testing.

This book examines intelligence as a product of history rather than an outcome of nature. This does not mean that I deny that some people do better on IQ tests than others. And it certainly does not deny that Louisa's particular struggles with the kinds of skills tested on an IQ test are a result of her genetic differences. But how we value intelligence and how those values shape our world can shift and change. This is a good thing, because if we want to create a more equitable future, we need to restructure how we value intelligence.

What follows is my personal (and therefore incomplete) attempt to understand the way IQ tests will shape my daughter's life. But along the way I discovered that the tests impact all of us. The psychologists who developed IQ tests in the early twentieth century did more than draft tools of assessment. They established the ways we still understand and value intelligence, who is and is not given opportunities to be successful, and who gets to have access to the best education possible. By making those origins clear, how our world still reflects the values and intentions of those earlier psychologists, I hope to inspire readers to evaluate some of their most deeply held assumptions about intelligence.

I did not write this book because I think Louisa is exceptional (although, as her mother, I certainly do). The scene I began with—one of parents and teachers meeting around a conference table to discuss an IEP—is particularly common. In fact, IEP meetings, however long, productive, frustrating, or tearful they might be, bring parents of kids with disabilities together like no other. Each child who is served by an IEP is different; each parent comes to the table with valid and meaningful perspectives. But the shared experience of the annual meeting bonds us in solidarity as we fight for our children to be seen as unique, capable individuals by a system that often struggles to do so. *More alike than different*, is one common way of putting it. The equity at the heart of this statement has been a particularly challenging goal because of the impact of IQ testing.

From the perspective of history, Louisa has a life that is fuller, happier, and perhaps even more common than those who developed IQ tests in the early twentieth century ever fathomed. This is in spite of the influence of IQ tests, not because of it. I am grateful for those who have fought against the bias of IQ tests to ensure that Louisa has the opportunities to grow and learn with her peers. Yet there is still so far to go. There are so many ways in which our world's conception of intelligence limits how she can pursue her potential. In writing this book, I hope to remind readers that change is possible, even though the way we think about intelligence continues to fail so many. The world I want readers to envision is one in which Louisa and others like her will be included as valued citizens, learning and living at its very center.

What the Test Tests

Years before that first IEP meeting, I processed the world through the lens of history. Late in my pregnancy, my doctor explained that my daughter had not dropped into a birth position and a C-section would be the safest way of bringing her into the world. So it was scheduled at thirty-nine weeks, presumably at the optimal time to have a baby. I was admittedly disappointed. I did not imagine birth as something I could schedule like a routine dental checkup. But leading up to the appointment, I also thought a lot about my historical good fortune. I asked my doctor how my current condition would be handled if I had lived a hundred years earlier, when mothers rarely survived C-sections. Would my baby grow inside me for extra weeks, becoming too large to make it past my pelvic bones? Exactly how long would I have to stay pregnant? She looked at me with a confused expression, as if wondering why I wanted to dwell on the past. "It would be a very painful birth," she said.

Thanks to a cesarean section and plenty of drugs, it was not a painful birth. I don't remember much about being in the operating room, but I do remember Louisa's coloring as she was taken out of my body and lifted over the curtain that separated the upper and lower halves of me. Her hair was bright orange and her skin was purple. She pinked up fairly quickly as she took her first wailing breaths and Andy laid her on my chest. The orange hair would last for her first few months, at first matching her father's curls, but eventually settling into the brownish blond that she has today.

Soon after Louisa was born, a doctor visited my hospital room and told me that she wanted to point out some features of our baby. At first, this struck me as quaint. In my daze of exhaustion and happiness, I somehow thought it a celebratory routine for a doctor to identify features of a baby like a salesperson going over the bells and whistles of a new car. The doctor showed me the crease in the middle of Louisa's palm, the skin folds in the corners of her eyes, her low muscle tone. Then she explained that these features led her to believe that our baby had Down syndrome, but no one could tell me for sure. The minimal prenatal testing my baby and I underwent had not revealed any reasons for concern. I did not fully accept this unexpected new reality until we looked at the blood tests at our first doctor's appointment a few days later. There they were. The three wiggly copies of the twenty-first chromosome that appeared in a karyotype offered visual proof.

After Louisa's diagnosis, my interest in imaginary time travel shifted. I no longer imagined the conditions of birth in olden times. Instead I thought about the life of someone with Down syndrome born twenty, fifty, one hundred years ago. The health and well-being of my daughter were, from her very first breath, a product of the conditions of the time and place in which she was born.

In 1967, *The Atlantic* published a very different birth story about Bernard Bard's son, Philip. A doctor pointed out certain features of Philip too. But after an examination, the doctor concluded that "the outlook is for an individual without a long life-span and not great mental development." In the next few days, Bard met with several doctors, who all recommended that Philip be placed in a private institution where, at the father's request, nothing would be done to prolong his life. No vaccines would be given against diphtheria, measles, or chicken pox, no ventilators would be used. A few hours after he arrived at the institution, Philip died of heart failure and jaundice. "Consider it a blessing," a doctor said.

This article, "The Right to Die," is framed as an ethical advice column, and another man absolves Bernard of the guilt of his decision. After the father tells his story, theologian James Fletcher claims that there was "no reason to feel guilty about putting a Down's [sic] syndrome baby away, whether it's 'put away' in the sense of hidden in a sanatorium or in a more responsible lethal sense . . . True guilt arises only from an offense against a person, and a Down's is not a person."

FOR MOST OF our modern history, intelligence and perceived capability have determined a person's worth. If Louisa had been born sixty years ago, it is likely she would have been put in an institution, whether I agreed with this decision or not. Children with Down syndrome were not seen as worthy of education or medical care. In such an environment, it is unlikely she would have lived past childhood. Now the average lifespan of a person with Down syndrome is sixty. It is hard to deny that the lives of people with Down syndrome have improved dramatically since the time of Philip Bard's death. But it would be wrong to see time as a steady march toward progress. I am grateful that my daughter was born when she was. No one ever suggested to me that I institutionalize her, although I know other parents whose pediatricians assumed that they would be putting their newborns up for adoption. Low expectations have not disappeared.

No matter what expectations we face when we are born—whether we are tracked to go to college or live in an institution—these expectations are shaped by the logic of the IQ test. They are how the test haunts us all.

*   *   *

ANDY AND I ate fish tacos for dinner on our deck the night before Louisa was born. It was a chilly evening in late May, but it seemed like we should savor the moment. Would we be able to eat outside when the baby is here? Would we be able to eat together? We didn't know exactly what it would be like tomorrow, but there was a sense that one chapter in our lives together was coming to a close and another was opening up. That evening I felt completely confident that I knew what to do to give my daughter what she needed.

"I wonder if she will go to Yale or Brown," I said to Andy as we ate and looked at the imposing trees in our backyard. I now realize that my question wasn't about the well-being or happiness of my future child. It was about status. *Brown, she'll definitely go to Brown*, I thought. *That's where the more creative, independent kids go. We will, of course, start saving right away to pay for this, but maybe she will be a National Merit Scholar. . . .* Andy teased me, "Maybe we should let her decide?" "Okay, sure," I replied. "But I bet you she'll go to one of those. And major in English literature, because she won't want to be an art historian like her parents." Remembering my words now, I am not disappointed that my expectations for Louisa's future have changed. And who knows. If I've learned anything it is to not underestimate my kid. Rather, I am ashamed of my narrow vision of success and my tunneled perspective on what her happiness and fulfillment might be like. I am not disappointed in her. I am disappointed in myself.

One of the only things I associated with Down syndrome before Louisa was born was low intelligence, although I did not know exactly what this meant. The ambitions of intelligence seemed far in the future, unrelated to the immediate challenges of breastfeeding and sleeping through the night. But I soon became aware of the continuum we occupied. More sleep meant more brain development, which meant a better chance of higher cognitive ability in the future. Being able to breastfeed meant stronger development of the muscles around Louisa's mouth, which meant the possibility of better speech. But breastfeeding wasn't working for us, and Louisa wasn't gaining any weight. We saw our pediatrician every other day for the first two weeks. She began to mention the phrase "failure to thrive." While waiting for an appointment, I read a pamphlet, which mentioned that breastfeeding could raise a child's IQ by six points. It seemed as if I couldn't give Louisa what she needed most. The failure, it seemed, was all mine.

Louisa's low muscle tone made it difficult for her to latch on to my breast. Not only did I not realize that this was the problem, I also did not know what it meant to have low muscle tone. I know now that it describes the general degree of tension in her muscles, which impacts how much effort it takes to accomplish most muscular tasks, like breastfeeding. I also know now that low muscle tone is an almost universal trait of people with Down syndrome, and infants with the condition are often referred to on medical websites as "floppy babies."

Louisa wasn't gaining enough weight and the pediatrician gently encouraged me to move on to formula. The doctor was clearly not familiar with my stubbornness. Doubling down, I refused to give up on the physical connection to my daughter I had imagined. The solution involved long hours of pumping and Andy's unflinching collaboration. Every three hours, round the clock, he gave Louisa a bottle of breastmilk while I bonded with the breast pump and its motorized hum. It was not exactly what I had imagined, but it was what I felt Louisa needed. Breastfeeding began to symbolize, in unreasonable ways, how much we would support her potential. I didn't care how hard it was. And eventually, we got the hang of it, or at least Louisa was no longer failing to thrive.

It was during these long nights that I began to think about how my daughter was going to fit into this world. My late-night internet research bounced back and forth between terrifying claims about people with Down syndrome and articles in parenting magazines such as "Raising a Smart Baby," "Boost Your Baby's IQ," and "How to Build Your Child's Brain Power." Medical websites described people with Down syndrome as having a wide range of developmental delays and physical disabilities. I read about a nine-year-old girl with Down syndrome who lives in Peru and loves horseback riding. I learned about a man with Down syndrome who lives in Albuquerque, New Mexico, and owns a restaurant. I also read about Ethan Saylor, a man with Down syndrome who died while being detained by police in a movie theater. One website described the correlation between the number of words a baby hears and her verbal IQ. I wondered what verbal IQ was, exactly, and if two attitudes toward the future—one of immutable fate and one of hope and potential—could somehow coexist.

Louisa took her first IQ test when she was five, but her development was closely monitored from the moment she was born. I keep a collection of reports from doctors and therapists, who noted developmental milestones like bringing her hands to her midline and pinching a Cheerio between her thumb and index finger. The records amount to a fastidious journal tracking Louisa's development, but I am never sure where they belong. Do they go with the tiny baby shoes and blankets on the top shelf of her closet in her room, or do they belong in the file cabinet next to the hospital invoices? It seems like they straddle the separate spaces of family memories and medical assessment.

It turns out that the logic of IQ tests was there from the beginning, even though I never thought of it that way until later. These records speak about Louisa's development on two separate tracks, her mental age and her chronological age, as if her extra chromosome had caused some kind of fissure in the space-time continuum that she occupied. Louisa's mental age was measured in terms of what milestones she had met, what tasks she had accomplished. As the months went by, these two ages seemed to slowly diverge.

I eventually learned that the French psychologist Alfred Binet first developed this way of expressing intelligence through age in 1905. With the psychiatrist Théodore Simon, Binet published a test that consisted of a series of thirty short tasks that related to basic expectations for comprehension and reasoning and could be administered to a child in about forty minutes. Children were asked to label parts of the body, to describe the difference between a fly and a butterfly, and to use scissors to cut a specified shape out of a piece of paper. Binet sequenced the tasks assigned according to their difficulty. A child proceeded through the exam until she could no longer complete the tasks. The age associated with the last task she could perform was her assigned mental age. This number was divided by the child's chronological age to arrive at an intelligence ratio, an early version of an IQ score.

At three months, Louisa received a set of flash cards from a therapist. The black-and-white cards had bold, clear pictures on them. Louisa rested her shoulders on a small pillow and worked to raise her head and focus on the target or monkey face on the card I held in front of her. "Come on, Louisa. You can do it," I whispered. Andy and I cheered her on as she strained her low-toned muscles in a kind of modified tummy time. The cards were supposed to motivate her physical development, but according to the therapist and many parenting websites, focus and attention stimulate cognitive development too. Black and white provides the strongest visual contrast, thereby sending the clearest signals to babies' brains. I was skeptical that this activity would have any impact. But it was better, I realized, to feel like I could help her. I needed to believe we could shape the course of her development. Perhaps, I wondered, it might be possible to suture this split between mental and chronological age I kept reading about in her progress reports. In any case, Louisa loved the pictures. In a couple of months, she was resting her chubby elbows on the pillow and able to control the weight of her upper body, ready to learn about the world.

Louisa and I worked on her tummy time and stared at her flash cards, but we did not leave our house much for the first months of her life. She slept a lot, although more during the day than at night. Andy held her on the couch while he read and tried to work. I held her in the beige, overstuffed armchair in our living room, my arms and legs gently folded around her. We worried if it was possible to hold her too much and that she would never want to sleep in her crib, but we never really wanted to let her go. We listened to the birds outside as the world turned green and warm around us. We dozed off while listening to Adele. We marked time by watching the noon and three o'clock games of a European soccer tournament. These non-activities of sitting, watching, listening, and sleeping were deeply rooted in the present in a way I haven't been able to re-create since. But my thoughts often drifted to the future, wondering how the world would look at my beautiful Louisa once we left the house. My mind swirled with fear about what her life would be. In these moments of fear, the circumstances of Philip Bard's birth and death seemed too close. I had very little experience with disability, and my preconceptions had nothing to do with the cuddly perfection of my daughter.

I grew up in northern Kansas City, Missouri, in a neighborhood entrenched in middle-class whiteness. I attended an elementary school that was a short walk from my house, passing other newly built, three-story homes with pools in their backyards. I do not remember interacting with many children who were not white, nor do I remember being aware of the city's rich Black cultural history as I grew up. Our field trips took us to the American Royal, the annual livestock show and rodeo, but never to the Negro Leagues Baseball Museum. I was not allowed to go to the 18th and Vine Jazz District, which I was told was in the wrong part of town. Difference was something my parents taught me to accept in theory, but I had little experience with the complexities and rewards of its realities until I moved away. I also never learned to interact with people with intellectual differences. Most adults my age remember the special education programs of their childhood elementary schools that kept kids like Louisa isolated and hidden away in separate classrooms. I never learned how to be their friend, but I remember staring at them when they entered the gym during school assemblies.

On a cold winter day when I was five, my father took me to a golf course near our house to go sledding. We bundled up to brace ourselves for the stinging wind and trekked to the field of pristine snow a short distance from our house. We were bounding over the hills and dips of the golf course on our sled when my father saw a boy named Nick trudging toward us. I recognized him from the swim team in the summer. When we took our team picture, he stood on the top row of the metal risers but did not stand straight and still like the rest of us. To my five-year-old self, his difference was terrifying. He had spots on his face. His arms and head did not seem the right size for his body. He always wanted to talk to me but I could not understand him, and it made my stomach hurt and my face turn red. I wasn't happy to see Nick on that cold day, but my father wanted me to understand that Nick needed our friendship. He insisted that I ride my sled down the hill with Nick, and I headed home in protest.

My father and I did not have many more chances to sled together. He became sick a few years later and died when I was eleven. In my memory, his impatience with my discomfort is tinged with urgency. He left me, my mother, and my sister in good financial shape, but I realize now that he was desperate to ensure my capacity for empathy and compassion before he died.

In *A Disability History of the United States*, Kim Nielsen writes that the languages of most indigenous communities of North America do not include a word for disability. The closest approximations are terms that emphasize community relationships. Impairment would be referenced if a person could not contribute to their community, no matter how minimal or simple the contribution might seem. The severing of a reciprocal relationship with a community was identified as a concern, not a particular cognitive, physical, or emotional difference. In my interactions with Nick, it seemed as if I had internalized at a very young age the way we sever relationships with people with disabilities. If I remember doing it to Nick, how could I not expect others to do the same to Louisa?

*   *   *

THE COLLEGE TOWN where Andy, Louisa, and I live is surrounded by cornfields. Its population is about 7,500, but swells to three times that when students dominate nine months per year. Many university faculty commute from Cincinnati, about an hour away, but those who live in town enjoy a thriving farmers market, a tight-knit community, and miles of hiking trails. When we finally began to leave the house, I walked with Louisa in her stroller while she napped. I steered clear of the student neighborhoods with sidewalks littered with red plastic cups and yards with cornhole sets and ping-pong tables. We headed toward the community park, where we felt the wind zip across the soccer fields.

We were never supposed to be here long. Andy and I had moved to Ohio after two years in Europe doing research for our dissertations. When he got a job at this university in the middle of cornfields, we thought it might be a good place to start while I finished writing my dissertation, before we moved on to more ambitious jobs at a more interesting school, presumably somewhere on a coast. We rolled into town in our U-Haul truck, which was filled with the boxes of books and some furniture we had stored in Philadelphia, our previous American residence, while we were abroad. I told myself to be positive, above all else, since I knew Andy was already anxious about bringing me here. It wasn't bad, just small.

Years later, we are still here. I got a job as a professor a few years after he did, and two tenure-track positions at the same university aren't easy to come by. I used to think it was unacceptable to live somewhere like this, without skyscrapers, subways, and proper bakeries. I miss looking around and seeing all sorts of faces, with only a few the same color as mine. But it is okay that I am not living in one of the cities I love the most. Here the puppet shows at the local library were free. I could walk on streets lined with towering black walnut and sweet gum trees as my daughter napped in her stroller. On clear nights we could look up and see a sky full of stars. In the fall, a full, harvest moon sat just above the horizon.

Living in a small town, I didn't have many people to talk to about my fears for Louisa's future after she was born. I began to wonder if other parents thought about the intellectual development of their children as much as I did. The internet led me to believe this was true. Many studies that I read tried to identify what circumstances foster the highest possible IQ. Such studies then inform parents' consumer choices, making it difficult to figure out where sound research ends and consumer advertising begins. Parenting a baby seemed to be about feeding the right foods, buying the right toys, and choosing the right daycare to ensure intelligence later in life.

The internet is filled with websites targeting parents who want to raise their child's IQ, presumably because of what such an achievement promises to ensure—happiness, success, prosperity. Some suggestions for raising a child's IQ seemed obvious, like reading and talking to your baby, and making sure she gets enough sleep. One study reported that eating fish is consistently associated with a higher IQ, and leafy vegetables lead to "better brain power." Every toy I considered buying ensured me that it would stimulate brain activity and development. And there wasn't a moment to waste. From sitting in a bouncy chair to playing with cups in the bathtub, all moments of babyhood are susceptible to commercially curated brain stimulation. Intelligence, it seemed, was something that could be shaped by parenting choices. But it also seemed that whatever I did, it would never be enough.

Parents have always felt anxious about their children's intelligence. Around 1900, Binet based his earliest research on intelligence on his observations of his two young daughters, Madeline and Alice, who were two years apart in age. He developed a series of activities to compare their behavior and mark the milestones of cognitive development. The activities often sound like the common attempts of parents to understand what is going on inside their child's head. Binet recounts a conversation with Alice in which she remembers her father killing a boy with his cane. They quibble over the distinction between real and dream.

Alice insists that the event was real, meaning that she really dreamed it. But she admits that she cannot lead her father to the site of the murder, telling him that "if you killed a boy in the courtyard, it would smell bad." Binet attempts to report his experiments with some emotional distance, describing "the little girl of whom I speak" rather than using a more sentimental reference. But he does admit an intimacy with their development, often marveling at how two girls from the same household and the same parents could be so different. In these brief, recognizable glimpses of parental awe, I see the possibility that intelligence could be described with the heart rather than statistics and standardized tests.

As early as 1896, Binet planned to develop a series of mental tests that would be so simple all parents could give them to their child over the course of an hour or two and determine their child's rate of intelligence. "To judge well, to comprehend well, to reason well, these are the essential activities of intelligence," Binet wrote in 1905. This is as close as Binet gets to defining intelligence directly, but he goes on to describe it as something separate from the sensitivity of the senses or the acuteness of memory. He also claimed that intelligence was something fixed and stable. Binet designed his test to reflect a child's capacity for reason and judgment, which he believed could not be taught in schools. Even now, psychologists tell me that they expect Louisa's IQ score to remain the same, reflecting a consistent comparison between her and her peers.

There were other ways that psychologists were thinking about intelligence when Binet was publishing his work. While Binet described a collection of diverse functions and processes that developed at different rates in different people, British psychologist Charles Spearman saw intelligence as more monolithic. There was a single source he referred to as an "engine" that fueled proficiency in all mental functions and tasks. Following Spearman's work, German psychologist William Stern introduced the idea of expressing intelligence as a single number. An IQ score is a measurement that aims to assess intelligence, but it is not equivalent to intelligence. Before long the distinction didn't seem to matter.

Testifying to how quickly the IQ score and the concept of intelligence became synonymous, an essay in the *New Republic* from 1923 declared that "intelligence as a measurable capacity must at the start be defined as the capacity to do well on an intelligence test." Already a common slippage had been normalized—a test score and mental ability became one and the same.

YEARS LATER, AFTER Louisa took her first IQ test, I combed through the library's collection of textbooks on cognitive assessment. I was looking for the information I needed to decide if I should let this testing continue. But the accumulation of information also felt like a way to defend against the catastrophically low expectations that led to Philip Bard's fate. If I knew more about the IQ test, then maybe it would help me prevent others from judging Louisa's potential because of her score. I learned that IQ tests are actually a series of subtests that target a range of different cognitive faculties. It is a strategy of inaccurate but overwhelming force rather than the precise identification of a target. Regarding his own strategy of gleaning a child's intelligence, Binet wrote in 1911, "It matters very little what the tests are so long as they are numerous." If several strategies are employed, one is bound to hit the mark.

Based on his parental experience as well as his work with children in the public schools of France, Binet eventually introduced a system of measuring intelligence based on age. Adopting a trial-and-error method, other psychologists presented a series of puzzles and questions and grouped these tests according to appropriate age levels. According to the Stanford-Binet exam, for example, 60 percent of children who were twelve years old in 1916 should be able to define three out of these five words: pity, revenge, charity, envy, justice. According to instructions, a child can define *pity* as "to be sorry for someone," but not "to help" or "mercy." A test administrator would time younger children while they fit a series of shapes into corresponding cutouts on a form board and string a set of beads into a prescribed sequential pattern. Another test presents a picture of a cat with whiskers on one side of its face and asks a young child to point to or identify what is missing. When about 60 percent of children at a particular age could complete an activity, then it was considered indicative of the expected intellectual capacity of that age group. Defining expectations for a particular age group involved finding activities that fit into the expected bell curve of normalcy—most could complete the activity, while a few could not, and a few could do much more. So, at least initially, an IQ test measured a child's capacity to complete a rather arbitrarily selected group of activities and compared that child's performance to others given the same tests. Early on in the development of IQ testing, a child's mental age was the age level associated with the most complex tasks she could complete on a test and was determined in relation to what other children could accomplish. In the words of one early critic of IQ testing, "The intelligence test, then, is an instrument for classifying a group of people, rather than a 'measure of intelligence.'"

The overall IQ score is determined by calculating and compiling scores on a number of different subtests. On the Visual Puzzle subtest of the WISC, the test given to Louisa at school, test-takers reproduce a geometric image by choosing three shapes from six options that can be combined to form that image. The Picture Span subtest requires children to view a page with one or more images for a minute. Then the child is asked to select the same images from another page with a larger group of options. The Coding subtest evaluates associative memory, requiring a child to associate symbols with particular numbers. Because the IQ score comes about indirectly, psychologists have debated whether the overall score is more important than the separate subtest scores. The relationship between a subtest and a particular cognitive skill is complicated. Many of the subtests are intended to assess more than one skill. Coding, for example, measures processing speed as well as short-term memory and attention to visual stimuli. People who are good at one subtest tend to be good at them all, which justifies the value of the IQ score as a marker of general intelligence.

In the early twentieth century, psychologists talked about intelligence as something to be revealed, something hidden that was made visible by this quantitative tool. Many believed that IQ tests visualized something that was present in our brains before the desire to measure it, like a heartbeat or a breath. Among psychologists who research intelligence today, there is a persistent belief that it *is* like a heartbeat or a breath. Since the mapping of the human genome, psychologists have searched for specific genes that are responsible for normal variations in intelligence. So far, it appears that if there is a relationship between genes and intelligence, it involves so many genes that the connection is too diffuse to be identified. In 2008, a genome scan of 7,000 seven-year-old children found six genetic markers that might be associated with cognitive ability. Together, these six markers explain just 1 percent of possible variance. But this has not stopped psychologists from emphasizing intelligence as a measure of a human trait based in our biology, rather than a social and cultural value.

The idea that IQ tests measure an innate identity trait is an alluring one. We love to tell stories about it. Movies like *Good Will Hunting*, *A Beautiful Mind*, and *Little Man Tate* are based on the fantasy of a naturally born genius in conflict with his (almost always his, rarely ever her) environment. The idea that genius is more a product of hard work and social circumstance is much less entertaining. And, in fact, the most boring foil to genius, being unequivocally normal, is equally built on fantasy and privilege.

The idea of *normal* developed in the early twentieth century alongside the modern language of intelligence. Disability studies scholar Lennard Davis explains that it wasn't until the mid-nineteenth century that *normal* took on its meaning as "not deviating from the common type." Previously, the word had meant "perpendicular," analogous to a carpenter's square, called a *norm*. In the burgeoning language of statistics, *normal* and *average* came to describe what the majority of the human population should be. Use of the term increased by over 800 percent between 1860 and 1920. Normal became a new ideal, and deviations constituted a difference from the cultural and social expectations of society. At the moment of Reconstruction and increased immigration, in which the United States was codifying its identity, "normal" also meant white and middle-class. IQ tests were normed for white, middle-class test-takers. In other words, their results were the ones considered normal, and other ways of experiencing the world were inadequate. Privilege grows from this understanding of normal, in which no other way of experiencing the world needs to be accounted for. Now you can't turn on a television show without a character who wants to be normal, just like everyone else. Though perhaps boring, normal is powerful. Every other way of being in the world is judged against it.

The nineteenth-century Belgian astronomer and statistician Adolphe Quetelet expressed this idea as a bell-shaped curve, which became a symbol of modern expectations for normalcy, as well as my framework for processing Louisa's IQ score, her development, and her physical growth. He also described someone who could be plotted at the very peak of the curve as the Average Man. Quetelet does not provide a picture of this abstract human, but I imagine him something like a modern version of Leonardo da Vinci's *Vitruvian Man*, a conflation of the two concepts of ideal and ordinary. While we might use *average* and *normal* to describe something or someone that is unimpressive, Quetelet saw his Average Man as perfection itself. "The average man, indeed, is in a nation what the center of gravity is in the body." Quetelet's praise for average was set off by his disdain for those who strayed from this mark. "Everything differing from the Average Man's proportions and condition would constitute deformity and disease," he wrote in *A Treatise on Man and the Development of His Faculties* in 1842 and described a utopian fantasy of normalcy. "Everything found dissimilar . . . would constitute Monstrosity." Conflating the ideal and the ordinary makes it next to impossible to disentangle the two and acknowledge difference. With the established conflation between the white middle-class and the concept of normal, this identity became the ideal.

Intelligence is usually visualized as Quetelet's bell curve, a graph in which the horizontal axis registers the IQ score, and the vertical axis records its frequency among a population. The average score on an IQ test is 100, and it is recorded at the peak of the bell curve. The shape slopes down at roughly the same angle on both sides of the peak. The farther away from the average score, either to the right or the left, the fewer people are identified with that score. The bell curve aims to sort us all into a fixed place in society. Those on opposite sides of the bell curve—the gifted and those with intellectual challenges—might seem worlds apart, placed into different educational experiences and socioeconomic futures. But, in fact, they are part of the same system. One could not be defined without the other, and any attempt to upend the bell curve would be, in Quetelet's terms, throwing a nation off its center of gravity. Someone demanding to be placed differently—or to not be placed at all—upsets the whole system and throws the legitimacy of other, more privileged places in the hierarchy into question. We are all part of the bell curve, although those placed on its ends feel its power the most.

The British philosopher Herbert Spencer, who coined the Darwinian phrase "survival of the fittest," described intelligence as the "continuous adjustment of inner to outer relations" in 1855. The language of evolution and the language of intelligence went hand in hand. High intelligence was pegged as the end goal of evolution. Intelligence was something fiercely competitive, defined as what is pursued through natural selection. Psychologists still consider intelligence to be synonymous with processing speed, focus, and memory. These traits are also essential to success in the modern world. They are the traits of the factory worker, the office employee—new jobs of the twentieth-century capitalist workforce—but less so the farmer, the blacksmith, or the artist.

Quetelet's Average Man and the bell curve were used to describe and predict much more than intelligence. They played an essential role in designing the values of the modern world. The culture of normal is also a culture of fierce competition that compares citizen to citizen, worker to worker. Karl Marx used the idea in his formulation of average wage and average labor in his study of capitalism. Other scientists used the bell curve to chart a range of features of human physiology. The bell curve became the way humans made sense of each other and modern life.

Even now, Americans know that to fall from the norm is to risk being left behind. About six months after Louisa was born, I joined a Facebook group for mothers of babies with Down syndrome who lived in the Cincinnati area, the city closest to where we live. We posted pictures of our babies and found support among other mothers who were adjusting to this new bilingual world of mental and chronological age. Some babies were having heart surgery; others were struggling to eat or nurse. Mothers in the group reported when their babies passed certain milestones—the first step, the first word, a bite of solid food—and we all celebrated because we knew the hours of therapy and hard work that it took to get there. But it was hard not to use the group as a tracking opportunity. I found myself comparing Louisa's development to what other moms reported about their children in order to make sure that she wasn't falling too far behind and that she was as normal as she could possibly be.

Quetelet's Average Man and bell curve also made it seem possible to predict a person's future. If humans are organized and classified according to certain shared characteristics, then useful predictions could be made by considering the patterns and outcomes of a shared group. If all members of a group behave in similar ways, then social scientists can make predictions about the salary, education, and intelligence of group members in the future. This new language of statistics, measurement, and averages dramatically changed the course of the burgeoning field of psychology.

German psychologist Wilhelm Wundt declared in 1862 that "It can be stated without exaggeration that more psychology can be learned from statistical averages than from all philosophers, except Aristotle."

The IQ test represents a historically specific attempt to define intelligence as something quantitative and measurable. Of course, no hint of this understanding of intelligence was presented to me when we met at Louisa's school to discuss her IQ test. It wasn't explained, but it was there in the quantitative and statistical data presented to me and Andy. It informed the way I was expected to take pride in my daughter's IQ score. And it informed the fact that I fulfilled that expectation. If there is one thing that this understanding of intelligence teaches us, it is that placement on the bell curve matters above all else.

If statistics are a language, then I have stepped onto foreign soil, frantically trying to pick up any cues of communication to figure out where I should go. The glimpse of human connection between parent and daughter that I sensed in Binet's earliest experiments in intelligence are long gone. In its place, statistics and charts impose a kind of authority that I find difficult to challenge. The IQ score, which is now the product of comparison with thousands of other children, seems to have a hold on aspects of my daughter's life experience, but it feels entirely divorced from the girl I love.

THE STRANGENESS OF the IQ score is that it is a ratio, but it is not expressed in recognizable units. Unlike other ratios borne from our need for speed and quantification in the modern world—miles per gallon or gigabytes per second, for example—an IQ score is not based on the commensuration of any concrete form. That is, intelligence has no shape or form outside of the test's number and a rounded bell curve. Its self-enclosed status is precisely what makes it seem so absolute and constant. It is a ratio based on an abstract average, but it is presented as if it is reflecting the amount of something inherently in one's body.

In her essay "The Pain Scale," writer Eula Biss points out that every scale of measurement needs a set of fixed points. Water freezes at 32 degrees on the Fahrenheit scale, which finds meaning in relation to 212 degrees Fahrenheit, or the temperature at which water boils. The pain scale provides a simple, although flawed, set of relative values. In the doctor's office, zero equals no pain. Ten equals the worst pain imaginable. Scales are attempts to map structure onto something that is otherwise difficult to communicate or describe. The statistical calculation of IQ and its shaping into a bell curve is no different. But unlike the pain scale, the meaning of an IQ score isn't fixed between limits, but around a norm. About 70 percent of all people score within 15 points of the average score of 100, between 85 and 115. About 95 percent of people have an IQ score between 70 and 130, which leaves 5 percent for the extremes. The limits of the bell curve, its outskirts and biggest deviations from normal, are harder to define. The distribution of intelligence means that 100 is normal. Two hundred is theoretically the highest IQ possible and 0 is the lowest possible score, but both are mathematical possibilities rather than lived realities.

According to editions of *The Guinness Book of World Records* published between 1985 and 1989, Marilyn vos Savant, a magazine columnist, had the highest IQ ever recorded. In an unbelievable coincidence, the word *savant* means "a person of learning." When she was ten years old, Savant took an old version of the Stanford-Binet that calculated her IQ in the way that Binet did on his earliest tests, mental age divided by chronological age. This gave her an IQ of 228. But now psychologists do not acknowledge an IQ score above 170. In 1990, *The Guinness Book of World Records* retired the category of "Highest IQ" after deciding that IQ tests were too unreliable to determine a single record holder.

The lowest IQ ever recorded has never been identified, because it is much less celebrated. The lowest possible IQ score is zero, but zero is nothing. No thinking and no life. The lowest scores discussed in psychology textbooks are around 40. Adults can mow lawns and do simple laundry with an IQ of 40, one chart tells me.

Louisa's IQ score is described as borderline, which was classified by psychologists for most of the twentieth century as "dull" or "feeble-minded." That same chart says that she will have a 50/50 chance of reaching high school and working at a store.

I read an explanation for the way IQ is calculated in a book on intelligence meant for non-experts like me. A chart attempted to clarify by translating the number into more recognizable predictions about an individual's future. A person with an average IQ is expected to graduate from high school "without much distinction" and attend community college. A person with an IQ of 85 is likely a high school dropout. The psychologist writing this book caps this person's future as a skilled laborer. He employs IQ as a predictive tool, which indirectly stereotypes and devalues certain professions and social classes. It draws a clear line from an IQ score to a certain future, without questioning whether certain economic, cultural, and social circumstances could be transformed to wrestle a future away from such a predetermined fate. This, I realized, is one way that history informs Louisa's future. Certain life paths are open to her, while others are not.

Thinking about IQ tests from the perspective of norms and the aggregate seems fundamentally incompatible with attention to individual human experience. I grapple with where Louisa's life fits in with such predictive determinism. I think I am realistic about my daughter's place in a world in which human worth is associated with intelligence, yet I still feel a deep pang when I see it so explicitly stated. If Louisa's future is fixed, what does that say about my role in her life, my deep desire to help her learn? In the end, will the breastfeeding actually have been worth it? What were those black-and-white cards for, I wondered, if Louisa's fate and social status were already determined as the IQ predicts? What opportunities will there be for my adventurous daughter who seems curious about every aspect of the world?

Such predictions also solidify a rift between what my life has been and what Louisa's life will be like. It seems like a betrayal to talk about my daughter's IQ score and not talk about mine too. I do not know my IQ, but teachers and therapists are able to know Louisa's. This is at the crux of the power dynamic the IQ test generates. I have the privilege of not knowing, but Louisa is forced into a diagnostic system in which her intelligence is quantified and tracked. It is deeply uncomfortable to face a system of measurement that I benefit from but which potentially limits my daughter's access to those same benefits of respect, autonomy, and consideration. Given these predictions, my resistance to Louisa's IQ test seems justified. It is difficult to trust the psychologists when they tell me that the IQ test could be used to help her. On the contrary, the IQ test reinforces the world's minimal expectations for her.

Parents often describe their children as small parts of themselves who walk around independently in the world without protection. I, too, see Louisa as an extension of me. Although I logically know that her IQ score was determined in large part by a third copy of the twenty-first chromosome, there is still a part of me that understands this number as a reflection of me, my parenting, and my love for her. This number, and the fact that it is possible to associate Louisa with a number at all, is also a reflection of history. Before Louisa, I had no reason to notice or question the social hierarchy that intelligence testing facilitates. I am a university professor and lifelong overachiever. Yet Louisa's opportunities for a full and happy life are limited under the logic of intelligence testing and its values that dominate the educational and professional systems in which I have succeeded my entire life. Louisa challenges what I thought was the best way of being in the world, which was being demonstrably and certifiably intelligent. Making space for my daughter's own unique way of being requires deprioritizing things I value. That act is a part of my maternal care, in all of its impossible challenges and rewards.

The DSM

A third copy of the twenty-first chromosome is part of my daughter's genetic fabric. It can be pointed to in a karyotype. But identifying an intellectual disability is more fluid. As Brian, the school psychologist, had explained to me, Louisa's IQ score made her difficult to classify, which might put access to certain systems of support at risk. So much seemed to depend on whether her behavior and test scores matched diagnostic descriptions. After the meeting with Brian, I looked up "intellectual disability" in the *Diagnostic and Statistical Manual of Mental Disorders* (DSM), an indispensable professional resource published by the American Psychiatric Association. Although encyclopedias have lost their authority since the mid-twentieth century, replaced by Google searches and crowdsourcing, diagnostic manuals remain resources of established truth.

Once a behavior or condition is named in the DSM, it becomes a problem that needs to be cured or treated. Psychiatry is a science of behavior rather than objective cause, and it depends on the DSM because of its evasive subject of study. There is no blood test or genetic marker to determine beyond doubt that someone is schizophrenic, autistic, or depressed. Diagnosis depends on a description of symptoms agreed upon by professionals. Those symptoms and the language used to describe them change. Authoritative resources like the DSM—not just individual medical doctors and psychologists—are responsible for the treatment and understanding of behavior.

Wading into the DSM is like reading a foreign language. Both are filled with unfamiliar words and meanings. I am not a psychiatrist or psychologist, but that doesn't mean I should ignore the influence of this resource. It will impact how my daughter sees herself. It will affect how the bureaucratic systems that will touch her life—health care, law, education—will judge her competence, independence, and even her human worth. I want to understand and prepare for that influence.

The DSM is an intimidating tome of professional practice, consisting of a labyrinthine taxonomy of categories and criteria. Although I could refer to it online, I wanted to sense its authority by feeling its weight in my hands. The fifth edition has 947 pages and weighs 3.7 pounds. It has expanded considerably since its first edition was published in 1952 as a thin paperback. Lining up copies of all five editions on my desk created a small staircase, and its swelling suggests its gradual dominance and an increasing need to define and pathologize deviant behavior.

In the DSM, intellectual disability is a subcategory within the larger classification of neurodevelopmental disorders. These disorders are characterized by "developmental deficits that produce impairments of personal, social, academic, or occupational functioning." Other neurodevelopmental disorders include autism spectrum disorder, and attention deficit / hyperactivity disorder. These conditions are grouped together because they all typically manifest before a child enters grade school and they often co-occur.

The DSM-5 states that people diagnosed with an intellectual disability have an IQ below 70, but that three categories must be met to validate the diagnosis: 1) deficits that would be defined through intelligence tests that assess reasoning, problem-solving, planning, and abstract thinking; 2) deficits in adaptive functioning that limit individual independence and social responsibility in everyday life across multiple environments;

and 3) the emergence of these deficits during the developmental period of one's life. The diagnosis is then broken down into categories based on the profundity of the impairment with a ranking of mild, moderate, severe, and profound.

Labeling gives legitimacy and form to subjects. It is not possible to diagnose, to treat, or to submit an insurance claim for treatment for a psychiatric condition unless it is in the DSM. Each of the hundreds of diagnoses in the DSM corresponds to a particular code in the International Classification of Diseases (ICD). The ICD was created by the World Health Organization and the inclusion of its coding in the DSM helps psychiatrists cross-reference, like translation between two languages. A mild intellectual disability is classified as 317, yet this diagnosis might be accompanied by others, such as a range of communication disorders (315.32–315.39), autism spectrum disorder (299.00), or the strangely vague "specific learning disorder" (315.0–315.2). Although she doesn't qualify for 317 on her IQ score alone, the other criteria—deficits in adaptive functioning and the onset of these deficits during the developmental period of her life—create enough diagnostic leeway for Louisa to be included in this diagnosis. The code 317 will give her access to Medicaid and living support when she is an adult. It will allow her to access higher education programs and federal financial aid specifically designed for people with intellectual disabilities, even if she does not complete secondary education in a traditional way. So, while the DSM feels like foreign territory, the diagnosis it provides is necessary.

When I read about intellectual disability, the familiar impulse arises in me to distinguish between how a professional sees Louisa and who my daughter actually is. The DSM is an impressive accumulation of knowledge acquired by experts, and there is something comforting about finding a diagnosis so thoroughly explained. But I am aware that she both matches and exceeds such a description. While I can't deny that my daughter has "difficulty in accurately perceiving peers' social cues" and needs "some support with complex daily living tasks," I also resist the implied conclusion that there is something wrong, something in need of treatment with these parts of her. Even though this diagnosis fits, it does not account for how she sits on the couch with her dad and looks at maps in an atlas for hours, how she loves her friends despite not sounding or acting exactly like them, and how she searches for crayfish in the creek behind our house.

GIVEN THE NO-MAN'S-LAND that Brian described to me, I wondered if we needed to be more precise about Louisa's diagnosis, and whether it was possible that more evaluation was necessary rather than less. By second grade, Louisa's teachers were starting to contact me about her behavior at school. She was struggling to stay on task and to keep her attention on her work when a friend would walk by her desk. Apparently, Louisa spent most of her time sharpening pencils, wearing down several each day. "Often she can become distracted and has trouble reentering the assigned task if she has become sidetracked, which makes simple tasks more laborious," one teacher told us. In a classroom setting, it seemed like the challenge was less with Louisa's understanding of the lessons than with her ability to maintain focus. But by now I knew enough about Louisa and intelligence to know that cognitive ability and attention weren't so easily separable. It seemed clear enough to me that she was talking with her friends and sharpening her pencil to avoid tasks that were hard for her. But Louisa was also having problems with self-control. She was constantly hugging her friends and tried to kiss some of them. The affectionate behavior she showed in preschool was less appropriate for second grade. Most kids didn't like it and some had responded with an unwelcoming shove. We needed some strategies to help Louisa stay on task and develop some social inhibitions. I contacted a psychologist in hopes that a professional could provide some answers. After all, psychologists should offer more than just diagnosis. They should also offer help.

We met with a psychologist for three sessions. The first involved a thorough interview with me and Andy about Louisa's behavior at home. Was she getting herself dressed? Was she using a fork and spoon at meals? We reported that Louisa struggled with transitions and resisted when it was time to stop doing preferred activities. We mentioned that she could be easily distracted and had a hard time staying on task. At the second meeting, Louisa worked through a series of IQ tests with the psychologist. And at the last meeting we discussed the results of Louisa's cognitive evaluation, which concluded that "despite having Down syndrome Louisa does not currently meet criteria for a diagnosis of intellectual disability."

The psychologist explained that the differences between people with Down syndrome and their peers often increases by the age of eighteen, and Louisa would most likely match the criteria for an intellectual disability in a few years. She showed us her report, which stated that "diagnostic observations indicate impaired language skills. The pattern of behaviors meets the diagnostic criteria for communication disorder." I suspect that the psychologist knew that communication disorder wasn't really an adequate diagnosis. But it would keep Louisa in the system, qualifying her for an IEP and school support. A diagnosis that captured some of Louisa's challenges was better than no diagnosis at all.

I found myself in the uncomfortable situation of wishing my daughter had, officially, an intellectual disability. The diagnosis would have put us on more stable ground, rather than navigating in between definitions. In the DSM, the criteria for a communication disorder are much more vague. "Disorders of communication include deficits in language, speech, and communication," it states. The entry goes on to assert that assessment must take into account an individual's cultural and language context. The diagnosis seemed only superficially relevant to Louisa, but I was willing to go along with it if it would give her the support she needs.

Giving a name to someone's difference is treatment itself. It offers legitimacy to suffering and validates experience. It also provides an explanation of someone's behavior, that someone with pyromania (312.33) isn't just a bad person but has a psychological illness that is potentially treatable. Diagnosis also shapes identity. Asperger's syndrome is a relatively new term, coined in 1981 and taken up by the fourth edition of the DSM in 1994 as *Asperger's Disorder* (299.80). It lists the diagnostic features as "severe and sustained impairment in social interaction" and "the development of restricted, repetitive patterns of behavior, interests, and activities." After its appearance in the fourth edition, support communities emerged and public figures like environmental activist Greta Thunberg shaped the group's cultural identity. But when I searched the fifth edition of the DSM, I could not find a similar entry on Asperger's syndrome. The only reference is a curt instruction to give individuals previously diagnosed with Asperger's syndrome, according to the preceding edition, the diagnosis of autism spectrum disorder.

Published in 2013, the fifth edition no longer acknowledged Asperger's syndrome as a distinguishable condition. One psychologist I talked to said that it had become "weirdly fashionable to have Asperger's instead of autism." The change in the DSM, she told me, was based on research that failed to demonstrate a clear distinction between the two. I found myself wondering which reality to believe, the world without Asperger's in the DSM or those who claimed the condition as a fundamental part of their identity. After the publication of the fifth edition, members of online communities of people with Asperger's syndrome began to wonder if their diagnosis was real. One participant asked, "How autistic do you have to be to be called autistic? How autistic do you have to be to be called Asperger's?" To many, the DSM's restructuring appeared to undercut the credibility of a cultural community. The manual was in conflict with their sense of self.

My curiosity grew as I looked back on earlier editions of the DSM and found entries that do not belong. Homosexuality was diagnosed as a "sociopathic personality disturbance" in the first edition and was reclassified as a "sexual deviation" in the second. I found no mention of homosexuality in versions of the DSM published after 1973. Later I learned that gay activists disrupted the 1970 and 1971 meetings of the American Psychiatric Association and eventually forced its members to acknowledge that homosexuality was a healthy part of human experience and not in need of treatment.

The DSM is a world that was made and then repeatedly revised. What does and does not exist depends to a large degree on what is written down, how it is described, and how it is organized. A diagnosis of intellectual disability is referred to as a descriptive term, which isn't a discovery of cause, but the best match between the language of experts and the experience of a person. The DSM attempts to define conditions that are personally experienced, and therefore it never precisely describes its subject. But by its very nature, the DSM tries to deny this. The language and ideas through which we navigate the world are always tenuous. The ground that we stand on shifts and gives way to larger systemic whims.

LIKE OTHER PEOPLE with or without Down syndrome, Louisa likes to talk to herself. Although, it's not exactly to herself. When she was about seven years old, she began talking to an imaginary baby she has named Baby Boomshalala. This baby seems to be with us more than I'm aware, as I'm often confused when she asks me, "Do you want to play with us?" I used to think that this was just a grammatical slip, but no, she is asking if I want to play with her and Baby Boomshalala.

I don't find Baby's constant presence particularly troubling. I see it as how Louisa processes new experiences. It's also a way for her to have a bit of control, as I think Baby will do just about anything that my daughter wants. Talking to herself can still pass as an endearing developmental quirk when Louisa is young. But if Baby Boomshalala stays around when my daughter is an adult, she could be judged as a sign of mental illness.

I obsessively ask Louisa each day after school who she played with at recess. I make a mental note if too many days go by when she mentions Baby Boomshalala as her only companion on the playground.

During our second session with the psychologist, when she gave Louisa a series of cognitive tests, I sat in the lobby and filled out a stack of questionnaires on Louisa's behavior. When we began this evaluation, I did not really understand that I would be part of the testing too. These forms were meant to round out the information that the psychologist obtained about Louisa, providing another perspective on her behavior and day-to-day life. The questions on these forms are relentless, an assault of suggested behaviors that often seem ghastly. If my eight-year-old was drinking alcohol or hurting small animals, I hope we would have more support than noting it by circling "often" on a checklist. Other descriptions of behavior seem subjective: "work is sloppy," "has poor handwriting," "is not a self-starter." These all seemed like traits that might describe any kid rather than symptoms of psychosis, and I wondered if these questionnaires were a tool to weed out those who did not meet our culture's high bar for perfection and productivity. And under these terms, Baby Boomshalala seemed troubling.

For most of the behaviors, I marked a 0, which means "not at all a problem," but some I marked a 1, "The behavior is a problem, but slight in degree." The form instructed me to "take relative frequency into account for each behavior specified. That is, consider this person with respect to others of similar age and sex, in general." There were multiple forms, and the questions often repeated themselves. They listed a behavior and asked me to rate how often Louisa does it on a scale of 1 to 4:

Becomes upset with new situations
Has trouble concentrating on tasks, schoolwork, etc.
Mood changes frequently
Acts too wild or "out of control"
Becomes too silly

Thinks too much about the same topic

Does not pay attention to details or makes careless mistakes with, for example, homework

Has difficulty staying focused on what needs to be done

Is easily distracted by noises and other stimuli

Is physically cruel to people

Has stolen things that have value

Has deliberately set fires to cause damage

Has forced someone into sexual activity

Feels worthless or inferior

Is sad, unhappy or depressed

I marked a 1, but maybe should have marked a 2, for:

Impulsive (acts without thinking)

Irritable and whiny

Yells at inappropriate times

Uncooperative

Does not pay attention to instructions

Demands must be met immediately

Cries over minor annoyances and hurts

The behaviors listed are like a thousand small cuts, not because they all relate to Louisa, but because of how invasive they are, how each assumes that this child is a problem and that every little misstep, every mistake needs to be evaluated. My answers were not consistent. On one form I marked "leaves seat when remaining seated is expected" as 1, which means she does this occasionally. Sometimes we play music during dinner and she gets up from the table to dance. I know she behaves the same way at school, as evidenced by the pencil sharpening. But is this something to be concerned about? On other forms I mark "0" for the same question, which means she never does this, by which I mean that

I understand the urge to dance and do not see spontaneous dancing as a problem.

One form asked me to rate whether Louisa's reading, mathematics, and written expression are above average, average, or problematic, which are labels I object to. I do not think Louisa's academic performance is problematic, but I know it is probably below average.

I could not evaluate whether Louisa "frequently" or "sometimes" puts away her toys after using them without considering how she might be judged unfairly. If I said she "frequently" forgets, did that mean there is something wrong? Do kids whose parents don't have to fill out these forms always put their toys away? Is it different from my behavior when I was a child?

My responses to other questions depended on what I was asked before and how defensive I felt in that moment about participating in my daughter's diagnosis and evaluating the slightest aberrance from normal as contributing to the definition of a problem. The forms asked me to measure Louisa's behavior by quantifying it on a scale of 1 to 4, but the fear that my answers would make it easier for others to judge Louisa unfairly could not be kept at bay.

We ate hard-boiled eggs with dinner after the tests with the psychologist. After tearing through one side of the jiggly white part to get to the yolk, Louisa held up what was left, an umbrella of egg with one side removed. "This looks like Bach's hair," my daughter said. And she was right! The smooth, white dome did resemble the powdered wigs of eighteenth-century composers she had seen on the album covers in her father's collection. The comment was astonishing in its wit (egg white as hair!), but it was also a reflection of her home environment and her parents. (And before it is assumed that my daughter is living in a bubble of rarefied culture, I should mention that she is just as excited by Taylor Swift, Bill Withers, and the soundtrack to *Encanto*.) While I laughed and looked at an egg white in a way I never had, I thought of the list of behaviors I had worked through earlier that day, how it seemed so lifeless and unnecessary in the face of a hard-boiled egg white creatively turned into Bach. This is the kind of behavior I want to value, I thought to myself. This is the world I want to live in.

I STARTED TO wonder how intellectual disability got into the DSM in the first place. By way of its inclusion, an intellectual disability is defined as a mental disorder in need of clinical treatment. Although I do not know for sure, I imagine other diagnoses in the DSM, like bipolar and anxiety disorders, are traumatic disruptions to one's sense of self and involve a significant amount of suffering and pain. Despite the sporadic appearance of Baby Boomshalala and frustration with the demands of school, I do not think that my daughter's intellectual disability causes her to suffer. I do not know yet how my daughter feels about it, but I do not want her intellectual disability to be cured. On the contrary, I want to help her navigate a world that identifies a problem where there is really only a difference.

Intellectual differences are often associated with mental health challenges and were isolated in the realm of fools and madness long before the development of IQ tests. American Isaac Ray, who in 1838 distinguished between idiocy caused by congenital defects and idiocy caused by lesions or tumors, published one of the first attempts to make a distinction between kinds of mental differences. But he also questioned the value of classification. "Such divisions," he wrote, "have not been made in nature and cannot be observed in practice." To Ray and others, classification seemed more useful for data collection than for treating patients. The federal government began collecting and publishing statistical data on the "idiotic and insane" in the census of 1840. The International Congress of Alienists categorized idiocy as one of seven forms of insanity in 1867. The Oxford English Dictionary defines *alienist* as an expert witness in court to assess whether a defendant is sane. The root of the term suggests that our legal system has historically seen those with mental differences as a foreign threat.

I decided to trace the history of intellectual disability in the DSM, starting with the first edition published in 1952. I hoped to uncover an origin story, how this diagnosis came to be and what parts of its past still linger in the present. The first edition classified what we now call intellectual disability as chronic brain syndrome. "Mongolism," which was the racist, phenotypic label given by physician John Langdon Down to what is now called Down syndrome, is listed as a cause in this first edition. The description in the first DSM states that chronic brain syndrome is a category formerly known as "secondary mental deficiency," or "mental disturbances" linked to a biological cause. I found three classifications of chronic brain syndrome associated with syphilis, but the entry associated with Mongolism is the only one for which an IQ score is mentioned.

Published in 1967, the DSM-2 lists mental retardation (310–315) as a main category of diagnosis and defines subcategories that specify severity (borderline–profound) with a rigid correlation between IQ score and diagnosis. It states, "The diagnostic classification of mental retardation relates to IQ as follows:

310 Borderline mental retardation IQ 68–83
311 Mild mental retardation IQ 52–67
312 Moderate mental retardation IQ 36–51
313 Severe mental retardation IQ 20–35
314 Profound mental retardation IQ under 20"

But in the editions of the DSM that followed, the information provided about each diagnosis was less focused on tracing the cause of a condition and increasingly preoccupied with the description and identification of symptoms. In the DSM-5, I read that, "The various levels of severity are defined on the basis of adaptive functioning, not IQ scores, because it is adaptive function that determines the level of support required." This implies that the conditions of a person's environment—how inclusive or oppressive it may be—can be considered as part of the diagnosis.

In its fifth edition, the DSM began to refer to *intellectual disability* instead of *mental retardation*. The change in label indicates a seismic shift in thought for the American Psychiatric Association, an institution that once pathologized homosexuality. The current definition of intellectual disability de-emphasizes the IQ score, or at least does so relative to the definitions in earlier editions of the DSM. It now considers other factors like adaptive behavior, environment, and health. The evolution in the definition indicates a slow transition from seeing intellectual disability as a condition to be cured to identifying a need to modify a person's circumstances to better suit her needs. In this way, Baby Boomshalala isn't a troubling sign of Louisa's deviation from normal. This conjured companion demonstrates Louisa's need for the time and space for imaginative play, an opportunity for her to develop her internal sense of self.

But psychologists still consider IQ tests to be one of their most important diagnostic tools, and the diagnosis of intellectual disability still leans heavily on the IQ score. In an article published in the journal *Intelligence* in 2010, psychologist Douglas Detterman defended how earlier systems of diagnosis linger in twenty-first century definitions of intellectual disability. "Measurement is essential to any good scientific definition," he writes. Detterman makes an important point here. Diagnosis should rely on objective evidence as much as possible. Otherwise, clinicians are forced to improvise, which opens up diagnosis to errors and bias. But it also seems impossible to fully eliminate the gap between measurement and judgment.

To support his case for the importance of the accurate measurement of intelligence, Detterman mentions *Atkins vs. Virginia*, the 2002 Supreme Court ruling that executing people with intellectual disabilities violated the Eighth Amendment prohibition against cruel and unusual punishment. "It can literally be a life-or-death issue at least partially based on clinical judgment," he claims. And thus, he believes, "we should complete the task begun by Galton, Cattell, Binet, and Goddard, and countless others of understanding exactly what general intelligence is." For these psychologists, the task was to establish a clear system for assessing intelligence. They believed that statistics could determine a person's fate.

This perspective seems common among psychologists. I once had a psychologist peg me as an "IQ skeptic," and reply to me in an email, "I find IQ testing 'skeptics' often have little understanding of how many things they are *not* skeptical of depend on intelligence testing—such as not subjecting people with an intellectual disability to the death penalty." The snappy retort demonstrated to me one of the most disturbing outcomes of the belief in intelligence as something that can be measured and absolute, rather than something shaped by bias and power. Certainly, I do not believe that people with intellectual disabilities should face the death penalty. But more to the point, I do not believe that anyone should.

Psychologists in the early twentieth century used IQ scores as a reason to intervene in the lives and bodies of their patients and segregate them from the rest of society. Using IQ tests as part of the diagnosis of intellectual disability—especially in the circumstance of the death penalty—does the same. Because of its perceived scientific certainty, the IQ score gives governments a false claim over the bodies and lives of people with intellectual disabilities. This claim does not consider whether IQ testing should be used as part of the government's unjust power to end the lives of its citizens in the first place.

Psychology manuals like the DSM describe a person with an intellectual disability as potentially a threat to self and others. They state that a lack of communication skills in people with intellectual disabilities may lead to aggressive behavior. Gullibility and lack of risk-assessment skills may result in exploitation, victimization, and physical or sexual abuse.

It is easier to blame a person than to correct structural injustice in our society. Turning our scrutiny away from the pathology of individuals and toward the systemic reasons why so many people with intellectual disabilities face poverty, segregation, and diminished opportunity would open up the possibility for social change. I hope this will occur within my daughter's lifetime.

LOUISA'S COGNITIVE EVALUATION came with a substantial plan of care, a list of suggestions to help engage her attention in the classroom. But most of the suggestions seemed so obvious it felt condescending for me to even bring them up when I met again with Louisa's teachers. *Eye contact should always be made when giving Louisa a task. Louisa needs to be seated near the teacher for instruction. She may also benefit from visual learning strategies.* These were things that Louisa's teachers were already doing. I began to see that Louisa wasn't going to be supported with a list of suggestions. Her challenges were caused by a bad match between the processing speed and attention expected in the classroom and who she fundamentally was. Solving this would take a larger structural shift in education.

I began to see the IQ test and the understanding of intelligence it generated as something made up, or at least no more or less legitimate than other narratives. Argentinian writer Jorge Luis Borges once remarked, "I wonder why a dream or an idea should be less real than this table, for example, or why *Macbeth* should be less real than today's newspaper. I cannot quite understand this." I first read Borges's short stories in college, and I kept thinking about them when trying to make sense of the DSM. One of my favorites, "Tlön, Uqbar, Orbis Tertius," is about a country whose actual existence is unclear. If the country is only described in an encyclopedia, does that make it real? How can we really know something if it is not archived, classified, and described through official channels? I found it telling that literature did more to clarify the authority of the DSM to me than the psychologists who use it. Borges's stories demonstrate how a great deal of what we can know and experience is determined by forces we might not even recognize. More than most, he understood literature's power as a tool to rethink what we know.

I am determined to provide a life for my daughter that is not ruled by the DSM and shaped by the narrative of its anticipated outcomes. My daughter's interaction with the world will be shaped by her assessment, diagnosis, and classification. But other stories, other narratives, including how I see my daughter and how my daughter sees herself, can be just as valid and powerful. Baby Boomshalala is real, and she is welcome to stay with us as long as she likes.

Mind Games

I was starting to believe that IQ tests had little purpose for Louisa besides reinforcing low expectations. But at the same time, I knew that they were required for school and helped secure essential educational support. The truth is, I had no idea what it was like to take an IQ test. Was it like a medical exam, seeing a therapist, or taking the SAT? In order to understand their power, I needed to be more familiar with the mechanics of IQ tests, not just their historical emergence but how they work pragmatically in the here and now.

So, on a morning in late summer just as the semester began, I walked across campus to the Psychology Clinic. Sitting in the lobby felt like waiting at a doctor's office. There were coffee tables with magazines and pamphlets about mental health. A reception desk was tucked behind a sliding glass partition. Harris, a grad student in his mid-twenties, wore neatly pressed khakis and a red button-down shirt and greeted me a few minutes after I checked in. "Nice to meet you, Professor Stetler," he said as he shook my hand. I insisted that he call me by my first name, but I appreciated his manners. Harris led me down a small hallway into a closet-sized conference room. We sat on opposite sides of a table as he explained that he would give me an IQ test over two, two-hour sessions and that he would write up a report that would be a way for him to practice writing up reports. He wanted to make sure I knew that this was not an official IQ test. Harris was practicing, gaining experience responding to the different scenarios that could occur when giving a test for real. For this reason, my test results were technically not valid. I did not learn my IQ, which was fine by me.

Psychology privileges certain ways of knowing that can only be accessed if you are a psychologist. But *how* we know determines *what* we know. How we know—what our expertise is—even shapes what we decide is knowledge. I wanted to learn what can be known about the IQ test—and about oneself—from the perspective of the test-taker. I also hoped that taking a test would be a way to stand in solidarity with Louisa. While my social, professional, and financial opportunities are not linked directly to an IQ test, Louisa's life potential could be determined by her performance. Taking this high-stakes test that would determine so much of Louisa's future would, perhaps, help me advocate for her. Neither of our test-taking experiences would have to stand completely without the other.

We started with a clinical interview that helped Harris decide how to modify the various subtests that followed. He asked me how I described my gender and what pronouns I used. "Can you tell me about your family history?" "What are the values that are most important to you?" "What has brought you to the psychology clinic today?" He seemed open to whatever I chose to share. He also explained that he would be writing behavioral observations while I took the various subtests. Whether I got frustrated or flustered or demonstrated complete apathy was part of the assessment, along with whether I got the questions right. In a clinical context like the one being rehearsed by Harris, an IQ score is one part of a larger context of observations and more qualitative assessments.

There are a number of different intelligence tests, and psychologists select the most appropriate one based on what they want to know. Harris prepared to give me the Wechsler Adult Intelligence Scale–Fourth

Edition (WAIS-IV), which is one of the most widely used intelligence tests for adults. It consists of fifteen subtests and provides information about specific cognitive abilities in addition to a general intelligence score. Pearson Assessment, the company that now publishes the exam, claims that it is the "most advanced adult measure of cognitive ability."

David Wechsler was a Romanian American psychologist who published the first edition of his intelligence test in 1939, known as the Wechsler–Bellevue Intelligence Scale. Wechsler believed that other versions of IQ tests focused too much on skills acquired through formal education and not enough on how well a person functions within his social and economic environment. For example, he knew one "native, white Oklahoman," who supported a family as an oil driller and earned $60 to $75 a week, a decent living at the time, but scored with the mental age of an eight-year-old on the Stanford-Binet exam. Wechsler's approach to intelligence testing, removed from the motivations to ground the practice in the social statistics of the early twentieth century, seemed more practical and human to me. According to Wechsler, intelligence tests measure "the capacity of an individual to understand the world about him and his resourcefulness to cope with its challenges." For Wechsler, intelligence wasn't just a measure of how well the mind works, but a way of describing the relationship between a person and the environment. An outlook like this makes me think it is possible to have a system where the IQ could be a force for good. It could help Louisa receive more personalized, specific care and support.

In 1932, he was appointed chief psychologist of New York's massive Bellevue Hospital, where he supervised the testing of thousands of patients. His intelligence test was the first tailored specifically to adults rather than children. Psychologists found that mental age scores did not increase after adolescence and therefore Binet's IQ formula (mental age divided by chronological age) was not sufficient for adults. As an alternative, Wechsler used the point-scale method that normed all IQ scores at 100 and converted IQ distributions for all age groups to have a standard deviation of 15. This way of expressing a person's IQ and comparing it to others proved so efficient, it was eventually adapted for IQ tests for children, too, although age equivalents for children are still provided.

Unlike the Stanford-Binet, Wechsler's test introduced a combination of verbal and performance-based tests. In this way, he intended to shape an understanding of intelligence based on a person's "ability to do things, as well as by the way he can talk about them." Later he admitted that other factors affect a person's ability to navigate his environment effectively, including drive, persistence, and curiosity. But Wechsler never developed a test to measure those qualities.

To test my ability to do things, Harris took several sets of blocks and spiral notebooks out of a sturdy black briefcase and arranged them on the table. Then he placed a spiral notebook in front of me and handed me a set of six blocks. The design of each block face varied. Some were solid red or yellow, others were divided diagonally with red or yellow triangles on either side. Harris demonstrated how the blocks could be arranged to reproduce pictures illustrated in the notebook. He handed me three more blocks and asked me to practice. "Are you ready to begin?" Harris asked. Then the test began for real, or at least fake real. "Ready . . . set . . . go." Harris started his timer and I began arranging my blocks to look like the pictures in the notebook. He pressed *stop* and flipped the page. I worked through a few more block arrangements until Harris said it was time to move on.

Given Wechsler's approach to intelligence as behavior rather than a quality of the mind, it was surprising to me how isolating it felt to take the WAIS-IV. Sitting in a windowless room with someone I barely knew hardly seemed conducive to accurately studying a person's "ability to do things." I took Wechsler's phrase to mean the ability to manage one's life—to make plans and keep them, to meet responsibilities, to adjust when routines change. How could forming pictures out of blocks possibly assess these skills?

I was growing more self-conscious of my behavior and how it was read by Harris. In the next section, he asked me to describe how two words are alike. "Bud and baby," he said. "They are early stages of life," I replied. "Music and tides." "They both consist of patterns and cycles," I answered. *Cycles? Was that right?* I wondered. *How could such an idiosyncratic association be judged or quantified?* The relationship between words became gradually harder to describe. "Allow and restrict." "They are both actions of authority," I said. "Tell me more," Harris replied. *Was I making this too complicated? Did I sound like I was trying too hard?* "They refer to the control of another person's actions," I suggested. Perhaps my association reflected my strong suspicion of authority, and the authority of this test in particular. Harris looked closely at his manual, possibly searching for a way to evaluate what I just said, but I couldn't really know for sure. He slowly nodded his head and said, "Okay," and we moved on to the next pair of words.

This was an unusual testing experience for both of us. So often the test administrator controls the pacing and direction of a test. The test-taker is subjected to the administrator's time frame and questions. But Harris and I politely battled for time control. I waited for Harris to write my answers down and follow the scoring guidelines in the manual. (I assumed he was doing this, but I couldn't actually see the manual. Asking to see it seemed like a breach of boundaries, and I didn't want to make him have to tell me no.) But I was taking notes, too, scribbling in a notebook to document the experience, which wouldn't have been allowed if this were a real test. Harris patiently waited for me to finish writing before moving on to the next question, but the silence as he waited and I wrote was heavy. I was disrupting the flow and rhythm of his work.

Harris recited an increasingly long series of numbers and asked me to repeat the numbers backward. The test gauged working memory, my ability to hold information in my head while using it to complete a task.

It was as if I were carrying too many glasses, stumbling to fit them all in my arms before they crashed to the floor, while Harris observed and did nothing. "Would you correct me if I got it wrong?" I asked. "I like how hard you are trying," he replied. After I recited about ten sequences, he said, "Let's try something else."

Cognitive tests ask us to stand alone and deny our instinct to connect to one another through affirmation and support. In a classroom, thinking happens through connection and positive feedback. But in this room the size of a large closet, none of these were offered. As Harris waited for my answers, I began to think about how the circumstances of testing were at odds with Louisa's social nature. There was no opportunity to feel excited about an idea or to connect to others, which were things that motivated her to think and answer questions in the first place.

I wanted Harris to validate me when I gave an answer, which is embarrassing to admit. It was important to me, I realized, that Harris thought I was smart. Intelligence holds so much power, but it needs to be demonstrated socially, outside of the mind. When I was a kid, I proved my intelligence through report cards, test scores, and incessantly raising my hand first in class to answer a question. Like many kids, I wanted to feel normal, but I also felt as if I had to be the best and most intelligent version of normal possible. The experience of taking an IQ test with Harris seemed surprisingly familiar in this way. It was as if I were back in high school, solving math problems and answering questions in class. My eagerness to perform intelligence—in high school and now with Harris—was also motivated by an urgency to demonstrate that I belonged, in calculus class, at a university, and in the broader middle-class world. The social anxieties I felt around intelligence made sense given Wechsler's way of defining intelligence. "Intelligence is an aspect of behavior," he wrote. "It has to do primarily with the appropriateness, effectiveness, and worthwhileness of what human beings do or want to do."

Wechsler does not acknowledge that the judgment of a person's behavior—whether it is acceptable—is determined by others, usually those who function in the privileged realm of normal. But he does admit that the assessment of intelligence is ultimately a judgment that it is consistent with the values of a particular time and place. The more questions I answered and puzzles I solved, the more I realized that IQ tests and the culture of academic achievement associated with them involve a policing of the boundaries of normal, an anxious competition to demonstrate belonging.

I recalled my dreams for Louisa to attend either Yale or Brown. This ambition was about me, not her. My desire to be the most outstanding version of normal meant that I wanted my child to succeed and belong in the exact same way. Having a child means that our desire to belong takes up more space in the world and that our sense of belonging is both in and out of our control. In problematic ways, the success and failure of our children impacts our sense of belonging as much as it does theirs.

WHEN LOUISA WAS nine, I signed her up to participate in a research study at Cincinnati Children's Hospital on how best to assess the cognitive abilities of people with Down syndrome. In this research study, a team of psychologists turned their scrutiny back on the tests, suggesting some doubt about how effectively they provide a good understanding of kids like Louisa. Given what I had learned so far about IQ tests, I made the decision to enroll her in the study with some trepidation. But I wanted to make sure I was doing all that I could to help her. And by participating in the study, I hoped that we might help psychologists more accurately measure the strengths and weaknesses of children with Down syndrome. We met every six months with Leila, a clinical research coordinator who gave Louisa a series of intelligence tests. Leila had well-kept red hair and dressed in blue scrub pants and a Cincinnati

Children's Hospital T-shirt. Before every meeting, she greeted us with a warm smile and handed me a bunch of forms to sign and an envelope with a debit card, which is how Louisa and I were paid for our time.

This research study was examining whether the cognitive tests were equally reliable for children with Down syndrome as for the rest of the population. The strategy reminded me of how Binet developed his IQ test more than a hundred years earlier—a process of trial and error to figure out which tests work and which ones do not. The study opened up room for skepticism about whether IQ tests could actually provide any meaningful information about Louisa's development and potential. IQ tests seemed to differentiate normal from not, but could they tell us more useful, individualized information about those kept out of that privileged concept of normal?

I felt ambivalent about Louisa's participation in the study. I was sure that these tests were not immediately harmful to her, but I felt guilty subjecting her to more of them than she needed to take. On the other hand, this was an opportunity to learn more about intelligence testing and help psychologists learn how to improve their assessment of Louisa's strengths and weaknesses. Although it didn't seem like much fun to me, Louisa liked meeting with Leila. "She is so nice," Louisa told me after each session. After our second meeting, I asked Leila if she might video-tape her next session with Louisa so I could study it, and to my surprise, she said yes.

"We're going to play the same games today," Leila said as Louisa took off her coat. Like my test with Harris, Louisa's intelligence test also con-sisted of a series of subtests, but for children they are described as games. They started off with a game Leila called "cat-dog." She showed Louisa a picture of a cat and asked her what it was. "Cat," Louisa answered. Leila repeated the question with a picture of a dog. Then she placed a piece of paper in front of Louisa with a grid. Each box contained a picture of either a cat or a dog. "Are you ready to go as fast as you can?" Leila pulled out her phone and started the timer. Louisa identified the animals while

Leila pointed to each one. Louisa's voice was engaged. She sat up straight and put her hands down on the table. "Ten seconds!" Leila exclaimed. "Wow, that's fast!" Louisa replied. "You're so fast," Leila responded as she made notes on the testing form.

"Remember the next part?" Leila said to Louisa and showed her the picture of the cat. "Remember what we say if we are silly?" "Dog," Louisa said. Leila showed Louisa the same grid of pictures, but this time Louisa was silly, reversing the identification of each picture to say the opposite. "Oh my goodness! You're a pro at being silly. Fifteen seconds!" Leila encouraged Louisa with feigned enthusiasm as she made notes on the test's worksheet.

Leila gave her a mix of cognitive tasks that come from several different test batteries, including the Differential Abilities Scales, the Developmental Neuropsychological Assessment, the Stanford-Binet Intelligence Scales, and the Wechsler Intelligence Scale for Children. Some of the games required Louisa to respond verbally. But others only asked her to point to the correct answer on a page in a spiral notebook, such as *point to something crunchy that elephants eat*. This acknowledges that not everyone can demonstrate their abilities through verbal means. Wechsler saw verbal and nonverbal tests as equally valid measures of intelligence. He believed that nonverbal tests reduced the risk of overdiagnosing intellectual disability due to tests that privileged verbal feedback. Individuals who have not had the chance to develop proficiency in English—either due to immigration, poor education, or hearing impairment—could still have a profound potential to learn.

Louisa was enthusiastic about test-taking in a way I was not. But like me, she was motivated by validation. Leila moved the pictures of cats and dogs to the side and took out a set of cards. "Now we're going to do color!" "Yes!" Louisa said. Leila asked Louisa to identify the colors on the flash cards. "That's a big clip!" Louisa said, looking at the binder clip that Leila had just taken off the laminated cards. "Go as fast as you can," Leila instructed. Many of the tests given to Louisa seem to be about speed, and the tests gradually got harder. Leila asked Louisa to identify the color and animal in a series of pictures on a page. She started off strong and then began to fade. Eventually she said "dog orange" instead of "orange dog" and slowed down, not matching the speed expected of her.

"DO YOU TELL people their scores?" I asked Harris at the beginning of our second testing session two weeks later. He explained that scores are normed by age and gender before they are shared with test-takers. The dictionary of the American Psychological Association defines a norm as "a standard or range of values that represents the typical performance of a group or of an individual (of a certain age, for example) against which comparisons can be made" or "a conversion of a raw score into a scaled score that is more easily interpretable, such as a percentile or an IQ score." In other words, test-takers eventually get to see scores and reports, but not raw data and not before the results are compared to others. Harris explained that clinicians will often "pump the brakes" on people wanting to immediately know their score, although they often want it. Psychologists treat IQ scores as complex data that must be interpreted and filtered through their own guidance and expertise. This seems like a responsible approach. But patients and clients often see the score as personal information that might influence how others see them, and want to control that information by knowing it right away. There is a discrepancy between how the expert and the non-expert value the test's score.

We began our session, and I tried to will a set of geometric tiles into the shape of a boat for a few minutes. "Do you have an answer?" Harris asked. I wasn't getting anywhere, and it seemed as if Harris was growing impatient. I thought I had it, then realized there was one point of a triangle sticking out, making my boat different from the one in the picture. "Let's move on," Harris said.

The next section assessed acquired knowledge. This part of the exam resembled a game of trivia:

Who was Martin Luther King Jr.?

What language has the most native speakers?

Who wrote *Hamlet*?

Who wrote *Alice in Wonderland*?

What is the measurement of the Earth at the equator?

What is the distance from the Earth to the sun?

For the last question, I responded, "I have no idea." "What's your best guess?" Harris replied. I rattled off a long number: 5,654,972 miles. Was this even in the ballpark?

I answered the questions as best as I could, but their cultural bias seemed obvious to me. Later on, Harris told me that his testing manual listed *the son of Martin Luther King Sr.* as one permissible answer to the first question, which made me wonder if clever improvisation and acquired knowledge were scored in the same way. Later, Harris told me that test scores are normed for a US sample, meaning that people who take IQ tests in France, India, or China are not expected to know the same information as people in the United States. But this still assumes that a country is an educational and cultural monolith, and that someone who knows who wrote *Hamlet* is more intelligent than someone who does not.

The expectation that an intelligent person would know who wrote *Hamlet* or *Alice in Wonderland* overvalues what the anthropologist John Ogbu called the "White middle-class ecocultural niche." Since IQ tests have been written primarily by white middle-class Americans, "the questions or tasks they use to elicit the intellectual skills in IQ tests are those that are familiar to the Western middle class." The bias apparently extends beyond questions about certain authors or scientific facts. According to psychologist Patricia Greenfield, even nonverbal tasks on IQ tests are culturally specific. In a study from 1998, she examined the Guilford-Zimmerman Aptitude Survey. One task on this exam asks the test-taker to identify an upside-down clock, rotate it mentally a quarter turn to the right, and then match the resulting visual perspective with one of five different drawings. Greenfield pointed out that the task is "extremely culture-specific." It requires knowledge of what a clock looks like. It also expects test-takers to be familiar with the visual symbol of an arrow and that its particular position on the test sheet means to describe the rotation of an object. It is easy to assume that a test-taker would know what a clock is, although perhaps this is less certain in the age of smartphones. Nonetheless, both Ogbu and Greenfield conclude that IQ tests assess how well someone functions within white middle-class American culture rather than some innate or universal intelligence.

While Harris recorded my answers, I thought about my own experience with how intelligence is asserted within my own ecocultural niche of white middle-class America, and why I quit the debate team in high school. During a tournament, the outcome of one particularly heated debate depended on what I said was the population of the United States. My answer would determine whether the solution to the nation's health care problems I proposed was financially possible. "Six million people?" I guessed. I knew I probably wasn't right, and the judge could not hide her contempt for my inept answer. "Six million people," she shot back. The opposing team snickered and my debate partner dropped her eyes to the desk and collected her notes. I felt utterly alone, as if I had just proved that I did not belong in the group of intelligent students that I was desperately trying to join. It was a moment of disempowerment, and I wondered if I had just doomed my future. Like most people who grow up with privilege, I was never really aware of it until it felt under threat.

As the other debaters got up and left, I sat down on a bench in the empty high school cafeteria. My cheeks burned with shame. I felt inferior because I did not have one factoid at my fingertips. In a similar way, Harris asked me to compute the earth's circumference and pressed me until I gave an answer. I knew my answer was wrong, and in that moment I realized that the shame I experienced in high school was because my belonging within the category of normal seemed under threat. If normal was ideal, I had strayed from normal, and it made me feel completely vulnerable and exposed.

My awareness of my compulsion to answer every question Harris asked as best as I could led me to realize that I didn't really have to. If I wanted to, I could have presented as someone entirely different than how I chose to identify. But it might not have endeared me to Harris if I made our few hours together into a full-on charade. So I didn't. I worked my ass off on that test for no really good reason except that it has been embedded in me to work my ass off on tests. It was the way that I felt like I belonged.

"UM, AFTER THIS I'm kind of hungry." Louisa knew the routine. At a previous testing session, Leila and Louisa took a trip to the vending machine after playing a few games and came back with some sort of packaged snack that I rarely allowed her to have. "Let's do a few more games and we can get you a snack," Leila said. "But you have to keep working hard." Leila explained to Louisa that she would say fifteen nouns out loud and she wanted her to remember as many as she could and say them back to her. Louisa recited back seven words and then put her elbows on the table and her hands over her eyes. She looked at her fingers, trying to remember more. "What else?" Leila prompted. I could see the timer on Leila's phone count the seconds, but Leila was looking off to her left, as if growing bored and restless like Louisa. "Can you think of any more?" Leila asked. She didn't look at Louisa and seemed lost in thought.

After a painfully long minute, Leila looked at her phone and said, "Time's up. Great job!" Leila glanced at her manual. "Guess what, Louisa? We get to do more!" Whenever Louisa got an answer right, or answered well enough according to the manual, she had to answer more questions. Louisa needed to get four in a row wrong before they could move on to another game. But her stamina was fading. "I'm supposed to have a snack," she retorted.

Halfway into the test, Louisa was still working through Leila's commands, but now she had her head down on the desk. She was getting squirmy. Leila asked Louisa to stand up like a statue at the edge of the table with one hand on the table and the other in a fist raised to her shoulder. "Eyes closed, don't move, don't talk until I say time's up, okay? Ready?" About ten seconds later, Leila fake-coughed. "Are you okay?" Louisa said. I realized that this was a test of whether Louisa could sustain focus. Her score, I knew, would be penalized for her interjection of empathy. A few seconds later, Leila tapped her knuckles on the table, and Louisa opened her eyes to see what made the noise. After a few more seconds, Leila told Louisa that she could sit down. "What's that?" Louisa asked Leila as she leaned over the table. "This is how I score you," Leila said. "How good of a statue you are. I think you're a pretty good statue." Louisa was curious about what Leila was writing, just as she was concerned if Leila was coughing because she was sick. But curiosity and moral compass are not part of the test's calculation.

Leila and Louisa left the room to visit the vending machine down the hall. Louisa returned from her break with a bag of Cheez-Its and seemed refreshed. But soon she couldn't keep her body still. She put her knees on the chair and rested her torso on the table. "I need you to list for me all the things you can think of that you eat or drink, like pizza or milk." "Pizza, milk, water, tacos." Louisa quickly slowed down, no longer interested in complying. She had lost focus and looked around at the other objects—a computer, dry erase markers, a telephone—stored in the room. For the next game, Leila showed Louisa a picture of a girl and they talked about which body parts were higher or lower on the girl's body. Leila recited sequences of body parts and Louisa had to repeat them, resequencing them from highest to lowest. "Mouth, nose," Leila said. Louisa looked at the picture and replied, "Nose, mouth." "That's right, Louisa. You went from highest to lowest." Shoveling in Cheez-Its,

Louisa seemed revived, and the visual cue of the picture was helpful. But the snack spoiled the pace of the test. "Elbow, wrist, hand," Leila recited, clearly trying to ignore Louisa's obvious exhaustion. Louisa glanced at her bag of crackers. "Hmm?" she said.

I cringed while watching Louisa squirm. I had internalized the expectations for focus and cooperation that were part of a system of intelligence that I wanted to fight against, and the conflict was about to make me burst. The research study was designed to evaluate the tests, and in that sense it was expected that many of the activities would not accurately measure Louisa's abilities. But Louisa was not taking these tests seriously, and unlike me, appeared to have no ingrained impulse to want to do well. As I watched Louisa squirm, unable to keep her body still after ninety minutes of testing, I found her behavior to be both frustrating and admirable. I was in awe of how she seemed impervious to wrong or right answers. Leila's company and encouragement were enough. But ultimately, I feared that these tests would have consequences, and I wanted Louisa to have the same opportunities and experiences as her peers who do much better on the IQ test than she could. Even though the concept of intelligence rooted in IQ testing was socially toxic, protecting the privileged inside its walls and keeping others out, I couldn't let go of the fact that I wanted Louisa to belong.

When Louisa finished the test, her capacity to pay attention stretched to its limits, I was waiting by the door. We hugged and I exhaled a tension I didn't know I was carrying. Although the research study was supposed to acknowledge that IQ tests do not accurately show the abilities of people with Down syndrome, I still wanted her to do well on them. Out of habit, I asked Leila, "How did she do?" as if Louisa was the one who was being evaluated, rather than the test itself.

"The assessment of intelligence inevitably is a value judgment," Wechsler wrote in 1975. In the tests that Leila gave to Louisa, speed, focus, and self-sufficiency were valued highly. These are the values of our modern society, the white, middle-class ecocultural niche. We are tested against those standards of intelligence, but I wondered if it would really be possible to judge other values as important too. Louisa performed about as expected on the tests, which is to say, badly. But watching the tests unfold gave me a different perspective. Her test scores may have been low, but I saw so many of the things that made her my favorite human. She was concerned when Leila coughed, she refused to sit still for more than forty-five minutes, and by god, she wanted a snack. These were not behaviors recorded in her test results. In fact, they seemed to be entirely overlooked, outside of the values that IQ tests assessed. If I hadn't seen Louisa take these tests, if I hadn't pushed for access to the tests in ways usually denied to parents like me, I might have never considered the bigger picture.

A Laboratory and a Garden

After Louisa finished the research study, I found myself wondering whether the ambitions of psychologists like Leila and her team at Cincinnati Children's were realistic. Was it really possible to use the results of an IQ test to help Louisa succeed and do her best at school? Given the ways in which IQ tests have helped classify and discriminate against people with intellectual disabilities, wouldn't it be better to reject them entirely? Binet's and Weschler's intentions were decent enough, but I had yet to dive into the ugliest parts of the IQ test's history. I needed a better understanding of this dark past to decide whether that history could be overcome. I decided to visit the Cummings Center for the History of Psychology at the University of Akron to study the papers of Henry Goddard, the psychologist who transformed Binet's relatively informal studies of intelligence into a systematic method of social classification. I had already read many of Goddard's published papers before making the drive to Akron, but I wanted to see his archive for myself. I hoped that looking at his drafts, his private papers, his letters, might give me a better understanding of how Goddard's research still informs Louisa's future, and how different her life can be from the lives of those who Goddard studied.

I left at dawn before Louisa was awake and drove an hour on flat, two-lane state routes until I reached I-70. Fields of corn stretched for miles until they met the delicate pink of the rising sun. Barns and old farmhouses popped up on the horizon. Farm equipment sat on brown dirt like alien spacecraft that had landed overnight. It was a cool morning in September after rain the night before. The corn was at its peak, just beginning to turn yellow at its tips. All the roads looked the same, each one surrounded by thick fields, and intersections seemed to arise from nowhere. A thick fog hovered above the wet pavement, settling into the bristles of corn. I could barely see the road twenty yards in front of me. After living here for more than ten years, I still get lost.

I finally reached the interstate and began to traverse Ohio. The cornfields soon gave way to long stretches of highway marked by billboards that alternated between advertisements for sex shops located at the next exit and announcements of the end of days, warning me to accept Christ or else. As I headed into the northeast corner of the state, industrial smokestacks and tract housing gradually replaced the fields and farms.

The Cummings Center occupies a five-story building in downtown Akron. The brick facade stays true to Akron's industrial roots as the rubber tire capital of the nation. A row of large glass windows on the second floor gives the building, which now houses a library, museum, and archive, a sense of lightness and transparency. I pulled into the adjacent parking lot and looked around. Another brick building with a facade of garage doors was across the street. Orange-and-white-striped construction cones stood on the far side of the parking lot, next to a chain-link fence. The campus of the University of Akron was just a block away, but I didn't see any students hurrying to class. It was midmorning, but the sidewalks and streets were nearly empty.

After I checked in for my appointment, I sat at one of the twenty large desks aligned in a rank-and-file grid. The archivist wheeled out several boxes of files on a cart and parked it near my desk. I opened a folder and a photograph of the Vineland Training School, where Goddard did most of his work, fell out of a stained and softened envelope. Buildings sat within a landscape that looked like the fields I drove through that morning. Dirt roads intersected to create a broad pattern over the fields of grass and trees. The photograph was dated 1898. The scattered buildings in a field I was looking at were probably what Goddard saw when he came to Vineland for the first time.

Goddard came late to psychology. A New England Quaker, he was a high school teacher and principal for six years before enrolling in the PhD program in psychology at Clark University. He then taught at Pennsylvania's West Chester Teacher's College. But his big professional break came at age forty, when he was named director of research at the Training School in Vineland, New Jersey. Edward Johnstone, the Training School's superintendent, invited Goddard to begin a scientific laboratory to study the children who lived there. The invitation marked a turning point in how institutions like the Training School characterized their purpose. Rather than serving only as a charitable hospice for children labeled as feeble-minded, the school became an opportunity to study human behavior in increasingly scientific ways.

At the Training School, Goddard redefined IQ tests as a diagnosis of how much a child's intellect strayed from normal, and managed to convince thousands of American teachers and school administrators that cognitive assessment was an essential part of education. By 1915, seven years after he first learned about Binet's test, he had distributed more than 22,000 copies of the exam to teachers in all parts of the United States. In the hands of Goddard, the IQ test morphed into a tool to identify genetic inferiority and degeneracy. "Stated in its boldest form," Goddard wrote in 1920 when the eugenics movement was sweeping the nation, "our thesis is that the chief determiner of human conduct is a unitary mental process which we call intelligence; that this process is conditioned by a nervous mechanism which is inborn." Goddard was a staunch believer in the hereditary nature of intelligence and fought ardently for the eugenic improvement of humankind.

The Training School consisted of several small cottages and Assembly Hall, the school's administration building, set among the bucolic fields of the rural town of Vineland, about thirty miles south of Philadelphia. These cottages were nestled together in the middle of flat farmland and housed around 300 children. Vineland was both a home and a school. One cottage included a playhouse, another included a piano for evening singing. It also included a farm with gardens, stables, carpentry, and cobbler's shops. Farm chores and manual labor served as a form of rehabilitation and job training for those who lived there. But the rural setting also hid its inhabitants at a safe distance from more populated areas and isolated them from the modern world.

The strange paternalism of the place was perhaps best captured by child psychologist Earl Barnes in 1903. "To me Vineland is a laboratory and a garden where unfortunate children are to be cared for, protected, and loved while they unconsciously whisper to us syllable by syllable the secrets of the soul's growth. It may very well be that the most ignorant shall teach us the most." Like plants in a botanical greenhouse, those who lived there were under the careful supervision of their caretakers, scientists and researchers who saw them as subjects to be studied and problems to be solved. But the garden metaphor seems particularly apt in another important way. Goddard's work with the residents of the Training School would be dramatically influenced by Gregor Mendel's scientific study of garden peas and the study of genetics that he sparked.

Hunched over my desk, reading these texts from the first decades of the twentieth century, I started to notice the use of words of striking opposition to describe the same place: laboratory *and* garden; repulsive children *and* happy places. Although we use different words to describe these places today, there are still so many ways in which people with intellectual disabilities are separated from their peers, presumably for the good of both groups. If IQ tests were originally developed to fulfill this purpose, how could they ever be used for anything better? Why should I trust Leila, her research team, and other psychologists to use them to help Louisa?

GODDARD HAD VERY little experience with people he referred to as feeble-minded before he took the job at Vineland. But he was intent on bringing order to the Training School by transforming the care of its residents into something more scientific. On a two-month trip to Europe in the spring of 1908, Goddard heard about Binet's test, but was unimpressed with its impact. "Binet's lab is largely a myth," he wrote in his diary. "There are no special classes in French schools, and only the worst cases are sent to institutions." The purpose of Binet's test was to identify children in the French public school system who would benefit from extra help in the classroom. But Goddard wondered if he might use the test to identify a child's inherent intellectual capacity.

Goddard realized that Binet's test could solve a persistent problem in psychological research. Those who lived in American institutions were previously categorized by appearance and symptoms. Diagnoses were often based on the intuition of a physician, but there were no objective measures to study and compare particular cases. The term "feeble-minded" was applied to most inmates of mental institutions. The same patient could be described as an "idiot" by one physician but as an "imbecile" by another. The language of psychology lacked precision. There were plenty of case studies, yet psychologists weren't talking about their patients in the same way.

When he returned from Europe, Goddard equipped his lab at the Training School with state-of-the-art research equipment, including an ergograph for measuring the energy used in muscular movement, a photography darkroom, an automotograph for recording involuntary movements of the hands and arms, and, of course, the equipment needed to administer Binet's test. Goddard relied closely on the form board test, which measured the time it took a child to arrange ten blocks in the holes that corresponded to their shape. Binet adapted the form board test from the research of Edouard Séguin, who first developed the exercise as a nonverbal assessment of intellectual ability in 1856.

While Binet described the intelligence of children by using the term "mental level," Goddard solidified the idea of mental age, which provided a more radical reframing of time. "Mental age" prioritized a linear sense of intellectual growth and progress measured in relation to their actual age. After giving Binet's test to children at Vineland, Goddard proposed that "idiot" would be used to describe those who had no higher intelligence than a two-year-old. Those who had intelligence "from three to seven years" would be imbeciles. For a third grouping, those with a mental age from eight to twelve, Goddard proposed a new term, "moron." This last group concerned Goddard the most because these children could slip through the cracks and most easily pass for normal. He describes how he considered other terms, too, like deviates, the almosts, or proximates. But these terms, according to Goddard, did not have the right sound. "Our public school systems are full of them," Goddard wrote, "and yet Superintendents and Boards of Education are struggling to make normal people out of them." The IQ test could more definitively identify this group and place them in institutions, where Goddard thought they belonged.

In 1910, Goddard published the tests proposed by Binet for children between the ages of three and thirteen. Three-year-olds are asked to identify their nose, their eyes, their mouth. Six-year-olds are shown a picture with the heads of six women in three pairs. "The one pretty and the other ugly or even deformed," Goddard wrote. "Which is the prettier?" "At six all choose correctly; at five about half." Goddard illustrated the pairs of crude line drawings. With the Eurocentric bias of the IQ test fully on display, the drawings of women with high cheekbones, dainty noses, and small mouths appear next to faces with bulbous noses, protruding jaws, and apelike features. The test affirms one conception of beauty, while others are discounted as incorrect. When looking at these drawings, I recalled the question about who wrote *Hamlet* when I took the IQ test with Harris and tried to imagine a young boy or girl taking this test in elementary school in the early twentieth century. Although they were more than a hundred years apart, both experiences conflate cultural bias with intelligence.

Goddard's influence spread quickly. In 1911, he boasted about the 2,000 pupils he included in his studies of intelligence, a number that seemed impressive at the time, but is now drastically overshadowed by the millions of children who have taken IQ tests since. Testing provided valuable scientific data. The more children who took the test, the more accurate the bell curve of intelligence would be. Schoolchildren were tested one by one by a team of trained examiners. In June, Goddard published the test results and reached two conclusions: that the Binet scale was "wonderfully accurate" and that "a child cannot learn the things that are beyond his grade of intelligence." Goddard described that the results fit into a "normal curve of distribution," with most children (78 percent) testing "at age," or "normal and satisfactory." Four percent of students tested are "especially well-endowed," or "gifted," and he said that these students should get the best teachers and most opportunities, the extra advantages that they deserved.

Goddard declared that 18 percent of the children tested were feeble-minded, and his recommendations set the stage for special needs classrooms for most of the twentieth century:

> Educationally the conclusion is forced upon us that it is very unfair to the normal child to keep these children in the same class with him.

They should be segregated and given a special teacher who understands their case and is allowed to train them as their mental condition will permit. Of course, ultimately they ought all to go to the institutions for the Feeble Minded where they will be cared for and prevented from contaminating society; but until this can be done, the special class for defectives is probably the wisest solution.

Soon after Goddard published his results, the New Jersey legislature passed laws that required public schools to give all students IQ tests and provide separate classes for those with low IQ scores, if they were enrolled in school at all. These classes, Goddard believed, were essential to the isolation of the feeble-minded and the next best thing to institutionalization, which the country could not afford.

In 1912, the United States Public Health Service invited Goddard to Ellis Island, where he administered Binet's test to the "great mass of average immigrants." The American Immigration Act of 1882 barred "lunatics and idiots" from entering the country. But as a new wave of southern and eastern European immigrants began to arrive at Ellis Island at the turn of the century, apparently a more scientific means of exclusion was necessary. As immigrants stepped onto Ellis Island, tired or disoriented from an unimaginably hard journey, Goddard and his team of IQ test administrators surveyed the crowds, looking for those who might be likely testing subjects. After some experience, Goddard's team acquired a discerning eye and were able to get "a sense of what a feeble-minded person is so that he can tell one afar off." The examiners' skills yielded shockingly efficient yet biased results. Ordinary doctors who were screening immigrants at Ellis Island were only catching 10 percent of "defective" immigrants looking to enter the country. "While with the Binet scale it was possible to get ninety percent," Goddard claimed. Goddard found that 79 percent of Italians, 80 percent of Hungarians, 83 percent of Jews, and 87 percent of Russians were feeble-minded. Rather than considering problems with the test, language barriers, or how transatlantic immigration might create traumatic circumstances for test-takers, Goddard declared that "immigrants were of surprisingly low intelligence."

The astonishing percentages of people who were categorized as feeble-minded in these early IQ tests was an outcome of bias, inadequate standardization, poor administration, and general growing pains of drafting the right tests. Nonetheless, the results did not seem to warn the public of the potential inaccuracy of information gleaned from an IQ test. Instead, it stoked the fires of a national paranoia that feeble-mindedness was on the rise and immigration and racial difference were the main causes. In 1915, psychologist J. E. Wallace Wallin called for the "compulsory official identification and registration of feeble-minded children" and their immediate segregation, "to investigate them with scientific thoroughness," which meant institutionalizing feeble-minded children in places like the Training School.

GODDARD KEPT INDIVIDUAL case studies of the children he worked with at the Training School. These descriptions helped me see beyond the test scores and statistics that Goddard was developing. They preserved some sense of the humanity of struggling children who found themselves at the Training School. But they also made it painfully clear that low intelligence was associated with deviance and misbehavior. In one case study, Goddard describes an eleven-year-old girl named Abbie who was "gluttonous, untidy, untruthful, indolent, sly, profane, obstinate, and stealthy." Mentally, she had the development of a seven-year-old. Looking back on her time at the Training School, Goddard regretted efforts spent on her education. Once it was possible to assess her intelligence with the Binet scale, it was clear to him that she had reached her intellectual limit long ago.

Among Goddard's papers, I found an unpublished daily record of Clarence Chambers, who came to the Training School on July 30, 1897, nine years before Goddard's arrival. Clarence often woke in the middle of the night screaming and singing, disturbing the others in his dormitory. To correct the behavior, Clarence was taken outside and a headmaster, Mr. Kilburn, forced him to dig dirt and throw it into a hole until dawn. On some nights, a quick slap to the face made him stop screaming. On others, Clarence was whipped until he was quiet. The screaming persisted for years. No real efforts to alleviate Clarence's distress are recorded, but the abuse continued. Those like Clarence and Abbie with low IQ scores were presumed to have limited capacity and therefore limited worth. It was this belief that allowed their abuse to be justified.

While reading the cold, clinical records of Abbie and Clarence and studying photographs of other children lined up on benches in the middle of fields at Vineland, dressed in well-kept dresses and neatly pressed suits, these children rose up as ghosts in my mind. I thought about how these children might have lived as apparitions for their families too. They still existed yet were kept away, out of sight and without a chance to really live, grow, and learn. As I looked at these ghosts, I felt an ache in my chest as I thought about Louisa and how painful it was to be separated from her, even for only a couple of days. *She is with me*, I told myself and imagined her at school as I sat in the archive.

BEFORE KINDERGARTEN, LOUISA attended a half-day preschool program for children with developmental delays. One morning Louisa, Andy, and I waited on a wooden bench outside the school bathrooms. A long hallway separated us from the classroom. The preschool aide was trying to coax a boy named Amal down the hallway to class. Amal was unwilling, and collapsed to the floor in the middle of the hallway in a heap. Some other parents and children were beginning to arrive, waiting for the teacher to greet us. We watched while Tracey, the aide, dragged Amal down the hallway by his legs for a few feet, until one of the preschool teachers heard Amal's screams and came out of the classroom. The three of us sat on the bench and my heart raced. I pulled Louisa closer to me and squeezed her hand.

I did not recognize what I should have done quickly enough. I think about what I saw frequently and live with the regret that I did nothing to help Amal. Why did I not get up and tell Tracey to stop? I had been socially conditioned not to interject, as if a child with behavioral challenges was part of a separate world. I did not know how to respond to a child who falls to the floor and screams. Amal was communicating something, but he was not being heard. Tracey simply saw a boy who would not cooperate. There was no reason, it seemed, to tend to his emotions or his needs. By being dragged down the hall, Amal—like Clarence at the Training School over a hundred years earlier—was experiencing a form of institutional power that diminished his dignity as a human being and reinforced, to everyone watching, the damaging belief that he was worth very little effort.

This aggression happens more often to children with intellectual disabilities, to boys than girls, and to children of color than children who are white. In fact, a study conducted by the Government Accountability Office in 2018 found that Black students, boys, and students with disabilities were disproportionately the focus of disciplinary action in public schools. Students with disabilities account for 11.7 percent of all public school students, but represent about 25 percent of students suspended from school for disciplinary reasons—an overrepresentation of about 13 percentage points.

Tracey doted on Louisa, fawning over her sweet smile and adorable clothes. Amal communicated his needs differently, in a way that Tracey was unwilling to deal with. But Louisa, I realized, was vulnerable to the same biases that Amal was. After all, Louisa will grow and not always be perceived as cute. What might happen to her then? I began to understand the way that Tracey fawned over Louisa diminished her human dignity as much as her abuse of Amal.

I cannot excuse Tracey's choice to physically drag an emotionally overwhelmed child down the hall, and I cannot excuse myself for sitting on a bench and watching it happen. But I know that someone with no training in early childhood education should not have such a crucial job. Our education system does not recognize the value of educational assistants. When Louisa was in preschool, it paid $11 an hour with no benefits. Some other parents and I eventually spoke up about what we had seen, and Tracey was removed from the classroom. But since we live in a small town, I still see Tracey occasionally. She walks by our house and mentions that she likes the Christmas lights that we string along our chicken coop in December. I say thank you, but keep Louisa far away from her.

I SPENT TWO days at the Cummings Center in Akron, delving into IQ testing and Goddard's efforts to segregate those who did poorly on it. When I left the archive after the first day, I noticed that I had missed a phone call from Louisa's school. I knew from experience that a call from school in the middle of the day was never good. Either Louisa was sick or in trouble. Panicked that I didn't know what was going on and school was over for the day, I called Andy.

"Apparently, Louisa pinched a friend in the classroom," Andy told me. The principal had called him when he couldn't reach me. With Louisa sitting in his office, the principal relayed to Andy that Louisa had repeatedly pinched until her friend finally cried out in help. Louisa was in the fourth grade, and this was not the first call we had received about her behavior. Andy knew the routine. The call to her parents was part of Louisa's punishment; she was supposed to feel ashamed that the principal had to call. Although we were grateful that the school communicated with us, it wasn't clear to me that Louisa needed to be punished at all. "Why did Louisa do this?" I asked Andy, convinced that something must have provoked Louisa to pinch her friend. "I don't know," Andy replied, "The principal said that Louisa wouldn't talk about it. She was sitting in his office with her head down, her hands covering her face."

I felt the frustration of getting information second- and thirdhand rise up in me. This time it was Andy's turn to take the call from the principal, and I wasn't sure what I would have said if I would have picked up the phone. Were we supposed to apologize for Louisa's behavior? What exactly did he need us to say? I knew that this was a moment in which Louisa needed an advocate, yet we couldn't get a sense of what had happened. And, of course, this happened on a day when I was hours away. It took a bit of coaxing, but Andy was finally able to get a fuller picture of the situation from Louisa after we talked on the phone. Her friend had repeatedly closed Louisa's computer lid. Their teacher had told the students it was time to stop working on their computers, but Louisa did not want to stop whatever it was that she was doing. Her friend was trying to be helpful but she overstepped, and Louisa didn't like it.

Recounting the details seems a bit silly, like it magnifies the importance of a relatively minor conflict. Such events are part of growing up, and learning to deal with peer conflict is a lesson everyone eventually must face. Louisa needed to learn to use her words. But it bothered me that she was sent to the principal's office and not her friend, who had somehow avoided a temporary removal from the classroom. I am sure that this was because Louisa didn't explain her actions clearly and immediately. Facing the pressure of disciplinary action, Louisa was silent, and the silence was read by the adults involved as an admission of guilt. Louisa was unable to communicate, to her friend, to her teacher, or to the principal, and this led to her temporary removal from the classroom.

The incident was not particularly serious, and Louisa was welcomed back to the classroom after her time in the principal's office. But removing a child with a disability from a classroom for behavioral reasons is an astonishingly frequent practice. According to the US Department of Education, there were 1,591,473 removals of students with disabilities from school during the 2019–2020 school year, and the number has remained consistent for a decade. This number was reached, presumably, before schools around the country moved online due to the pandemic, and it is likely that even more removals occurred in a less formal way. These removals often involve a call to parents reporting that their child has caused a disruption in the classroom and must be picked up immediately. Parents must abandon their work commitments to pick up their child. Sometimes the removal is only for an hour or two; sometimes it is longer.

Valerie Williams, the Director of the Office of Special Education Programs in the Department of Education, has argued that removals occur when school personnel lack strategies to mitigate disruptive behavior. In other words, schools often see behavior as offensive and dangerous rather than the communication of a particular need. The removal of a student from a classroom often comes with a longer punishment, in which a child must earn their way back. This discriminatory practice places the burden on students to act normal and fit in, rather than calling on educators to develop appropriate intervention and inclusion practices.

There are efforts underway in Williams's office to minimize this practice through preventive strategies that better prepare educators to meet the behavioral needs of all of their students. But it is equally important to acknowledge where this instinct to segregate and remove originates. The practice is rooted in Goddard's beliefs that it is best for everyone if those with intellectual differences are removed from the classroom. According to Goddard, those students with low IQs are not worth any real effort precisely because their capabilities are fixed, as he claimed to demonstrate with the case of Abbie. Each removal means time away from teachers, peers, and friends. It perpetuates the same message, to people with intellectual disabilities and to their peers, that Goddard spread one hundred years earlier. It tells the world they do not belong.

* * *

IN ADDITION TO bringing order to the classification and study of the feeble-minded, Goddard also applied Gregor Mendel's theory of dominant and recessive genes to the concept of intelligence, and theorized that "feeble-mindedness" was caused by a single recessive gene. Based on Mendel's experiments with pea plants, Goddard's approach to IQ suggested that if both parents passed a single gene along during reproduction, then the child would be feeble-minded. If that person was allowed to reproduce, then a single gene would potentially cause generations of mental deficiency.

With a codified language in place, Goddard soon focused his laboratory experiments on questions of eugenics to prove that Mendel's law of heredity applied to human intelligence as well as plants and animals. The Training School provided the ideal conditions to find an answer to such a question. Per an article in the *Popular Science Monthly*, "This institution has comparatively few children (390 in all), and many of these come from wealthy families whose ancestry is known or from families who have lived in New Jersey for several generations." The apparent stability of New Jersey's wealthy families provided a kind of experimental control of economic and racial status, which allowed Goddard to approach feeble-mindedness as a genetic characteristic that could be traced with as much clarity as height or eye color. Mendel's hybrid pollinations provided the framework for this extreme form of determinism, in which humans are helpless to overcome their immutable genes.

America's interest in eugenics began before Goddard's work at Vineland. In 1895, the legislature of Connecticut passed a law prohibiting people deemed to be hereditarily unworthy from marrying. Indiana authorized forced sterilization in 1907. But Goddard's work with Binet's IQ test married statistics to discrimination, providing a scientific logic that supported eugenic sterilization. As Goddard described, "feeble-mindedness" was a vague term used to describe the marginalized and the dispossessed. But by using the IQ test to "prove" its heritability, it gave blatant discrimination the aura of scientific validity. It also lumped those marginalized due to disability, race, or poverty into one indistinct group. "Feeble-minded" was the most common way to describe anyone who did not do well on an IQ test in the early twentieth century, no matter if the performance was due to genetics or a lack of education.

Goddard wove the heredity of feeble-mindedness into one family's history. "One bright October day, fourteen years ago, there came to the Training School at Vineland, a little eight-year-old girl." This is how Goddard began *The Kallikak Family*, his most popular and influential study on the heritability of feeble-mindedness. The widely popular book framed Deborah Kallikak as the living legacy of a family's chronic unemployment, criminal tendencies, feeble-mindedness, and general threat to "racial hygiene." Goddard explained that Deborah was given the Binet IQ test when she was twenty-one. "By the Binet Scale this girl showed, in April 1910, the mentality of a nine-year-old child with two points over . . . This is a typical illustration of the mentality of a high-grade feeble-minded person, the moron, the delinquent, the kind of girl or woman that fills our reformatories. They are wayward, they get into all sorts of trouble and difficulties, sexually and otherwise." She failed the tests that involved counting money, vocabulary, and reading comprehension. She rhymed *storm* with *spring*. Despite the best efforts of her teachers, Deborah seemed unable to learn. How do we account for this individual? "Heredity," Goddard answers. "Bad stock."

According to school records, Deborah was brought to the gates of the Training School because she did not get along with the other children at school. She was of average size and weight. She could wash and dress herself and was described as a good listener. She could not read or count, which should not have been surprising because she had not attended school regularly. Deborah had grown up poor with an unstable home life. Despite these conditions, Goddard was convinced that her IQ apparently uncovered something genetically inherited, rather than reflecting childhood poverty.

Goddard's genealogical study of Deborah Kallikak's feeble-mindedness begins with her great-great-grandfather Martin Kallikak, a soldier in the American Revolution who sired the offspring of an allegedly feeble-minded barmaid. Martin apparently turned his life around and married an upstanding Quaker woman, producing another line of descendants who, according to Goddard, were "respectable citizens, men and women prominent in every phase of life." By uncovering this genealogy, Goddard could set up a kind of experiment to prove that feeble-mindedness was heritable and best cut off at the source.

Goddard enlisted a group of field workers between 1909 and 1910 to determine the intelligence of Deborah's parents and grandparents. According to Goddard, field workers would ask relatives a series of questions to gauge their intelligence and the intelligence of earlier ancestors. "Three generations back is easy," Goddard boasted, "and six is not impossible." Goddard narrates an example, in which a field worker asks an old farmer, "'Do you remember an old man, Martin Kallikak, who lived on the mountain edge yonder?'" "'Nobody'd forget him,'" the farmer replied. "'Simple, not quite right here (tapping his head) but inoffensive and kind.'" Goddard then rhetorically asks his reader, "Is there any doubt that Martin was feeble-minded?"

Goddard's evaluation of the intelligence of a person's ancestors, and therefore his theory of the inheritance of feeble-mindedness, is based on indirect recollection. Scholars have tracked Goddard's original research on Deborah's ancestry. Unsurprisingly, they have found that both the "good" and the "evil" side of the family included success and hardship. In this way, the IQ test served as a cruel measure of circumstance, a way to quantify a person's misfortunes at the hands of our brutal system of social power.

The last chapter of *The Kallikak Family* asks, "What Is to Be Done?" But Goddard is not concerned with how Deborah can be helped. He means what can be done to protect people like him from people like her. Indeed, it is the moron, who can stealthily integrate into society, who is the most dangerous. Goddard suggested "segregation and colonization" as the most reasonable plan. Such colonization would reduce the population of feeble-minded by a third in a single generation. Goddard suggested "asexualization" or sterilization as another solution. The process, Goddard wrote, is "as simple in males as having a tooth pulled. In females it is not much more serious."

The suspect nature of evidence for feeble-mindedness in Goddard's time is appalling. When coupled with the quantitative data of the IQ test, it turns dangerous. Yet there is evidence that the ways in which children are placed in special education programs today are just as unscientific. In 2007, the US Department of Education indicated a three-to-one ratio of being identified with "mental retardation" for African American students to Caucasian students. These students have a higher probability of being categorized by schools with this label than being categorized with any other high incidence disability. It is often assumed that special education primarily serves students who have intellectual disabilities, or vision or hearing differences. But a research study conducted by the National Center for Education Statistics during the 2020–2021 school year discovered that only 10 to 15 percent of all students in special education programs are associated with one of these three categories. The most common (32 percent) categorization of students in special education is specific learning disability. These students, according to Kalman Hettleman's *Mislabeled as Disabled: The Educational Abuse of Struggling Learners and How We Can Fight It*, are struggling learners who have been failed by general education and are "dumped" into special education and slighted because of low to average IQ scores.

Margaret J. McLaughlin, a professor of special education at the University of Maryland, has described a need to "take special education policy back to its roots as an educational law that pertains only to students with clear and evident disabilities . . . as opposed to having special education programs provide compensatory services for students whose only 'disability' has been poor or insufficient general education." McLaughlin draws attention to the consistent conflation of disability and socioeconomic disadvantages. Yet reading about Goddard made me skeptical about whether there was a better special education policy to return to and whether determining who does and does not have access to a regular classroom could ever be done in an equitable way.

My trip to the archive revealed that the biases associated with distinguishing a psychological diagnosis from socioeconomic impoverishment have always been present. It also suggested that IQ tests have been consistently used as a tool of social classification and segregation as much as scientific diagnosis. What really, I began to ask, is all this for? Why do researchers and psychologists hold on to the potential of the IQ to help children like Louisa? After days in the archive, I still couldn't find a satisfying answer. It seemed as if intelligence assessment never really helped teachers meet the needs of all students. It prevented one classification of children from interacting with another. It justified the neglect of those who needed help the most.

IN THE FACE of the feverish spread of IQ testing, some psychologists did voice concern and call for a more coherent picture of intelligence. According to one psychologist, Goddard turned the IQ test "into a fetish to be worshiped and protected from all doubt and attack, particularly in the educational field." In 1922, journalist Walter Lippmann wrote a six-part series of articles examining the claim, "now widely made and accepted, that the psychologists have invented a method of measuring the inborn intelligence of all people." Lippmann did not have much respect for the methods of IQ testing. He claimed that psychologists "guess at a stunt which might indicate intelligence" to design an

IQ test's content. He also pointed out that the IQ test favored certain types of abilities. "The type of mind which is very apt in solving Sunday newspaper puzzles, or even in playing chess, may be specially favored by these tests," he wrote. But he was most concerned with how susceptible results were to misinterpretation. "The real promise and value of the investigation which Binet started," Lippmann wrote, "is in danger of gross perversion by muddleheaded and prejudiced men."

In the year after he called for a national registry of feeble-minded children, psychologist J. E. Wallace Wallin had a change of heart about the accuracy of the Binet test. He gave the test to the most American of demographics, a group of Iowa farmers. "Not a single one of these persons could by any stretch of the imagination be considered feeble-minded," he wrote. But based on their IQ scores, every one of the farmers tested would be considered as such. The results suggested to Wallin that psychologists were playing "fast and loose with such vague and undefined concepts as 'defective children,' 'mental deficiency,' 'mental defect,' 'defectiveness,' 'subnormality,' 'feeble-mindedness,' 'monornity,' and 'criminal imbecility.'" But when new immigrants to the United States were the ones labeled as feeble-minded, Wallin voiced no objection. The intelligence of Iowa farmers was the only kind that counted.

These warnings were not heeded. In 1927, the US Supreme Court ruled that the forced sterilization of those with low IQs did not violate the Fourteenth Amendment's equal protection clause. In his majority opinion in *Buck vs. Bell*, Justice Oliver Wendell Holmes declared that those with low IQs "sap the strength of the State" and "three generations of imbeciles are enough." The ruling allowed the eugenic sterilization of Carrie Buck, who had lived at the Virginia State Colony for Epileptics and Feeble-Minded since 1924. Her foster parents left her there when she was seventeen and pregnant. As Adam Cohen explores in his book *Imbeciles: The Supreme Court, American Eugenics, and the Sterilization of Carrie Buck*, Holmes's ruling delivered a "clarion call" to Americans to identify those who were feeble-minded. "It is better for all the world," Holmes wrote, "if instead of waiting to execute degenerate offspring for crime, or to let them starve for their imbecility, society can prevent those who are manifestly unfit from continuing their kind." As cruel as Holmes's words may seem to us today, denying the impact of them on social policy for the rest of the twentieth century was not so easy. This Supreme Court decision has yet to be overturned.

The Kallikak Family became a national bestseller. In *The Mismeasure of Man*, evolutionary biologist Stephen Jay Gould called it "the primal myth of the eugenics movement." Perhaps *The Kallikak Family* gained such national attention because of its purported ties to American roots. As a soldier in the American Revolution, Martin Kallikak represented two paths for the future of the new nation, and it was up to all Americans to choose the right path. *The Kallikak Family* went through multiple editions and was reprinted in Germany in 1933, the same year that the Nazi government passed the "Law for the Prevention of Offspring with Hereditary Defects Act," which was modeled on the eugenics laws of Indiana and California.

In 1945, long after he left the Training School and retired from his position as a professor of psychology at Ohio State University, Goddard published an article called "A Suggested Definition of Intelligence." After the catastrophic damage done to humanity at the hands of eugenics by the end of World War II, Goddard could still only tentatively suggest a definition of intelligence. "No one has produced a definition that satisfies," he wrote, admitting that the conception of intelligence rests on shaky ground. Nonetheless, Goddard offered the following: "Intelligence is the degree of availability of one's experiences for the solution of his present problems and the anticipation of future ones." To demonstrate what he meant, Goddard described Clarence, perhaps the same boy whose screaming was logged in the daily record at the

Training School decades earlier, but there is no way to know for sure. Clarence was forced to stay with Goddard in his laboratory one afternoon for reasons not provided. But Clarence wanted to leave. Goddard shut the door to his laboratory and locked it. Clarence, perhaps agitated from his forced containment, tried the door repeatedly but never considered the lock. For Goddard, the anecdote illustrated Clarence's lack of problem-solving skills. But to me, the scene gets to the cruelest way of defining intelligence—as a form of power, control, and forced submission. Clarence becomes the laboratory experiment, and Goddard sees his uncooperative behavior as a sign of his lack of intelligence. I wonder how long it took Clarence to internalize his own oppression, knowing what punishment might come to him if he kept trying to escape.

WHEN HITLER'S ATROCITIES were discovered at the end of World War II, America's eugenics fever did not break. The segregation of Americans with intellectual disabilities in institutions became common policy, as the case of Philip Bard's short life told by his father in *The Atlantic* demonstrates. Children with disabilities were not guaranteed access to a public education in the United States until 1975, when President Gerald Ford signed the Education for all Handicapped Children Act. Although surgical sterilization would become less common in the 1950s, forced sterilization in the name of eugenics continued for the rest of the twentieth century. Oregon ordered its last forced sterilization in 1981. But the practice continues in other countries around the world.

By the end of 2021, three states had voted to pay financial reparations to the living victims of forced eugenic sterilization: North Carolina, Virginia, and California. More than 60,000 people were sterilized in thirty-two states during the twentieth century under legislation that permitted the practice in the name of the improvement of the human race. Only a handful of those who underwent forced sterilization are still alive. In Virginia, eleven survivors were known when the legislation passed in 2015.

Despite these efforts to address the history of eugenic sterilization, the profession of psychology also played a significant role in the use of IQ testing to turn the segregation and discrimination of people with intellectual differences into a justified practice. On October 29, 2021, the American Psychology Association issued an apology to people of color for its role in promoting and perpetuating racism and human hierarchy in the United States. But it has never issued a similar apology to people with intellectual disabilities for the field's role in eugenics and the use of IQ tests to perpetuate such a deeply immoral approach to psychological research.

It was the end of my second day, and the reading room was about to close. I put the folders and envelopes back into their sturdy boxes and arranged them in their correct order on the cart next to my desk. Louisa's experiences at school, the attitudes of her teachers and the psychologists that we have worked with, were different from what I saw and read about in the archive. The national policies on the education of people with intellectual disabilities have changed dramatically too. But as I packed up my things, I thought about Amal. I thought about ways in which people with intellectual differences are still segregated today.

I got in my car and headed across Ohio, leaving behind the industrial northeast for the rural southwest. Both seemed equally stuck, clinging to a vision of America that was rooted in the past and that I wanted to escape. As I reached the outskirts of Akron, I passed a tall, white van filled with passengers leaning against the windows. At that moment, the segregation and cruelty of Vineland seemed present, spilling out of the archive and into highway traffic, like ghosts rising up from the past.

I pressed on the gas pedal. Louisa would be getting home from school soon and heading off to gymnastics class, where she jumps and tumbles and does her best side by side with other kids her age. I couldn't wait to hold her close and see her glowing smile. As I passed the van, I screamed in sadness, alone in my car.

Functioning

The trip to the Cummings Center in Akron rattled me. I was shaken by the history I had confronted and I feared how my daughter's life could be shaped by it. I wanted to leave it alone, but I kept noticing ways in which our understanding of intelligence in the twenty-first century still held on to the ideas of the past.

I began to recall earlier conversations about Louisa that now seemed casually informed by IQ tests. When Louisa was about two, I was talking to a student in my office about a paper assignment when I noticed her glancing at Louisa's picture taped to my file cabinet. It had been given to me by one of her caretakers at her daycare, Mr. Paul. In the photograph, Louisa is about one year old. She sits on a brightly decorated rug with a toy car at her feet, hands resting on her chubby thighs, her tuft of baby hair combed forward. Mr. Paul took the photograph to celebrate Louisa's latest accomplishment, sitting up independently. He must have been on the floor with her and managed to get low enough for the camera to meet my daughter's curious gaze straight on. She is a chubby, Buddha-like mound with one sock on and one off, studying the camera in front of her. It is still one of my favorite photographs, not only because of the baby face it preserves. It also reminds me of the care and support of the nurturing Mr. Paul.

Louisa is dressed in one of her best outfits, a pair of green cotton pants dotted with flowers and a matching top. I loved buying baby clothes for Louisa. It was an implicit way in which I asserted my desire for belonging to those who saw her. *Look how well-groomed this baby is*, I wanted people to think. *Clearly, she has good parents. This child has a bright future ahead of her.* I hated it when Louisa's diaper leaked at daycare and she would come home in other clothes. Their laundered smell, different from the scent of our family's clothes, irritated me. The borrowed pants were often too big, feeling like a betrayal of how I wanted Louisa to be seen.

"Your daughter has Down syndrome," the student gasped. "My brother does too. He's grown-up now." Thrown by the personal connection, I managed to say something about how well Louisa was doing, how she was born with a small hole in her heart. No surgery was necessary; the cardiologist determined that the hole would heal on its own. Fifty percent of babies with Down syndrome are born with congenital heart defects, I told the student, trying to maintain some sense of professorial command. But she didn't seem interested in this statistic. "My brother has to have a peanut butter and jelly sandwich for lunch every day or he will flip out," the student replied. "Is your daughter high functioning or low functioning?"

Two years into motherhood, I didn't really know. Her heart was functioning, which was what mattered the most. Describing my daughter in terms of functioning felt like acquiescing to the values of the modern world. Progress and development are valued above all else, even in babyhood. I tried to think of Louisa as simply *being*, learning how to be in this world. But would she be able to talk? When would she be able to walk down stairs by herself? Would she be potty trained by the age of five? I wasn't really sure.

The student mentioned her brother's sandwich preference casually, but the detail stung. In my mind, I jumped to the conclusion that this student assumed a daily peanut butter and jelly sandwich was in Louisa's future too. It seemed circuitous, non-progressive, as if Louisa would never learn to try new things. The student's comparison of my daughter to her brother annoyed me, even though I had never met him. Was she implying that Louisa's fate was sealed? Was my daughter's future filled with nothing but simple routines? For me, the eternal return of the peanut butter and jelly sandwich meant a lack of development, change, and exploration. Perhaps this routine suited my student's brother, but I had to believe that more was possible for Louisa.

Louisa has never really cared much for peanut butter sandwiches. She likes chocolate, eggs prepared in all ways, and almost all varieties of fruits and vegetables, though not squash or sweet potatoes. She also thrives on routine, but no more than Andy and I do. There is a common belief that all people with Down syndrome are alike, or at least have the same kinds of differences from normal. High or low functioning classifies people in monolithic categories and overlooks a person's uniqueness for the sake of a quick and efficient description. I bristled at the idea that Louisa and my student's brother were the same. They are two distinct people who may or may not have anything in common.

As I stumbled to try to answer her question, *"Yes! Very high functioning! She's sitting up and everything!"* I recognized a need to subtly claim a prognosis. In other words, what I think the student meant was how my daughter was expected to function later in life. Whether or not it was accurate, claiming that Louisa was high functioning put the present on stable ground, anticipating that everything in the future would be okay.

PEOPLE WITH INTELLECTUAL disabilities are evaluated in terms of their independence and productivity. Although anyone might struggle to set goals, hold a job, meet appointments, and pay their bills, people with intellectual disabilities are under particular scrutiny to demonstrate how well they function, to show that their lives are meaningful. Even when Louisa was a baby, I noticed my own need to prove to the world that she was on a promising trajectory. When someone asked me, "How is Louisa?" I was on high alert to respond with a checklist of developmental milestones. Saying three-word phrases? Check! Stringing a series of beads together? Check! I eventually realized that I was sharing more information than the innocent question meant to solicit. The truth was that my overcompensation was meant to defend against pity. It was also motivated by fear that Louisa would not be able to function as our world expected her to. To function is to belong. If she can't function, I feared the lonely consequences she will suffer in a world that often seems so demanding and inflexible.

IQ tests attempt to quantify and predict functioning. Those who take them are scored, rated, and judged on efficiency and processing speed. A degree of functioning, high or low, typically corresponds to a person's IQ score. Yet functioning translates an abstract number into a socially pragmatic shorthand. It describes how values like speed, productivity, and planning—assessed in theory on an IQ test—become meaningful in various real-life scenarios. Functioning is both a term of psychological classification and an obsession of our capitalist world. It is the assessment of how well a person meets the expectations of our society. High or low functioning often precedes diagnoses like Down syndrome, autism, alcoholism, and depression. It describes a person's ability to fit in, to pass for normal, and to mask their differences in order not to disrupt the routines and flow of the everyday lives of the rest of us. High functioning suggests self-sufficiency, but also that a person's need for support and care doesn't get in our way.

In the early twentieth century, Henry Goddard considered what IQ scores could tell him about functioning. As part of his hierarchy of intelligence, Goddard identified the moron, a high functioning person with a relatively high IQ, as the most dangerous. "Society is facing a tremendous problem in this high-grade feeble-minded child," he wrote in 1910. Those with lower IQs and lower functioning were easily separable from society, but "high-grade" children were the real threat to society because they could function well enough. These children who sat beside others in public school classrooms were "exactly like the high grades in institutions," Goddard wrote. These were the children who could pass for normal and elude separation into segregated classes.

Functioning was eventually tested in ways that augmented the assessment of IQ. The Vineland Social Maturity Scale was developed in 1936 by Edgar Doll, who trained with Goddard and eventually took his place as Director of Research at Vineland. In line with his mentor's pursuits, Doll sought to better articulate the difference between "feeble-minded subjects of high intelligence and normal subjects of low intelligence." Social inadequacy—disruptive behavior in the form of anything considered not normal—was often the first indication of mental deficiency, Doll believed, and could be evaluated even before an official IQ test might be possible. Like Goddard, Doll claimed that feeble-mindedness was previously determined by vague concepts and subjective evaluation. The standardization and quantification of social behavior would put such inconsistencies to rest.

A person's score on the Vineland Social Maturity Scale was determined in a method much like Binet's IQ test. Certain tasks were normed to a particular age-group and sequenced in order of difficulty. A total of 117 tasks were grouped by the age in which a person was expected to accomplish them and standardized on a scale for normal subjects. By two years old, a child should eat with a spoon and pull off her socks. By four, a child should button her coat and wash hands unaided. Eight-year-olds should comb their own hair and should have disavowed Santa Claus. As a person gets older, the criteria for sufficiency become vaguer. Adults in their twenty-fifth year should be performing skilled work, promoting civic progress, and creating their own opportunities. When test-takers reached the limit of tasks that they could complete, their proficiency was identified as their "social age" in a way that was nearly identical to "mental age" determined by an IQ test.

Doll found a high correlation between mental age and social age (0.80, about the same as the correlation of height between parents and

their children) and concluded that the two scores are mutually dependent. And since he believed IQ to be highly dependent on genes, he concluded that social competence must be too. "The environmentalist will
find but little comfort for his point of view in these results, while the
geneticist will find correspondingly much satisfaction," he wrote.

Doll's scale has been revised since the early twentieth century,
renamed as the Vineland Adaptive Behavior Scale, and is currently in
its third edition. Those who revised Doll's original work chose to maintain the nominal reference to Vineland, and its persistence is a chilling
reminder of the institution's legacy in how psychologists evaluate functioning today.

When Louisa was in second grade, the school psychologist asked
me to fill out the Adaptive Behavior Assessment System (ABAS),
third edition. Its relationship to the Vineland Scale is analogous to the
Stanford-Binet's relationship to the WISC; they are two different formats for measuring generally the same thing. The front page of the form
asks, "Does the child being evaluated have any disabilities or other limitations?" I was growing impatient with these forms, which insisted that
I scrutinize Louisa's every action and forced me to see her every move
through a diagnostic lens. My response was prickly: "I do not agree that
a disability is necessarily a limitation, but I know what you are asking.
Louisa has Down syndrome." I noticed many similarities between the
ABAS and Doll's earlier survey. It did not ask me whether Louisa still
believed in Santa Claus, but it did ask me to rate about 200 ways of
assessing Louisa's adaptive behavior, such as "refrains from telling a lie
to escape punishment," "orders own meal when eating out," "checks for
correct change when buying an item," "calls for help if someone is hurt at
home," "is well liked by others his or her age," and "talks about realistic
future educational and career goals." It asked me to judge her proficiency
in these functional skills on a scale of 0 (not able to) to 3 (always, or
almost always, when needed).

The rating of future career goals made me particularly anxious. Louisa mentioned many things she wanted to be when she grows up, such as a farmer, a flight attendant, an astronaut, a ballerina, an artist, and a teacher. These all seemed reasonable aspirations for a seven-year-old. But I wondered if Louisa was expected to see the limitations that the world put on her and create her goals accordingly. Her sense of her future, I believed, should not be limited by what most people, including the psychologists who drafted this questionnaire, might see as realistic for a person with an intellectual disability. Her aspiration to be an astronaut seemed no less realistic to me than other seven-year-olds, even though the question focused attention on a divide between what is expected of her and her peers.

Doll argued that the assessment of social maturity must be given in tandem with an IQ test in order to obtain "a complete diagnosis of mental deficiency." These days psychologists do not make a diagnosis of intellectual disability on IQ scores alone. It is determined by an IQ score below 70 and limitations in adaptive behavior skills. The diagnosis must also originate in the developmental period, usually before the age of eighteen. In the realm of psychological diagnosis, social functioning is evaluated in terms of adaptive behavior, or "the level of everyday performance of tasks that is required for a person to fulfill typical roles in society, including maintaining independence and meeting cultural expectations." In Doll's survey, people being evaluated were never asked to self-report due to the risk that they "might overstate their own abilities." Now, adaptive behavior is assessed through standardized questionnaires completed by caregivers, teachers, and the person being evaluated only if older than sixteen. But as Goddard established, the burden remains on people being evaluated to conform to how their world expects them to behave. None of these questionnaires, past or present, consider that "cultural expectations" could, or should, change to better adapt to the needs of a person. Rather, it assumes circumstances are normal and just.

Forms for summer camps and after-school activities often prompt for explanations or notes. *Is there anything we need to know about your child?* I have honed my response. "Louisa has Down syndrome," I write, "but we expect her to be included and follow the rules like any other kid." It is best, I have decided, to address issues when they arise rather than preemptively navigate the expectations of what Down syndrome and high functioning means to people reading the form. I worry that a lengthy addendum would make caregivers expect that Louisa is high-maintenance, taking up too much of their time and resources. Better, I believe, for them to meet her first and see that she is worthy of any extra attention that she might require.

In our social system, still influenced by the Vineland Training School, inclusion depends on functioning. Those who are low functioning are often isolated, segregated in separate classrooms and work environments. High functioning means easier inclusion. I haven't had to fight to include Louisa in most social contexts because she can keep up without needing too much support. But I fear that there will be more pressure to remove Louisa from mainstream classes as she grows older. Inclusion is more common in early education than in high school. One reason for this might be how the purpose of education changes. Classes become more focused on college prep, AP credits, and success on standardized test scores. So it's not really my daughter's relationship to her peers that might change; it's the growing chasm between what our world expects for her and for everyone else. Another reason that inclusion occurs less as kids get older might be that parents are worn out by the time their children reach high school. As any parent who's done it knows, advocating for inclusion takes stamina. "I wish it wasn't easy for people to give up," one parent of a child with Down syndrome reported. "For some, they can't fight the system anymore."

When Louisa talks about her future, she conveys her excitement for the process of growing up. By December, she is already anticipating the following school year, and the next one, and then the one after that. She tells me and Andy that after fifth grade she will be in middle school, and then she will be in high school. She tells me that she is looking forward to studying biology, geology, and maybe French. She also says that she will have the same friends, but maybe a few more. I can tell that she is wondering what it will be like to be so grown-up at school with all her friends. I don't know what that will be like either. But the thought that any of this future will be a disappointment to her, something ruled more by what others assume about her than what she actually wants, is unbearable. I fear that it might take more than stamina to give my daughter the future she deserves.

A FUNCTIONAL CLASSROOM is a term for a classroom that is separate from spaces for general education. Functional, in this context, refers to the focus on life skills instead of academics, improving a child's ability to adapt to social settings and teaching social and daily living skills that might come more easily to others. I know parents of kids with Down syndrome who believe that a functional classroom is the best environment for their child. A separate classroom has increased learning and reduced disruptive behavior, these parents tell me. But to me, functional classrooms seem suspiciously convenient for educators, not necessarily what is best for the students in them. I cannot accept that the most I can ask of Louisa is to function, follow routines, keep organized. I do not mean to diminish the importance of these skills, or what it takes for kids to accomplish them. But prioritizing functioning has led to the separation of those who do and do not thrive within our fast-paced, productivity-obsessed world. Ironically, I seem to hold on to the idea of Louisa being part of this world, even though it seems to make no one happy, no matter what a person's IQ score is.

Research consistently shows that inclusive education is the best way to educate students with learning differences. Despite what Doll claimed, social functioning is something that can be improved by environment and educational circumstances. Research has consistently identified a variety of benefits when students with intellectual disabilities are educated in inclusive classrooms. These include increased student engagement, improved communication, improved expressive language and vocabulary, more satisfying and diverse friendships, less disruptive behavior, and more social competence. One study that tracked 11,000 students with a range of disabilities reported that time spent in inclusive classrooms correlated with better outcomes after high school in employment and independent living.

I feel a constant tension between advocating for the world I want for Louisa and navigating the reality in which we live. I have been taught to value independence and avoid asking for help at all costs. For this reason, I feel a great deal of guilt and anxiety about how much support Louisa needs in the classroom. She has an educational assistant, a whole other person whose job it is to help Louisa stay on track. Still, I worry about how much time Louisa's regular classroom teacher must spend with her and how Louisa's needs pull attention away from the other kids in the class. I wonder why I feel so guilty asking that my daughter get what she needs to learn, and I realize it is because of the history of the IQ test—the way that Goddard, Doll, and other eugenicists used it to establish that normal is how a person should be. To be anything below normal is wrong and inconvenient to everyone else. The guilt subsides when I remember Goddard and his efforts to make anyone who did not meet the standards of normal intelligence feel as if they did not belong in classrooms or in the United States. What I feel is in large part due to that abhorrent history. No matter what it takes, Louisa deserves to learn among her peers.

Thankfully, many of Louisa's teachers know that dependence isn't a problem. It's what makes us human. One of Louisa's most extraordinary teachers once told me, "Her best is not perfect, nor is it like anyone else's perfect. Would it help to know that some of my kids thoroughly exhaust me on a daily basis and some days I wish I could trade them for more

Louisas?" I took this as a reminder that we are all dependent on each other, for support, for learning, for survival.

Inclusion is equally beneficial to students without disabilities, providing opportunities for collaboration and the acceptance of differences. Studies have found that educating students with and without disabilities in the same classroom made a positive impact on the academic performance of all students. I wonder how I would have felt about climbing on a sled with Nick on that cold winter day when I was child if students with varying abilities had been in classrooms with me. Research shows that students without disabilities have less fear of human differences and more growth in their own social empathy and awareness if they learn in an inclusive environment. In fact, there is no research conducted in the last fifty years that supports the value of segregated special education classrooms. But the fear and prejudice that Goddard and the IQ test shaped persists, and it is difficult to change course. Despite the overwhelming research support for inclusion, only 17.9 percent of children with intellectual disabilities spent more than 80 percent of their day in a mainstream classroom in 2022. Statistics don't always give a full picture, but it's hard for me to believe that this is how it ought to be, so many kids spending most of the day separated from their peers. This situation limits opportunities for students of diverse abilities to make friends and learn from one another. It perpetuates a value that is a shameful cornerstone of Goddard's vision of American identity—that it is more important to be productive and compete than to practice patience, empathy, and social support. Functional classrooms also serve as a self-fulfilling prophecy. Those segregated at school are much more likely to live isolated from their peers in adulthood.

As education experts have argued, inclusion is not a place or a threshold to be met. It is a systemic approach that addresses all forms of student learning and social engagement as connected within one whole community. Inclusion impacts everyone. Here are some examples of what inclusive education looks like: Louisa insists on getting to school a little early each day so that she can help hold the doors open for the kids getting off the buses. I am told she gives everyone a high five as they walk in the door. She spends most of her time in a classroom with her peers, but also spends forty-five minutes a day in another classroom with a smaller group of students, working with an intervention specialist on skills that are taking her longer to learn. At recess, Louisa desperately wanted to traverse the monkey bars. But it was harder for her to make it all the way across. Two good friends held her feet, awkwardly supporting her as she flailed and reached for the other side. In the cafeteria at lunchtime on Fridays there is an open mic. Any student who wants to can climb up on a small stage and sing a song. Apparently, Louisa takes the lead on most days. She hushes the crowd and then selects from her diverse repertoire, which includes the greatest hits of Taylor Swift, Ella Fitzgerald, and Bill Withers. Teachers tell me that when she finishes, the student crowd goes wild. Her unabashed confidence has inspired many of her peers to give it a try. And yes, inclusion also looks like her friends over-helping and mothering her, figuring out how to help Louisa while still respecting her autonomous choices. It hasn't been without its challenges, but separating Louisa from her friends and community would have made all these moments of friendship and community impossible.

The concept of functioning involves plenty of normative ideas about how minds should work. It is assessed in relation to a system of values that we hold onto like a security blanket. Comparison goes hand in hand with functioning. It is measured against what others are doing and how fast they are doing it. It very easily becomes an obsession. Louisa's teachers try to suggest to me that she isn't the only one in her class who finds it difficult to stay on task, manage time, and organize work. It is a comforting perspective. But more important, the gentle suggestions remind me that there are many people out there who struggle to meet the expectations of functioning. Evaluating who should learn where and who should do what by how well someone functions does not create a just or caring world. We stick to the old system because it is easier, even though it only ever worked for some. And this system, which benefits a few but leaves many others feeling inferior and without value, gained scientific credibility thanks to the methods and example of the IQ test.

THE STRUGGLE OF students with intellectual disabilities to be included does not go away in adulthood. Segregated education solidifies expectations that shape our perception about employment and professional opportunities. The research on what adulthood looks like for a high functioning person with Down syndrome is terrifying. The eleventh edition of the terminology and classification manual of the American Association on Intellectual and Developmental Disabilities (AAIDD) has a chapter about people with intellectual disabilities who have relatively high IQs. Its conclusions feel like a punch, reminding me of the deceptive allure of the high IQ and the naive pride I felt during the meeting with the school psychologist when he implied that my daughter was at an advantage. The handbook states that references to a mild or high functioning disability can often be misleading. Real-life challenges can be equal to and sometimes greater than those with lower IQ scores. "Expectations for performance are higher for people with higher IQ scores than those with lower IQ scores; the tasks given to them are more demanding because of the higher expectations; and a failure to meet those expectations is frequently met by others blaming the individual or the individual blaming him or herself." This is followed by a list of common characteristics of the everyday lives of people with intellectual disabilities who have higher IQ scores: "low rate of employment . . . low career success . . . high poverty and low access to good housing . . . higher obesity . . . and high risk of loneliness."

These characteristics are not that different from a person who scores lower on the IQ test, but it also seems like these challenges are not necessarily caused by what people are capable of. Rather, they emerge from what others expect of them and how high functioning is perceived.

Depression and self-blame are caused by pressure to meet the expectations of a society obsessed with functioning. It's hard not to read this as Louisa's fate and assume that her IQ directly correlates with this kind of life that I do not want for her and that she does not want for herself. Asking Louisa what she wants to be when she grows up can solicit a variety of answers that usually depend on context. If we are in the car listening to music, her answer is most likely that she wants to be a singer. When we were on a plane to Italy one summer, she said she wanted to be a flight attendant. Once, when we were at the hospital getting her blood drawn for a test, she said she wanted to be a nurse. Because she has two parents who are professors, she often says she wants to be a teacher. All of these possibilities seem wonderful to me. Of course, I have no idea what she will be when she grows up. It is the fact that she believes she has possibilities that matters to me most.

Research tells me that the intellectual development of people with Down syndrome decelerates with time. In adulthood, the intellectual gap between people with Down syndrome and those without grows wider. This is a comparative perspective, and it is unclear whether the gap is caused by cognitive decline or the decreasing opportunities for social interaction and intellectual stimulation for people with disabilities in adulthood. Although the decline might be caused in part by socially implemented limitations, cognitive decline does seem to be in large part genetic. Research has found that Alzheimer's disease is "most likely universal" in older individuals with Down syndrome. More than 80 percent may experience dementia by age sixty-five. But it seems wrong to claim that this decline is entirely genetic when there are so few opportunities for people with Down syndrome to function socially in adulthood.

There are moments when I glimpse the kind, loving adult that I know Louisa will be. I am not a morning person, and Andy and I usually wake to the sound of Louisa's shuffling feet on our floor. I open my eyes, and she presents me with a card. It's nothing elaborate, a sheet of folded white paper taken from her art table. She has written "Happy Birthday, mama.

Love, Louisa" on the front and has drawn a picture of a chicken on the inside. My birthday is in six months. I add it to the stack of similar cards on my nightstand. Sometimes she goes into my office and grabs an envelope. She draws a stamp and puts her return address on the outside. On the inside is a small fluorescent sticky note. "I love you, mama," it says. I take some comfort that she knows how to address an envelope, and I try to remember if this was a skill mentioned on the behavior assessment forms I have filled out. But more crucially, I recognize the enormous privilege to be greeted with such love by someone I love so much.

Before I can go to the bathroom and put on my glasses, Louisa begins fixing herself a scrambled egg in the kitchen. She gets out a bowl and breaks an egg without any traces of shell. Then she adds some milk, grabs a whisk, and fluffs it all together. I usually walk gingerly into the kitchen just in time to turn the stove on and add a pat of butter to the pan. Then Louisa pours the egg into the pan, grabs the spatula, and moves around the eggy mass. When it's done, I turn off the stove and help her pour the egg into a dish. I wonder how many seven-year-olds can do this. I don't remember whether *make a scrambled egg* or *cooks semi-independently* have ever been listed on an adaptive behavior survey that I have filled out for Louisa. Nonetheless, this seems promising. Someday, when I'm not there to cook for her, she can make a scrambled egg.

It is important to me that I face Louisa's future with my eyes wide open, fully aware of her potential and realistic about what I can do to prepare her as much as possible. But this perspective on the future leaves me feeling helpless. I cannot stop the eventual tide of cognitive decline, and its resulting isolation, no matter how functional Louisa may seem in the present. And despite the early intervention and support in public school, support for adults with intellectual disabilities is harder to find. Other parents describe it to me as being shoved off a cliff.

*   *   *

EMPLOYMENT SERVES AS a clear marker of how someone is functioning. I have heard a story of a couple who received a prenatal diagnosis of Down syndrome and went to meet with a geneticist about their options. The geneticist told them that people with Down syndrome have more opportunities now. "The young man who sacks my groceries has Down syndrome," he said. I'm not sure how this couple responded, but it seems like an awkward moment. The geneticist was trying to help the couple envision an uplifting future, one that was different from the institutions and decisions informed by eugenics in the past. I have had similar experiences when well-meaning friends have tried to suggest possible futures for Louisa. "She seems really into babies. Maybe she can work in a daycare when she's older," one friend once offered. These suggestions are not necessarily what Louisa wants; they are what society permits under its rigid, ableist framework.

There is, of course, dignity in all work and there is nothing wrong with bagging groceries or working in a daycare. Fifty years ago, people with Down syndrome would have never been prepared for or given such opportunities. But the specifics of Louisa's future are beside the point. Since that evening before Louisa was born, when I asked Andy whether he thought our daughter would go to Yale or Brown, I have learned that prioritizing how well Louisa functions will not lead her to her best life. I would rather no one imagine Louisa's future in terms of how productive and high functioning she will be. I would rather we had a world that prioritized how well she can serve her community and how well her community can serve her.

The geneticist painted an optimistic picture for the couple of their child's potential to function as an adult. But the truth is that only 18 percent of people with intellectual disabilities are employed in the United States. Many who are employed spend their days in sheltered workshops, which isolate people with disabilities from the general workforce. The Fair Labor Standards Act is most well-known for establishing minimum wage. But it also created 14(c) certificates, which allow employers to pay people "whose earning capacity is impaired by age or physical or mental deficiency" at a rate below minimum wage. In 2020, Americans with disabilities working under 14(c) certificates earned less than half of the federal minimum wage per hour.

Functioning is a diagnostic trait, yet how much we function and how people of certain identities are allowed to function are shaped by socially constructed and historically shaped circumstances. The Fair Labor Standards Act was passed in 1938, when eugenic sterilization was still a widely accepted practice and the segregation of adults with disabilities from the rest of society was considered the best solution for everyone. A world based on valuing perfection over inclusion, progress over opportunity, still persists. Although Louisa is an important part of her school community now, I feel the constant threat of that disappearing in the future. Despite her dreams for her future, she could be denied the access to the educational and employment opportunities that she deserves.

There is no limit on how little employees working under the conditions of 14(c) certificates can be paid, but wages are often determined with a brutal calculus that values productivity above all else. The Fair Labor Standards Act states, "The commensurate wage of a worker with a disability who is 75 percent as productive as the average experienced nondisabled worker, taking into consideration the type, quality, and quantity of work of the disabled worker, would be set at 75 percent of the wage paid to the nondisabled worker." In other words, the productivity and value of a worker with a disability can be measured against a standard of normal. The act also suggests that time trials might be used to determine the productivity of an individual with a disability, putting the burden on the workers to prove how they can function in a system that was set up to ensure their failure.

These time trials are an explicit way in which we measure human value against one another. We compare ourselves to each other to find what is normal and make decisions about how we care for others with that sense of normalcy in mind. This conception of functioning and productivity is grounded in statistics and quantitative comparison. The calculation of productivity of those working under 14(c) certificates has quite a bit in common with the statistical calculation of IQ in the hands of those like Goddard. Both tests evaluate functioning in terms of productivity. Both statistically quantify human value. Imagine if all of us had to undergo such an explicit determination of our productivity and functioning, how demeaning it is to a sense of human value.

As I write, eighteen states have passed legislation to phase out 14(c) certificates. Legislation has been introduced into the US House of Representatives to do so at the federal level. The Department of Labor is currently reviewing its policy on subminimum wages. The number of people working in sheltered workshops has steadily decreased in recent years. But the full elimination of 14(c) certificates has been slow, meeting resistance from politicians, rehabilitation service providers, and caregivers who still view 14(c) certificates as a justifiable system of employment for people with disabilities. The resistance to efforts to eliminate them often takes a charitable tone that echoes the perspective of those like Goddard and other eugenicists of the early twentieth century. Here is how one member of the Kansas legislature defended the status quo when the state began to consider eliminating 14(c) certificates:

> They [those who work in sheltered workshops] are people who really can't do anything. And if you do away with programs like that, they will rot at home. There is no place for them to go. They're taken care of. They're fed. They have a place to go and be functionable and they're happy. But when we come up here and we start dragging them [sheltered workshops] through the mud, I don't support this amendment because I think we need to support those companies.

This elected official values companies that exploit the labor of people with disabilities over equal respect and equal wages. Human potential is created by the opportunities and conditions in which we function. Low functioning, the label that describes someone who "can't do anything," ensures that a person's potential and life worth will constantly be under-valued. People should not be pushed into employment situations where they are not comfortable. Everyone should be able to choose where they work. But all people deserve to be paid minimum wage.

The perception that people with intellectual disabilities "can't do anything" is shaped by a world that values productivity above care and self-fulfillment. It is also an expectation that is solidified at an early age. I talked with Kyle Stumpf of Dubuque, Iowa, about his experience in school. "At times it felt like they just warehoused him," Bill Stumpf, Kyle's father, told me. Bill fought for his son's place in a regular classroom in elementary school, but as Kyle got older, the fight with teachers and administrators to meaningfully include his son became harder. "You just get beaten down," Bill said. "I finally thought, *Okay, let's just get through these next few years*," and they moved Kyle to a segregated classroom. After high school, sheltered workshops seemed like the only option for Kyle. It was difficult to see that Kyle might be capable of more if differ-ent opportunities were in place. But eventually, Bill saw a presentation on competitive integrated employment, regular work with support for at least minimum wage, and began to believe more was possible for his son. Kyle, now in his thirties, has worked at a Papa Johns restaurant for almost ten years. He makes more than minimum wage, and with his earnings, Kyle likes to go out to eat and visit microbreweries. He is also putting some of his money in an ABLE account. When I asked Kyle which job he liked better, the pizzeria or the workshop, he broke into a wide smile. "Papa Johns," he said softly. The manager now calls Kyle in to work hours in addition to his regular shifts when they are busy. His job has also generated meaningful friendships with coworkers. "It's real-life stuff," Bill told me. "They're looking at his worth."

A capitalist society values high functioning above all else and defines this functioning in terms of productivity, having a job, and making money. There are, of course, other things that can be valued about a job—a sense of purpose and importance to community, offering your unique perspective to the world. Yet having a job is a rare accomplishment for someone with an intellectual disability. On average, those who are employed work for about fourteen hours a week, and earn about $140 per week. When people with intellectual disabilities are hired, they often work in entry-level service jobs with low wages and minimal benefits. This is hardly enough to support oneself independently.

The same system that penalizes people with disabilities for not being functional enough discourages them from being functional. Not only is it possible for people with disabilities to be paid less than minimum wage, but those who do find employment at a sufficiently high wage risk losing social security benefits and the Medicaid that comes with it. How high is too high? The "substantial gainful activity" threshold in 2024 is $1,550 per month, which means that people with disabilities who depend on social security benefits and Medicaid for health insurance may only earn $18,600 per year. If they earn more than this, they risk losing their health insurance, housing, and any support they might need. People with disabilities who need support are thus caught in a trap. They are forced into poverty, which compounds the limitations that are put on them by an ableist world. There are ways to work around the employment income threshold. Special needs trusts allow us to save for Louisa's future without penalizing her. ABLE accounts are a kind of savings account that allow a person receiving disability benefits to save up to $18,000 a year. Neither of these options, however, addresses the way in which Louisa's integration into society will depend on her ability to function in the future.

Under these constraints on work and judgments about functioning, it is no wonder that depression is a common characteristic of people with intellectual disabilities. It is also not surprising that so much attention is paid to what people like my daughter can and cannot do. Those with intellectual disabilities are not likely to contribute in valuable ways to capitalism's cycle of production and profit. We usually see this non-productivity as a deficiency in the person. But given our current discontent with the inhumane demands of work and its tyranny over our lives, it might be time for our values of productivity and high functioning to shift. Those who are deemed "normal" or "functioning" might just be those who are able to most easily acquiesce to capitalism's demoralizing demands.

WE SAT WITH friends at dinner and talked about parenthood as a long journey of letting go, of preparing them for independence and preparing for the day when they will no longer need your guidance, your comfort, your care. Our friends have three kids and are understandably daunted by what sending them to college will mean financially. I nodded along as if I understood, though I was silent. I do not know what the future will look like, but it is possible that Louisa will always need our care. Although I am astonished by how quickly she has grown and changed, I am not preparing myself for a day when she will no longer need me. I am preparing for a future when she will always need me. And I am trying to prepare for a future in which I will no longer be there to take care of her.

Grasping for some common ground, I mentioned how concerned Andy and I are with saving, not necessarily for college, but for the rest of Louisa's life. "I know I'm ignorant," our friend said, "but I thought that the government kind of takes care of people like Louisa." It was a moment in which I felt a deep rift of parental difference. I realized that Louisa's ability to function could never be truly evaluated or predicted by a test. Her functioning was entangled in a mess of historically determined systems based on prejudice and bad science, and explaining this to my friend would be far too difficult for dinner conversation. My concerns over functioning and dependence didn't originate in unrealistic expectations or a denial of Louisa's challenges. They were grounded in how labels like low or high functioning determine what opportunities would be extended to her. I want Louisa to find work that makes her feel like a valuable member of a community. I want her to feel like she is making a contribution to the world around her. But I also obsess about her future with the greatest urgency because I want Louisa to be able to take care of herself after Andy and I are gone.

What might this future look like? It would require employment not evaluated and determined by productivity. A more person-centered approach in which all adults are considered worthy of employment on the terms that work best for them, a job that matches Louisa's interests and strengths, rather than assuming what she can't do. Support and self-determination would need to coexist; one would not disqualify her from deserving the other.

ONE SUMMER EVENING Louisa, Andy, and I packed a picnic dinner and took it to the park. It was a warm, humid evening and we set out our sandwiches and watermelon on a picnic table not far from the swings and monkey bars where Louisa liked to play. A mother sat at a nearby table and watched her daughter as she climbed up the slide and squealed in a high-pitched song, expressing something in between words and emotions. Before we could find our forks, the mother began talking to us. She shared too much about her daughter's diagnosis. She guessed that our daughters had the same intervention specialist at school. She asked if I knew other kids and their mothers whose names were not familiar to me. She asked about Louisa's IEP. She told me more about her own daughter than I was comfortable with. "She got up yesterday and made scrambled eggs for her father and me," the woman said. "Maybe she will be able to take care of herself when she's older after all."

I was not interested in chatting with this woman, but she didn't seem to pick up on my signals. I wanted to talk to my husband and watch Louisa climb. But I couldn't help noticing the story about scrambled eggs and how that experience meant something about the way our kids are measured, evaluated, and judged. As I swallowed a bite of watermelon, I had to admit that this mother and I shared something meaningful. No matter how well we function, we are all part of the same system. Louisa was more interested in playing than eating, and she headed for the swings. Soon Louisa and the other girl were playing together, chasing each other in their own version of tag. I turned to the mother and smiled. "Yes," I replied, "I know exactly how you feel."

Nature Nurture

One afternoon when Louisa was in third grade, I picked her up from school after the first snow of the season. We strapped on our snow gear to sled down the formidable hill in our backyard. Snow was still falling and green tips of grass peeked through the thickening blanket of white. We trudged up and down countless times, taking turns on solo trips and sitting together on our purple plastic sled. Eventually our toes turned numb and we headed inside to start her homework. So far school hadn't been easy, but Louisa amazed me with what she had learned. Due to the pandemic, which had started the year before, we were able to put off the IQ test a while longer, and Andy and I hadn't brought it up with the school psychologist. We were more focused on the daily challenges of learning. Louisa struggled with mathematical concepts like regrouping when subtracting multi-digit numbers, but I tried to help her keep up. Progress was slow but hard-earned, and I constantly reminded myself how well she was doing considering the expectations for a kid with Down syndrome.

Louisa's teacher asked all her students to read for twenty minutes every night and to fill out a homework log, which asked questions about their chosen book. "What can you infer about a character or event in your book? What evidence do you have to support your inference?" the worksheet asked. I'm sure Louisa's teacher explained these questions to the class. But Louisa couldn't tell me what *infer* meant, and my attempt at explaining it was absurd. "It is something you intuit but isn't said explicitly," was my pathetically academic way of describing this concept to an eight-year-old. My inadequacy as a teacher and mother felt fully on display. The more Louisa struggled, the more I feared for her inclusion. What would happen if she couldn't read along with her peers? Would she be put in another classroom? Would her inability to do an assignment be interpreted as some behavioral defiance? I could not help my daughter understand the concept, and I certainly could not help her provide an inference about the book she read, the hilarious *Fox and Crow Are Not Friends*. A familiar sense of helplessness lodged itself in my chest, and I wished that Louisa and I were still in the backyard, free and light as we slipped across the snow, taking off without any driven purpose and just experiencing the thrill of the ride before we ended up somewhere at the bottom of the hill.

Times like these are when the claim that nature is stronger than nurture creeps up on me. Francis Galton, the British scientist and founder of modern statistics, coined the phrase "nature and nurture" in an 1875 essay about twins. The essay describes a series of anecdotal mix-ups by parents and teachers he interviewed, lighthearted confusion that anticipated the shenanigans later immortalized in movies like *The Parent Trap* and *Double Trouble*. These cases of mistaken identities and misplaced punishments proved to Galton the persistence of the traits we are born with. His sample size is far too small to draw any meaningful conclusions. Nonetheless, Galton positioned nature and nurture as two separate forces, and this is generally how we still think about them today. The phrase "nature and nurture" caught on, but it eventually evolved to "nature versus nurture," to capture the supposed conflict between what we are born with and the environment we are born into.

"Nature is far stronger than nurture," Galton wrote. Based on his anecdotal evidence, Galton concluded that nurture is unable to affect a person's natural potential. It can do nothing "beyond giving instruction and professional training." For Galton, *nurture* refers to a person's upbringing, the circumstances into which people are born. He never asks how one's nurture might be changed to improve intelligence. For him, the question is not important because nature overrules nurture. But now, *nurture* implies a much more fluid state of assisted emergence. It is the act of caring for each other. We nurture plants to bloom and nurture the infirm to health. The outcome of this nurturing is unwieldy, impacted by conditions that cannot be predicted or statistically accounted for.

Nurture is also the realm of the maternal. I nurtured Louisa when she was inside me and every day since, hoping to ensure her happiness and the richest human experience possible. To downplay the process of nurture is to diminish our broader charge as humans to tend to one another, even though I cannot be sure how the ways I have nurtured Louisa have made any measurable difference.

But when we struggle with homework, I question whether my attempts to help Louisa learn are just a symptom of a stubbornness I can't abandon—a delusional belief that I can help Louisa overcome her genetic limitations through hard work. It is helpful for me to try to remember how hard assignments like this are for her. They involve a coordination of cognitive processes that most of us never have to think about because we can summon them almost automatically. Writing out a response to reading assignments requires Louisa to sync up various tasks that each have their own challenges. She must remember what she read. She must understand the prompt, including the meaning of words like *infer*, and keep it fresh in her head while she recalls what she read. But the assignment is not asking for direct recall. It demands decision-making skills and reasoning to find a plausible answer. Once she plans an answer in her mind, she must embark on perhaps the most complex coordination of tasks yet—the physical act of writing. This involves fine motor skills, the effort she must undertake to hold a pencil correctly, not to mention the extra considerations of spelling, capitalization, and putting spaces between words. She must focus, or at least make the effort to refocus after being distracted by the sound of the washing machine finishing its cycle or the snowplow as it charges by outside. As her mind attends to the coordination of grammar and fine-motor skills, she has to remember her answer, what she is trying to communicate in the first place. She tries to squish a few more words into a centimeter of space at the end of a line. She gets frustrated. I get frustrated. She forgets what she was trying to write. We take some deep breaths and start again. Breaking down all the tedious steps reminds me that learning is an astonishing process, and Louisa's hard work in particular is something to be celebrated as a feat of human determination. Galton was convinced that we cannot overcome our nature. But parsing nature from nurture ignores the wonder of learning, however it gets done.

FOR MOST OF the twentieth century, psychologists followed Galton's lead and believed that education had little impact on improving IQ. Instead, they saw IQ scores as indicative of whether a child deserved an education. A good education could help children with an intelligent nature, usually those of the privileged social class, reach their innate potential. But for those with lower IQs, it was a complete waste of time. English psychologist Cyril Burt likened intellectual capacity to a standardized measurement. "It is impossible for a pint jug to hold more than a pint of milk," he wrote in 1911. "It is equally impossible for a child's educational attainments to rise higher than his educational capacity permits." To Lewis Terman, the psychologist who developed Binet's early work into the pervasive Stanford-Binet IQ test, the special classes for "backward children" in the public schools were really just a futile experiment in whether it was possible to improve intelligence. "No other pupils in our public schools are taught in such small groups or by such able teachers," Terman declared in 1922. "Rarely do the IQs of children given these special advantages show significant improvement. Generally speaking, once feeble-minded, always feeble-minded."

As a great admirer of Galton, Terman posed his own questions about the origins of intelligence. "Is the place of so-called lower classes in the social and industrial scale the result of their inferior native endowment, or is their apparent inferiority merely a result of the inferior home and school training?" After giving IQ tests to about 500 schoolchildren, Terman concluded that children who performed better did so because they had genetically inherited stronger intellectual abilities.

The issue for Terman was which comes first. Are successful people just naturally more intelligent? Or do IQ tests only ensure the success of a specific type of person? Would those who score poorly on an IQ test do better if their potential was nurtured? According to him, the intellectually privileged were "the nation's finest asset" and should be treated as such by giving these children every possible advantage. In Terman's logic, the alignment of the gifted and the professional classes showed that democracy was working. If all people were given equal opportunities, then they would find their natural place in society according to their intellectual capacity. This natural alignment of success and intelligence was proven, according to Terman, by the demographics of IQ scores. Fifty percent of gifted children, Terman reported, belonged to the professional classes. According to him, this was a sure sign that privilege was a natural and just outcome of high intelligence.

Terman's assessment offered a blow to the lofty ideals of the American dream. "Even the most extreme advocates of 'free will,'" he wrote, "do not believe that the feeble-minded could successfully will to become intelligent, the tone-deaf to become musical, or the psychopathic to become stable." I once associated the early twentieth century with the renewal of

American promises, like everyone is created equal, we all deserve a fair shot, success is an outcome of hard work. But this social and economic optimism was matched by an undercurrent of genetic determinism in the logic of IQ testing in ways that the country rarely acknowledges.

By insisting on a genetic cause for intelligence, Terman reaffirmed the hierarchy that IQ tests buttressed since Goddard's work on Ellis Island and in public schools. White males have the highest IQ scores, and since we supposedly live in a meritocracy, they are the ones who achieve the most. The logic is tautological, creating a self-affirming spiral. IQ tests are normed for white, middle-class test-takers. They do the best on the test, which purports to measure innate ability. Therefore, white, middle-class test-takers are inherently more intelligent than non-white, socially underprivileged test-takers, and deserving of the most advantages.

This is the crux of the "nature versus nurture" debate among psychologists, whether IQ tests measure something as fixed and genetically transmissible as height and eye color or something that can be shaped by different socioeconomic environments and opportunities. Is success determined by environmental conditions or genetic inheritance? It involves debating what IQ actually measures—some innate and unchanging ability or the effects of a person's environment. For parents, teachers, social workers, and really anyone who believes in the potential of children, there is a lot at stake in this debate. Is it possible to improve a child's potential for success and happiness? Or are any efforts to do so overshadowed by the dominant forces of nature?

LOUISA'S TEACHERS EMPHASIZE her gains and describe the progress that she has made. But the story of Louisa's place in a classroom looks very different on her report card. Here it seems like Louisa is barely holding on. When assessing her ability to "spell correctly in written work" or "understand and use appropriate grade-level vocabulary," Louisa's scores are well below her peers. I try to greet the tinge of disappointment with a reality check. It is easy to forget how hard Louisa has worked to write her letters, to come close to navigating the arbitrariness of English spelling, to focus attention long enough to remember the word she is writing. But looking at the assessments and standardized tests alone, it is hard not to worry that her place among her peers is constantly under threat.

In a parent-teacher conference, not long after that first snow of the year, Louisa's occupational therapist complained about her lack of attention. "I can't get her to face the front of the classroom," she told me. "She can't sit still for long periods of time." Louisa's lack of attention is treated like something to be cured. The therapist writes her IEP goals in this way: "Louisa struggles to remain focused in the sensory rich environment of a general education classroom." But this is not a goal. Terman's statement, *once feeble-minded, always feeble-minded*, rings in my ears, and I read the therapist's comment as a warning. *Louisa doesn't belong in this classroom*, is what I believe this is telling me. *She is taking time and resources away from other children. If she doesn't shape up, this experience is going to be taken away from her.* I don't deny Louisa's lack of interest in paying attention to many tasks. But focusing on deficit sets up certain assumptions about her peers—as if all the other eight-year-olds in her class have razor-sharp focus for hours of the day. It is the demands we place on children to sit still that might be questioned or modified, rather than the kids themselves. In other words, perhaps the problem lies in her environment, rather than with her nature. Besides medication, there seems to be no effective therapy to increase attention, or at least none that the occupational therapist has offered besides constantly harping on Louisa to pay attention. In other words, there is no way to make Louisa change who she is, even though that might make the therapist's job much easier.

I used to believe that I could improve Louisa's intelligence, or at least I thought that trying to was my responsibility. I thought that the best way to prove that the conclusions of those like Terman were wrong was to show the world how smart Louisa really is and how well she could function. I now realize that this was at the heart of the pride I felt when the school psychologist told me that Louisa's IQ is high for a child with Down syndrome. It felt as if we had overcome something and that doing and buying everything I could to boost Louisa's "brain power" had paid off.

But I have learned, more through experience than research, that the best way to stick it to Terman is to reject the modern premise of IQ testing and bell curves entirely and work toward a world in which those with intellectual differences are not disadvantaged and all of us aren't working so hard to be normal. The answer to Terman's entrenched determinism is not to shape Louisa into a test-taker on par with her peers. This would only affirm the power of the IQ tests to control and define who she is.

The best way I can nurture Louisa, I realized, is to try to work against a regime of intelligence that gives her no space to be herself.

SCHOOL IS WHERE I feel the pressure between nature and nurture the most. But there are other places where I catch a glimpse of a world without such tension. Well into the winter, I sit in a metal fold-out chair in the waiting area of our local dance studio and watch Louisa's ballet class. There are a few other parents reading, working on computers, looking at their phones. Dance bags, ballet shoes, and water bottles are scattered on an old area rug. Two young boys play with a set of giant plastic puzzle pieces in the corner. Their toy tower eventually crashes to the floor. A mother looks up from her computer screen and stares at them, concerned about the noise. The boys giggle and begin reconstructing the tower. The studio's building is old and the heating pipes above my head clang forcefully. I strain to hear the music through the distractions and hope that Louisa can focus on the music, the ballet steps, her teacher's instruction.

Louisa started dance classes when she was five. Always a music lover, the combination of self-expression and physical movement suits her. I watch as she stands at the front of the room, facing a large wall of mirrors and gripping the ballet barre with her left hand. The delicate piano music begins and her head and spine curve down as she watches her right foot point and flex in front of her. Her head moves back and forth from her foot to the sharpened toe of the teacher as she tries to imitate as best she can. Louisa raises her right arm to her side. Her fingers stiffen in an attempt to extend the line of her arm in a graceful ballet curve.

Louisa is about two beats behind the coordinated movements of the rest of the class, but that doesn't really matter. Eventually the ballet barres are put away and students are taught short combinations of steps to dance across the floor. They start at the far side of the studio. Louisa does a waltz step, a *piqué* turn, a *pas de bourree*, a *pas de chat*. She pauses before each step, taking an extra second to consider which leg moves first, to decide how best to negotiate between accuracy and fun. She reaches the other end of the floor and turns toward the waiting area. I give her a thumbs-up and she performs the sequence again for me, this time ending with a deep and full-hearted curtsy.

I glance to my right and to my left. None of the other parents' faces wear the same unbridled smile that is on mine. They are looking at their phones or trying to make sure their son isn't making too much noise. I look down at my phone, too, because watching Louisa dance is like looking at the sun. Her radiance, simply that she participates in this class, fills my chest with such warmth and happiness I can barely stand it.

Known for its ethereal grace and physical demands, the intellectual efforts involved in dancing are less appreciated. Ballet is an exercise in short-term memory. Dancers must remember a combination of movement and absorb it in their bodies. Then there are all the parts of dance that demand mental coordination—balance, quick muscle movements, the anticipation of what movement comes next, pattern recognition, body and spatial awareness. In the midst of these challenges, Louisa's ability to remember combinations of steps is remarkable. She seems completely in her element. Rather than sitting in a chair, movement seems to help her focus. This environment, this studio, is a place where she does her best learning.

The culture of dance, especially ballet, is known for its rigid perfectionism, elitism, and exclusivity. But as I watch Louisa, I think about all the ways she is nurtured in this class. Her teacher emphasizes expression over perfection. She reminds Louisa to point her feet, but most of the time they are soft and bent, which doesn't really seem to bother anyone too much. She stands too close to the other dancers, often vying for a spot right next to the teacher. She is on the wrong foot. I suppose that many might see Louisa's way of dancing as a failure. Her movement isn't quite coordinated with the music. Her arms can't find that sweet spot between tension and grace. But none of this matters. Louisa makes a space for herself in this class. There is room for her way of dancing, and her movements are an expression of unbridled joy. Her toes may not be pointed and her legs may not be straight but she dances in a way that connects movement to something deep inside her. This is why I'm smiling. I want others to see it too. I'm watching what is possible when we give up ambition, perfection, and potential to take care of those around us.

IT IS REMARKABLE how little the terms of the nature versus nurture debate changed during the course of the twentieth century. There is now some consensus among psychologists that intelligence is dependent on environment to a meaningful degree, and that a distinction between genetically inherited intelligence and education is more muddled than Terman suggested. But the appeal of the heritability of intelligence persists and has supported some ugly conclusions. In the 1960s, Arthur Jensen, an educational psychologist at the University of California,

Berkeley, argued that the US government needed to reconsider its design and funding of compensatory education programs aimed at closing the achievement gap between disadvantaged, mostly non-white children and their white, middle-class counterparts. Achievement, of course, was measured in IQ scores. Such programs were not meeting their goals, he claimed, and their failure was because IQ scores—and the innate intelligence they claimed to measure—were immutable.

He also asserted that the importance of intelligence and our definition of the term were determined by societal demands. But that did not make the skills we associate with intelligence—processing speed, short-term memory, reasoning—any less based on genetics. He suggested that if educators really wanted to narrow the achievement gap, they should focus on teaching specific skills rather than trying to increase intelligence. This was a deeply pragmatic approach to the purpose of education. Schools should learn a child's IQ and then teach basic skills that a student will need to get a good job after graduation. A student's opportunities, in other words, are determined by IQ because we live in a world that prioritizes the skills that it tests. Jensen's approach to intelligence reinforced a kind of caste system, in which social mobility was only possible if an IQ score says so.

Jensen also offered an explanation for racial differences in IQ scores. On average, people who identify as Black score fifteen points lower on IQ tests than people who identify as white. While these statistics illustrate the bias of IQ tests for many, those who believe in the genetic basis of intelligence double down, suggesting that this provided evidence of the intellectual inferiority of non-European, non-white races. Jensen claimed that there is a genetic correlation between race and intelligence. He explained the generally lower IQ scores of people of African descent in this way: "There are no 'black' genes or 'white' genes. There are intelligence genes, which are found in populations in different proportions, somewhat like the distribution of blood types." Published in 1969, his theories clashed with a moment of intense civil rights protests across the country that demanded that everyone should have a right to the opportunities afforded to those with high IQ scores.

The late twentieth century brought efforts to remove systemic discrimination, like the Americans with Disabilities Act and the Individuals with Disabilities in Education Act. But progress was challenged by the cyclical return of Jensen's claims, which were originally the claims of Galton, Terman, Goddard, and others. Ideas about genetic determinism, the rule of nature, were perennially revived by the belief in the irrefutable objectivity of statistics. In 1994, Richard Herrenstein's and Charles Murray's *The Bell Curve* resuscitated Jensen's argument that IQ scores explain—rather than cause—who gets ahead in society and who is doomed to a life of dependency. It was an enormous popular success; more than 200,000 copies were sold weeks after it was published. The book describes "the cognitive class," those who have the highest IQ and are rightfully destined for a life of privilege. They exist at the top of a caste system that is structurally stable, according to Herrenstein and Murray, because our genes make it so. Those placed at the bottom of the caste system are genetically determined to stay there. Put another way, poor people are poor because they have low intelligence. *The Bell Curve* argues that low intelligence is a reason why Black Americans are disproportionately poor, incarcerated, and dependent on government welfare. It cited IQ scores as evidence for these claims, as if IQ tests were objective indicators of human value rather than the apparatus of a system of discrimination and suppression. "For many people," they write, "there is nothing they can learn that will repay the cost of teaching." Following Jensen's work, *The Bell Curve* claims that federally funded programs like Head Start and Help Me Grow—the preschool program for children with developmental disabilities that Louisa attended—are a waste of time and money. The policy suggestion was consistent with eugenicists of the early twentieth century, like Terman's belief that "imbeciles" should be removed from classrooms to avoid squandering resources or Jensen's belief that IQ tests help everyone find where they belong in the social hierarchy and, presumably, stay there.

MANY PSYCHOLOGISTS THINK intelligence tests predict things, but it is the general liberal position to believe otherwise. Prediction pigeonholes its subjects and contradicts the American sense of free will, that each of us can control our own life path. *The Bell Curve*'s unfounded conclusions about what is to be done about genetic differences still resonate in our own hyper-polarized political moment, in which free will seems to be under threat to so many. In 2017, months after Donald Trump was sworn in as president of the United States, Charles Murray was invited to speak at Middlebury College by a politically conservative student group. Murray was shouted down by students in attendance. When he took the stage and began to speak, the crowd stood up and turned their backs to the stage while reciting a chorus of prepared comments. The media portrayed the event as a shocking example of the inability of liberal young adults to listen to opposing viewpoints. Their behavior was juvenile. Students in the audience shouted and booed every time Murray's name was spoken by Middlebury's president and other introductory speakers. But I don't blame the students for asserting a limit to how far patience and tolerance should be extended.

There is still no evidence that the disparity in IQ scores among racial groups is due to genetic differences, as Jensen, Herrenstein, and Murray led us to believe. One reason for the lack of evidence seems obvious to me. Race, much like intelligence, is a cultural invention. Almost all Americans have a racially mixed genetic profile, complicating any effort to define precisely what is meant by correlations between racial identity, genetic heritability, and intelligence. After all, it is possible to accept the scientific evidence that intelligence—one's ability to perform well on an

IQ test, one's ability to excel in the kinds of tasks on an IQ test—might be related to genetics and also acknowledge that those genes have nothing to do with the cultural construction of race.

Decades of research has now found that Head Start and other early intervention programs improve educational outcomes, increasing the probability that participants will graduate from high school and attend college. Putting aside for a moment the fact that *The Bell Curve*'s conclusions are based on strikingly threadbare evidence, something about the return-on-investment mentality in *The Bell Curve* reminds me of the approach to education—especially higher education—today. If learning or education is not going to yield a direct, measurable outcome as IQ points or post-education salary earnings, then why do it? Why nurture, why try, if nature ultimately wins? We make decisions about education in terms of what it will yield in the future. But we might consider what is lost in the present. We miss opportunities to nurture and care for one another as a deeply valuable way of living now, if we are constantly expecting the payoff to emerge in the future.

MANY PSYCHOLOGISTS TODAY still believe that nature is far stronger than nurture, although most do not agree with the social policy conclusions of *The Bell Curve*. There is a general consensus among psychologists that intelligence is about 80 percent heritable, meaning that a person's IQ score is determined in large part by their genes, while only 20 percent is determined by environmental factors like socioeconomic class, access to good schools, and clean air and water. Intelligence is heritable, like many other aspects of human behavior. But the effects of genes on intelligence are not nearly as clear or assertive as Galton, Terman, Jensen, Herrenstein, and Murray claimed.

The persistence of Terman's genetic determinism explains some of my devotion to Louisa's education. I admit it is deeply ingrained in me that everyone can overcome their most formidable challenges, just like the grit and determination claimed in the Charlie Brown poster. Overcoming adversity through hard work persists as a belief at the core of being American. We are all equal, Americans are told; what matters is how hard we work. But living in a country that elects and rewards the privileged while oppressing those without such advantages has shown me otherwise. And still, part of me deeply believes that hard work pays off and challenging circumstances can be overcome. The dream of universal opportunity shouldn't be abandoned. Rather, access to opportunity should be expanded.

But there comes a point when the question of whether it's possible to change an IQ score loses sight of what matters. My point is not to raise Louisa's IQ score or to find loopholes and quibble with the details of tests until I have convinced her teachers that she should have a much higher score. It is clear to me that the IQ test was set up knowing exactly how someone with Down syndrome would perform. It was designed to put her behind the curve. Obsessing about improving her score would capitulate to the power of the IQ test to determine her place in this world. When we shirk the power of the IQ test, we can focus on how she might access knowledge, human experience, reflection, community involvement, all the reasons why we should nurture each other in the first place.

To me, both sides of the nature versus nurture debate come up short. Those on the side of nature say that a person's fate is in large part predetermined. Hard work, good choices, and free will only takes us so far. Those favoring nurture say that we should all be fully in control of our fate. Our destiny is entirely a product of our environment and the opportunities it makes possible. This perspective glosses over real genetic differences and overlooks the circumstances of people with Down syndrome, in which intellectual differences based on genes cannot be denied.

I feel a dizzying ambivalence toward these views when parenting. I am aware of how difficult it is for Louisa to keep focused on a task, but I still lack patience when I'm waiting for her to get in the car because she won't stop wiping the snow off the window with her mittens. My head feels like it will explode when I don't know how to help her, even though all I want to do is say the right words, find the right strategy to make a task easier for her. Galton and his followers overlook that it is possible to accept a person's particular way of being in the world and also nurture her to be her best self. It is possible to accept her for who she is while also wanting her to learn and know about the world in its most profound complexity and beauty and derive intense pleasure from it. Learning is not just about institutional resources, expenses, and a return on investment. Education improves a person's life. That is nurture.

Louisa is a walking, dancing, singing, laughing, joking, learning testament to the reality that genetic determinism was cruelly overstated. Andy and I are her greatest champions, yet even I never imagined what she would be capable of doing. She rehearses for dance recital performances, memorizing choreography to be performed onstage. She practices long division in a classroom with her friends. Thanks to the help of audiobooks, she can now read the Harry Potter series and talk to her teachers about Hermione Granger and her spells. Yet listing all of her accomplishments only proves that she is able to play by the rules of the intelligence game, checking the boxes of what a child is supposed to be able to do. And if she could not do these? Would she somehow not deserve to be nurtured and included?

I cannot deny that my daughter's differences are not just socially and culturally determined. Louisa is an only child, and I don't spend that much time around other kids. But when I do, I am often shocked by the differences between Louisa and her friends. Louisa seems less mature, less self-conscious than other kids her age. Her extra chromosome is a significant genetic difference, but the outcomes of that genetic information are also dynamic and malleable. Despite this difference, I am also shocked by her ease among her friends, and the ease of her friends around her. I keep waiting for her friends to separate, more interested in their own sense of normalcy and belonging than making space for Louisa. But so far, this hasn't happened. There is difference, but there is also love and inclusion.

What is more remarkable than her accomplishments is that she proves that the rules of intelligence, achievement, and skill acquisition aren't nearly as important as the opportunity to have the richest life experience possible. To be included in a dance recital, to work with a peer on math problems and sense how they might understand differently. Over and over again, Louisa shows me it is the nurturing that makes life richer.

When we define intelligence as a product of nature, IQ tests serve as a measure of one's genetic perfection. But even entertaining the concept of genetic purity—a way of being fully isolated from environmental influence—strikes me as a fantasy with particularly hazardous undertones. To isolate genetic identity means to make things less messy, enabling scientists and anyone else to identify who is truly genetically superior and who is not. We are closer to the disastrous pursuit of this fantasy than I would like to admit. Companies who have invested in gene-reading technology are selling parents predictions about their baby's innate aptitude and future. Gene-editing technology might someday soon be able to rewrite our genetic code to do more reliably what some scientists claim eating more fish can, boost brain function. Nurture will no longer be needed. This future is particularly terrifying for people with genetic differences like Louisa, who will face even greater challenges finding a place in a world that so deeply values genetic perfection.

What exactly is nature? What does it look like? Nature, in Galton's sense, is the most unnatural of ideas. There is no form of our being and development untouched by each other and our environment. Another way of saying this is that there is no moment of pure expression of a person's genetic orientation. Galton's proposed division between nature and nurture is a myth. What nature is, without our intervention, is entirely unknown. But quite a bit of care has been sacrificed for the sake of preserving this notion of genetic determinism. Our intelligence may well be determined in large part by our nature, but we can choose to take care of one another, which will inevitably lead to a better world.

PEOPLE WHO MEAN well tell me and Andy that Louisa is lucky to have us as parents. If this is true, it means that she has benefited from the blocks and cubes we used to help teach her place value, our insistence that she take art and dance classes in her community with her peers, a focus on reading that may seem obsessive, our flexible jobs that allow us to spend quite a bit of time with her. My resistance to such comments, which are certainly meant as compliments, is more than just modesty. To look these people in the eye and respond with a confident, "thank you," would align all too closely with what I felt during that pre-kindergarten meeting, when the school psychologist told me that Louisa's IQ was high for a child with Down syndrome. That comment, too, I believe, was meant to be a compliment. We are doing a good job, they say. Louisa is doing so well. "Whatever you are doing, keep it up," a doctor told us at one of Louisa's recent checkups.

These comments are meant to be supportive and encouraging, and I am grateful. But to fully agree would mean that I am somehow in control. I'm sure our particular idiosyncratic approach to parenting has had an impact on Louisa, like all parents on their children. But admitting an especially beneficial environment for Louisa is deeply uncomfortable to agree with. It would suggest that there are ways to improve Louisa. That her disability is something to be overcome or cured. This associates me with a kind of constant effort to improve the functioning and intelligence of my child that I work hard to resist. It would also imply that kids who are not doing as well as Louisa or perform differently on cognitive tests are less lucky to have the nurturing caregivers that they have. And I am sure this is not the case. But the opposite position—that Louisa is who she is because of her genes, and that those genes determine her score on an IQ test—is equally uncomfortable. This would mean siding with the eugenicists and believing that there is nothing to be improved about the lives of people with intellectual disabilities. It would mean that I am unable to meaningfully nurture the life of the person I love the most. It would mean that people like my Louisa are unteachable and unable to learn, and I know that this is not true. Better, I think, is to believe that the truth of what makes Louisa so marvelous is probably somewhere in between. Where exactly in between? We will never know.

Testing Moms

Whether IQ tests measure nature, nurture, or something in between, parents want to control the results. They often buy IQ test materials on eBay, attempting to ensure the placement of their child in the best schools possible. In 2007, Harcourt Assessment Inc., the company that at that time published the WAIS and the WISC, asked eBay to remove the testing materials from their website. But eBay denied the request, stating that there is nothing illegal about selling them. Still today, eBay sells a wide variety of IQ testing material to consumers for anywhere between $100 and $900, encouraging parents to expand their options for "fun at-home activities."

eBay was right; IQ tests are not legal documents. But the fact that some parents feel the need to prepare their child to do well on them suggests something more is going on here than just finding a bargain price. A high IQ score is meaningful because parents often perceive it as a ticket to their child's privilege and success, no matter how that number is achieved. eBay is filling a demand, providing parents with access to testing material that they aren't really supposed to have but feel determined to obtain. Parents care about their child's IQ score because their identity, their core sense of self, seems implicated. Beyond providing information about cognitive ability, IQ tests serve as symbols of status and belonging within that privileged concept of normal—white, middle-class America—that the tests empower. As Goddard and Terman established, high intelligence and social privilege go together. The former secures access to the latter. And to many parents, this sense of belonging is worth doing whatever they can to achieve it. This is what our parenting culture tells us nurturing is—buying and doing whatever it takes to help your kid win the intelligence game.

Accessing IQ tests from sources other than eBay is not easy. Pro Ed Incorporated, the company that publishes the Stanford-Binet exam, sells the test on its website for $1,361. Even if I wanted to spend that much, I would have to submit credentials to the company before I would be allowed to see a more detailed list of the testing materials it offered for purchase. I consider myself both a parent and a researcher, but neither identity provided me with access to IQ tests through the company's website.

One of the reasons why psychologists discourage the circulation of IQ tests is because they don't want people to practice. In theory, IQ tests are supposed to evaluate a person's innate intellectual ability rather than what that person has learned or prepared. But this distinction is difficult to maintain. And early on, psychologists acknowledged and attempted to navigate the overlap between testing and play. Samuel Kohs developed the Block Design test while a psychology student at Stanford in 1923. Kohs based the test on Color Cubes, a widely available game produced by the Milton Bradley Company, in which children construct patterns and designs from a set of sixteen wooden cubes painted in bright colors. In his instructions, Kohs advised his fellow psychologists that the blocks "may be secured at any of the large department stores." Psychologists soon recognized that children who had played the game at home were noticeably better at it and advised that some test-takers be given time to practice to offset the advantage of children who had a set of the blocks at home.

Once intelligence becomes measurable, it also becomes a game to win. Even in its early days, parents and psychologists alike understood what could be gained with a high IQ score. It is no coincidence that Color Cubes became one of Milton Bradley's most popular games of the twentieth century. The sets of blocks are now produced by companies that specialize in "brain building" toys, such as Learning Resources and ThinkFun. After all, parents are just as anxious about their children's intellect today as they were in 1923. According to these companies' marketing descriptions, toys help young children visualize, think critically, and problem-solve.

A kind of self-satisfying circuit emerges, one that reinforces capitalism's power to define and market good parenting. Toys resemble activities on IQ tests; some are even marketed as "Mensa approved," appealing to those who find value in the exclusivity of the high-IQ society. Parents find out what games most closely resemble the problems on an IQ test (possibly with the help of eBay) and want to buy them for their kids, sparking a cottage industry of test-preparation through toys. As Koh realized more than a hundred years ago, children with access to these games do better on IQ tests. His observation hints that perhaps there is no way to access intelligence without cultural influence, if it exists in some pure state at all. What they do measure is whether a person has been exposed to the games, puzzles, and cultural references that are baked into the tests.

In order for IQ tests to have any clinical validity, psychologists need to guard testing material against coaching. But the barrier to access also fosters an authority based in secrecy. It discourages non-specialists from asking questions and minimizes the perspective of other forms of expertise in conversations about cognitive ability. Should a test have so much power that parents are willing to intervene in their children's performance or spend too much money on too many toys to prepare? Is the value of IQ tests compromised if they promote such a culture? Such questions highlight that IQ testing isn't just a tool of psychology. It is a big business. Companies and the psychologists who develop testing material want to control the circulation of their tests to protect their efficacy, but they also want to get paid for them.

* * *

SINCE THE DEVELOPMENT of mental tests in the late nineteenth century, the public has been willing to pay to take them and to know the results. Nine years after he published his essay declaring that "nature is far stronger than nurture," Francis Galton set up his Anthropometric Laboratory at the International Health Exhibition in London. Some 9,337 visitors stopped by Galton's lab and paid three pence to undergo a variety of physical measurements and tests. Galton noted that the door to his laboratory was "thronged by applicants waiting patiently for their turn." Adults and children alike could receive a copy of their test and choose to register their results with Galton's office in South Kensington for future reference and follow-up testing. Capitalizing on the excitement about the new science of statistics, Galton hustled people into paying him for the data he needed to measure the differences between them. A familial cousin of Charles Darwin, Galton used the data to produce one of the first bell curves of human intelligence and propose ways in which intelligence could be improved through eugenic pursuits.

World's Fairs were a mix of trade exhibitions and popular entertainment that celebrated technological and scientific progress. Displaying mental testing alongside other wonders of modern advancement, such as steam turbines and car batteries, legitimized psychology for the public. Anthropologist Franz Boas organized a program of anthropometric measurements to be carried out on visitors to the World's Fair in Chicago in 1893. The guide to the exhibition pitched the tests to the public as if psychologists were providing a service to them for a small fee. Not only were these tests offering valuable information, but each score would stand among the pantheon of test-takers on laboratory walls.

Data collection at World's Fairs also served as another way to advance racially motivated research. Boas and his team attempted to test as many foreign visitors as possible. He also tested members of the Native American tribes who were put on display for paying visitors to watch like zoo animals. Like Goddard at Ellis Island two decades later, Boas collected data from people whose first language was not English. Both Boas and Goddard administered mental tests to confirm preconceived beliefs about racial inferiority.

Psychologists were eager for the white public to be comfortable with mental testing, but they also wanted to protect their territory and assert their authority and expertise. It wasn't long before the IQ test administrator was codified as a trained expert. In his 1916 study, *The Measurement of Intelligence*, psychologist Lewis Terman declared, "It cannot be too strongly emphasized that no one, whatever his previous training may have been, can make proper use of the scale unless he is willing to learn the method of procedure and scoring down to the minutest detail." Psychologist Harlan Hines took an even more protective tone seven years later when he warned, "Put into the hands of untrained examiners, intelligence tests are dangerous tools." Hines's warning is remarkable considering how dangerous the tool had become by 1923 for immigrants, people of color, and those with intellectual differences in the hands of purportedly trained examiners.

A World's Fair seems like a strange circumstance in which to be measured. The social interaction of public exhibitions was quite different from the private, clinical office in which I took the IQ test with Harris. But like parades and Ferris wheels, mental testing served as a form of entertainment, which suggests that it provided the public with more than just data from the beginning. In its non-clinical formats, mental testing still stages an opportunity to stroke egos and affirm superiority, no matter what a person's social status might be. Today, other forms of entertainment provide opportunities to win the intelligence game—online IQ tests, which are completely unscientific but instantly satisfying, trivia nights at local bars, or even television game shows like *Jeopardy*.

* * *

To GODDARD, ONE of the most appealing benefits of Binet's IQ test was its ability to predict the future. It could tell parents, educators, and lawmakers if it was worth spending the time and resources to educate a child, if a child should be placed in an institution, or if the child was a particularly promising investment. In Goddard's words, the IQ score explained "what the child is capable of in the way of training and development—the one thing that we in institutions wish to know, and the one thing that the public is clamoring to know, the one thing that parents ask when they come to us." IQ tests promised to quell or confirm anxieties felt by parents, while at the same time creating the fear that stokes such anxieties in the first place. They seemed to get to the core of what keeps parents up at night. Will my children be okay when they grow up? How best can I prepare my child for the future? It is easier to answer these questions if a child's potential seems straightforward and legible. And if you know a child's future, then it seems like destiny, and out of your hands.

By the 1920s, Goddard was receiving a steady diet of letters from parents seeking advice about their children's education and upbringing. In one letter, Mrs. Ruth Cole begged Goddard for a fifteen-minute appointment to follow up on his previous advice about her son Maynard's education, which was to keep him out of school if at all possible. The problem of Maynard's education, she explained, rested entirely upon her. Surely Goddard could understand that she didn't want to make a mistake.

On March 16, 1927, Mrs. Thomson wrote to Goddard soon after she finished reading *The Kallikak Family*. She and her husband planned to start a family and she wanted to know whether their child could potentially be "feeble-minded or a moron." Mrs. Thomson explained that both she and her husband were "normal and intelligent." In fact, she thought it was fair to say she was above average. She had graduated from high school with honors and had the highest marks on stenographic work of all the pupils in the whole school. She was not saying this to be vain, she explained. Rather, she believed this information could help Goddard advise her case.

Her husband's side of the family, however, included some relatives of concern. His sister looked intelligent and was fairly good looking, but "there is certainly something abnormal about her." Another brother never learned to read or write. According to *The Kallikak Family*, such evidence among relatives was indeed cause for worry. Goddard replied and ran through several possible genetic scenarios, but concluded that Mrs. Thomson had very little to fret about. In the cases of the brother and sister, it was most likely that "the procreative power had simply grown weak."

Goddard's research on intelligence appealed to a broader audience than just other psychologists. Parents believed that psychologists like Goddard could provide important information about what they could and should do to raise their children. When I read these letters, what bothered me the most was the trust that they put in Goddard and his pernicious ideas. That mothers were making parental decisions based on eugenics was horrifying enough, but these women also seemed completely lost without Goddard's authority. They were not just seeking advice. They were fully willing to submit to the power of IQ tests. I'm not sure we do much better today. Still, parents look to test scores to quell their anxieties about the unknown future of their children. This is why glancing at Louisa's test results makes my heart sink and my ears burn red. It appears to give me information about her future. And thanks to technological advances in genetics, we seem to be moving to a world in which future parents can be assured of the genetic "perfection" of their children even before they are born.

IQ testing managed to create the very anxieties that Goddard and others claimed that it quelled. Of course, parents had always been concerned about their kids' well-being. But now, with the measurement of intelligence, parents could measure sibling against sibling, cousin against cousin, neighbor against neighbor and make important life decisions accordingly. IQ tests provide parents with a satisfying sense of stability about the identity and potential future of their child, while locking them into an endless cycle of need and validation.

"Is MY CHILD a genius, a moron, or somewhere in between? Most parents would very much like to know." I am watching an episode of *The Gesell Report* from 1960, a weekly television program that provided parenting advice to the public. A man in a suit seated at a desk with a book open in front of him begins the episode with this question. The frankness of his words—*genius, moron*—hit my ears like a slap. But the host presses on, reading questions submitted by parents to Louise Bates Ames, Director of the Gesell Institute of Human Development, who answers them.

Dr. Ames was a research assistant to psychologist Arnold Gesell at the Clinic of Child Development in New Haven, Connecticut. In 1950, she became one of the founding directors of the Gesell Institute of Child Development. She wrote a number of syndicated newspaper columns for mothers and popularized the study of childhood development in the 1960s. In the two decades that followed, she wrote a series of books on child development, with volumes devoted to the ages and stages in a child's life. Other books in the series address common parental concerns about school. *School Readiness, Stop School Failure*, and *Is Your Child in the Wrong Grade?* testify to the growing concerns about school success among parents. The series established the public role of the child psychologist in telling mothers what is normal and what is not. After all, parenting is mostly an intuitive practice, and it is deeply affirming to have an expert on your side.

I did not read Dr. Ames's book series when Louisa was a baby, but I read many others that seemed to have the same approach. In most cases, parents just need to be reassured that everything is fine. Worry is something parents do to fill the void of the unknown, and Ames and other experts willingly took on the role of putting parents, crazed with self-doubt and sleep deprivation, in their place. And while I include all parents, I actually mean mothers. Ames's guides are traditional in the way she assumes that her readers are mostly mothers but rarely fathers. And although our co-parenting looks nothing like Dr. Ames's model or the ones our parents provided, I don't recall Andy ever opening up any parenting guide to quell his anxieties as I often did.

"I think that my thirty-four-month-old son is a genius." The host begins reading the first letter to Dr. Ames. "But nobody wants to do anything about it. How can I find out what his IQ really is? All I get is evasive answers, and they don't believe me that he can read without trouble." As the moderator recites the mother's question, Dr. Ames lowers her chin and smiles politely. She wears a dark, short-sleeved sweater and a bold, geometric necklace. Her wavy hair is pinned back, and her face is thoughtful and plain behind an assertive pair of cat's eyeglasses. Dr. Ames says casually that the mother can go to any child psychologist to have her son's IQ tested. "However, my advice to this mother is not to find out her son's IQ," she continues. She speaks in a confident voice that is enriched with a New England accent. "If the child was defective it would be important to find out. But if all you're worried about is whether your child is a genius, why not just enjoy it and not worry very much." Dr. Ames chides the mother a bit more. "It is kind of tiresome to professional people when a mother says, 'Now my IQ is this, my husband's IQ is this, my three children's IQs are this, and I want to know the IQ of this other one,' because it's just not that important to know. It's especially not important to know if she's going to go around boasting about it, which this mother is. She is making too much of it. The IQ is one measure of human behavior, but it is one small measure."

Watching Dr. Ames dole out her confident advice, I was struck by how little has changed. She is right that the IQ test is only one measure of human behavior, one that has become grossly overvalued. But she parsed the difference between the meaning of the IQ test for psychologists, "professional people," and the meaning of the IQ test for the mother, as if they have nothing to do with each other. I noticed similarities between the way Dr. Ames downplayed the importance of IQ testing and the way that the school psychologist told me that Louisa's IQ doesn't really matter. My reasons for asking questions about the IQ test may be different from this mother's motivations, and I assume that Dr. Ames would have thought it was important for me to know Louisa's IQ. But I recognize a shared tension underneath the annoying vanity of the mother's question, as Dr. Ames perceived it. This mother and I both seemed to be confronting the same conflicting messages. IQ is important, but also not. It is a way to learn more about your child, but also something that is specialized information that is too complicated and beyond our reach to grasp.

Despite our differences, I recognize a bit of my own reaction to Louisa's IQ in this mother's question. I admit that I was rather proud that Louisa's IQ seemed high for a child with Down syndrome, without really understanding why it mattered. But I also understand Dr. Ames's impatience with mothers who fret over a few IQ points. I find it hard to hear these quibbles and find empathy. I presume that this mother's child will not face the kind of intellectual discrimination that those who lived at Goddard's Training School experienced. Her son will not be labeled "feeble-minded" or "defective." Desperate to solidify her and her son's exceptional nature, this mother doesn't seem to realize how grave her concerns could be.

PERHAPS THE MOTHER who wrote to Dr. Ames sensed that economic and educational opportunities were growing increasingly dependent on IQ tests. Many parents wanted to know how they could help their children do better on them. In 1958, David Engler, a teacher from

New York, had his finger on the pulse of parents and wrote *How to Raise Your Child's IQ.* "We live in what has been called the era of 'mass man,'" he begins the introduction, "a time when people are thought of as statistical averages and not as individuals." In an interview in the *New York Times*, Engler admits that his title is a facetious hook. He agrees with many psychologists that "it may not be possible to increase a child's basic potential in the intellectual sphere." But the test, he believed, "cannot plumb the depths of basic potential; it can only measure its surface indications." Schools were becoming increasingly crowded, and the IQ test provided a convenient shorthand, Engler admitted, to determine where a child should be placed. "Just a few points may determine whether a child is selected for an enrichment class or, at the other extreme, placed with 'slow learners.'" It is therefore encouraged, if not required, that parents do whatever they can to improve their child's test score. The system is set, it seems. The only thing that can be changed is the pecking order, what advantage your child might have over others.

Engler imagined a number of different scenarios in his book, in which the life paths of various children would have been completely different if they had only scored a few more points on an IQ test. Bobby, for example, is "as bright as a button," but only has an IQ of 89. He is placed in a class with a "watered-down curriculum." At the end of the two years, Bobby's IQ will be even lower. Eventually, he will be rejected for training as a radar technician in the armed forces. There's also poor Marsha, who has an IQ of 128 but will not be hired for the research position she applied for because her IQ is two points below the minimum for the job. To avoid similar situations, Engler offers his parent-readers a series of exercises in the last third of his book, which are similar to but not exactly like what appeared on the most widely used intelligence tests in the 1950s. Engler claimed that the exercises were designed to increase both speed and accuracy. He stressed that children should not be made to feel that their IQ is inadequate, but older children might be motivated if parents explain to them the importance of IQ tests in schools.

Engler described an educational system in which IQ scores were casually traded among teachers and school administrators as a kind of shorthand for a student's life potential. Yet these scores were never shared with the students or parents, Engler reported, thus creating a world of insiders and outsiders. Teachers relied heavily on the convenient expression of intelligence in an IQ score, yet parents were not privy to or in control of such information.

So much research on IQ scores has been done since 1958, but the system that Engler described has only solidified and grown more entrenched. More research, more testing has attempted to classify and track students into particular learning environments with more precision. But the system and the ends it tries to achieve have not really changed, and Engler's approach marked a historical moment of no return. He advised that, whether we like it or not, whether it was good for society or not, the regime of IQ testing was here to stay. What parents could do was game the system, teach to the test, and work on raising that IQ score. Since IQ tests impacted the kind of education their children would receive, parents should have the right and the responsibility to do something about it.

Intelligence testing sits on a precipice between public and private information. It positions us in relation to our peers. Intelligence feels personal, a character trait that is ingrained in our very DNA. But in fact it has been shaped by very impersonal societal forces. It is easy to understand why parents reading Engler's book in the 1950s might have understood the IQ test as a consequential game, a hoop to jump through that could determine the course of a child's entire life. But IQ scores determine children's futures because we let them. Rather than providing some natural prediction, IQ tests became a sorting system, and parents felt powerless to stop it.

*   *   *

ENGLER COMPARED THE addiction to IQ scores in modern education in the 1960s to the cigarette-smoking habits of many Americans. Both were addictive and pervasive. But if you assume that the obsession with IQ that Engler describes is only related to the culture of chain-smoking, postwar America, think again. Most twenty-first-century parents are still hyper-aware of the threat of determinism that accompanies standardized tests. Public schools are now legally required to share test results with parents, yet it has made parents no less anxious.

A website called TestingMom.com ("Involved Parents, Successful Kids") offers twenty-first-century parents what Engler did more than seventy years ago. The website offers a hundred free practice questions and then offers thousands of others for a fee, "to help your child build the skills and familiarity to walk into Test Day with confidence." The website states that the purpose of the WISC is to determine whether or not a child is gifted, although I'm not sure David Wechsler would have agreed with such an assessment. TestingMom.com markets to parents who want to see their children get ahead, because the only reason imaginable to a Testing Mom that their child would be taking such an exam is superior intellect.

In a brief video on the website, Karen Quinn, aka "The Testing Mom," reassures anxious parents that they can help their child prepare to take a test like the Cognitive Aptitude Test (CogAT) to access a gifted program, despite what they might have heard from other parents or well-meaning teachers. She stands in front of bookshelves filled with colorful spines and strategically placed boxes labeled "IQ Fun Pack." Quinn informs parent-viewers that many of their child's classmates are at an advantage because their parents took action, "just like I know you'll take action," she calmly assures.

The website includes all the necessary caveats. The questions that TestingMom.com provides are practice questions, not the exact questions on the exam. It concedes that IQ tests are just one tool in a larger assessment process. But still, I can't help but think that this isn't the way it should be. As I watch the Testing Mom video, I keep returning to the question of what this is for but to classify and create social hierarchies. Those children with parents who have money and time to spend on practice questions will do better on the test. It is a system in which I believe parents are desperate to step away from. But parents are also afraid to let go of the value of tests for reasons that Quinn demonstrates. Every other parent is working on boosting their kid's IQ, she tells us. If you don't, your child will be left behind.

Believing that tests like the WISC and the CogAT will guarantee a path to success and privilege, Testing Moms are damn sure that their kids are going to nail that test. But the results of such efforts impact the entire community. As students are tracked into gifted and honors courses, they spend less time interacting with students who might not be sorted into such programs. Given that more than 60 percent of students enrolled in gifted education programs in the United States are white, the opportunities that these programs provide reinforce racial hierarchies of power in our education system and ultimately solidify the social and economic power of the mostly white middle-class.

And by the way, where are all the Testing Dads? As Dr. Ames showed us, the responsibilities of raising a child's intelligence falls on the shoulders of women, just like other traditional child-raising duties. The company's choice to call its website TestingMom.com makes it clear that this gendered role has not disappeared. I began to see these test scores, and my anxieties about them, as part of the work that is put upon mothers. Reinforcing the regime of testing—preparing our kids for it, making sure their potential is recognized—has become part of the maternal role, a distortion of our responsibility to actually nurture our children. We reinforce the power of tests by working so hard to ensure that our children live up to their expectations. There are other typical roles of the mother that I have been able to pull back from. I have refused the guilt of not volunteering for every holiday party and not always sending Louisa to school with lunches that are both healthy and cute. Yet the labor of being a Testing Mom has been harder to shake.

BEFORE LOUISA BEGAN fourth grade, we received a Family Score Report for a standardized test in English Language Arts that Louisa had taken the previous spring. Like many states, Ohio has a Third Grade Reading Guarantee law that states, according to the piece of paper sent home in Louisa's backpack, "schools must give extra help to struggling readers." The specifics of the extra help were not provided, but it did say that Louisa is not keeping up with her peers. Her test scores indicated that she had a limited ability to answer questions about what happened in a story and to find the main idea of a text. She was having trouble organizing facts and writing for a purpose.

The score wasn't exactly surprising, yet my rational understanding of her intellectual differences was not reflected in the heaviness in my chest and tears welling up in my eyes as I stood in my living room, staring at this piece of paper. I could not understand why I was having this response. Louisa read every day and found deep meaning in what she read, but that understanding and purpose wasn't seen on her test results. What she could do and understand wasn't good enough.

On some mornings, Louisa climbed into our bed with a picture book as I tried to cling to the last moments of sleep. Louisa was an early riser, and we usually had time to read before other thoughts and plans finally pushed me onto my feet. Despite the early wake-up call, these brief moments of reading became my favorite time of day. Louisa loves books. Andy and I read to her from her earliest days, starting with Sandra Boynton's *Belly Button Book!* and gradually working our way up to picture books about more complicated and subtle topics. Louisa and I read alternate pages and took time to look at the pictures. "What do you think the music that the man on the bus is playing sounds like?" I asked her. She hummed a silly tune in reply.

When we received her Third Grade Reading Guarantee report, the attention and focus needed to read on her own had not yet emerged. I tried to hook her on books like *Lola Levine*, which tells stories from the life of a precocious girl with a Jewish father and Peruvian mother, or *Ivy and Bean*, which follows the adventures of two friends with very different personalities. Louisa seems to prefer biographies. Perhaps the choice is an extension of her sociable nature and interest in people. But I admit that I must have influenced her reading interests. As the daughter of two art historians, she knew more about Georgia O'Keefe, Sonia Delauney, and Frida Kahlo than most third graders. Yet nothing seemed to rocket Louisa onto a course of independent reading.

Maybe I should have been immune to such bureaucratically communicated information about her reading, but I still felt a tightening weight in my chest. With all the work and time we put into reading, this was where we were. With all the work and time I put into thinking outside the regime of intelligence and assessment, this was still my response. I think that I don't really care about these tests until the knot in my gut reminds me that I do. I was disappointed in myself, and maybe a little in Louisa too. She seemed uninterested in taking such tests seriously. Her teachers reported that it doesn't take long for her to start randomly filling in the circles on her exam during test time. I see this as a form of protest that is both frustrating and admirable. How can I recognize that these assessments do not properly assess what Louisa knows and feel tearfully disappointed that she does so poorly on them? How can I hate these tests and want her to do better on them at the same time?

In most scenarios, Andy is much less likely to spiral into a vortex of fear and anxiety about the future than I am. While I believe that worry keeps me on my toes, prepared to deal with a future that can seem so unpredictable, Andy tends to take things one day at a time, not looking too far ahead into the unknown. The balance of our two perspectives usually works for us. He manages to stay in the present while I have a plan for when the unpredicted strikes. But worrying is exhausting, and at my worst, I read Andy's steadiness as apathy, a naive contentment to ignore any storm on the horizon that is heading our way. And I'm sure to him it seems as if I'm often inventing problems when maybe it would be easier if I just let things be.

Andy told me to throw the test results away. "If we know that they aren't showing us what she knows, then why do we care?" Andy never feels the sting of Louisa's test scores like I do, and his question was annoyingly reasonable. Yet to me, throwing them away only seemed to reinforce their power, like a bomb that needed to be destroyed before it truly hurt us. In their official envelope (*To the parents of . . .*) and their infographic, the report had an air of authority. But what I was supposed to do about the information it presented was unclear. And so, the report sat on our kitchen counter for months tucked inside its ripped envelope, with the savings plan statements, tax forms, and all the other pieces of paper that remind us we are adults with responsibilities.

I talked with friends who have kids with forty-six chromosomes about our shared anxiety concerning test results. "It feels gross," one of my friends admitted. Her daughter found a set of standardized test results when they arrived in the mail and had a good look at the jumble of charts and graphs with her name on them. To my friend, it seemed like one of those moments in which children learn about a world beyond the bubble that parents try to keep them in, like when they see violence on the news. Her daughter's test results were excellent, my friend told me, yet she didn't know what to do with them. Her husband told her to throw them in the trash, too, as if they needed to be removed from the home environment before any serious damage was done. But this seemed wrong to my friend, as if it was irresponsible to throw away such official information.

Parents want to be nonchalant about standardized tests until it is their kid's future that is determined by them. The power and meaning of the IQ tests shift depending on who holds the information. In the hands of ambitious parents, their kid's high IQ is much more than a scientific measurement. It is a validation of their own lifestyle and understanding of success. But in my hands, and I suspect the same is true for other parents of children with intellectual disabilities, it is a reminder of how my daughter will struggle to find a place in this world. In a world that measures intelligence in this way, she does not belong.

I have considered taking steps to opt out of these standardized tests. I brought this up with one of Louisa's teachers and she said that often parents choose to opt out for mental health reasons, although I'm not sure if she meant the mental health of the student or the parent. But on the other hand, opting out means that Louisa's test scores will not be part of the school and district report card as issued by the Ohio Department of Education. This would mean that the school district is not held accountable for Louisa's test scores. The more parents with kids who struggle on these exams opt out of taking them, the less accurately these school and district report cards represent the range and variety of learners in their classrooms.

When Andy and I meet Louisa's teachers, I constantly feel obliged to perform my involvement and interest in making sure Louisa is learning. I've realized that I do this to assert that I am different from what I assume most parents are like—not reading the notes that come home, not reading with their child, not taking an active role in their learning and modeling that learning is important. I want them to be sure that Louisa's challenges are not due to my lack of involvement.

But time and again, my assumptions have been wrong. We all seem to relax and be more comfortable with each other after I mention that how fast Louisa can recite her multiplication facts is not important to me. Louisa can take her time; I just want her to know them, eventually, maybe. And I don't want anyone to doubt her potential. I tell them what I believe is true, that supporting Louisa does not mean helping her do better on tests. It means making sure that she knows that it's okay not to. Whoever she is, and however she expresses it, is fine.

Teachers are guarded about their assumptions and try to approach all parents without prejudgment. But I've realized that they don't assume parents are uninvolved. They assume parents are overinvested in their child's test scores and assessment markers. They do not think I might be uninvolved. Their guard is up when they think I am a Testing Mom. "Some of the ways that we broadly assess things in a school setting are not accurate reflections of what students know or how it is used in real life," one of Louisa's teachers once told me. "We live in a world of numbers and comparisons and it's not good for anyone." This seemed to me to be an apt evaluation of a world shaped by IQ tests. They are linked to capitalist forces in pernicious ways that have distorted our ideas about what we should do to help our children live happy lives. We have been sold the idea that making our kids into good test-takers is a form of nurturing. But actual nurturing would disavow the pecking order and predictions that IQ tests have established. We need to ask how we can help our kids be more unique and self-fulfilled people who are connected to a diverse community. This would be nurturing at its best.

The best teachers, I've realized, push against the standardized assessments and cognitive tests and try to find the individual in their midst. Thanks to the human intervention of her teachers and school principal, who realize there is more to development and learning than a test score, Louisa was promoted to fourth grade, where she continued to joyfully underperform on all standardized tests.

Gifted

"Would you like to buy a cake roll to support my trip to Space Camp?" There was a girl standing on our porch holding a clipboard and a pen. I recognized her from a recent choir concert at Louisa's school. I could barely hear her above the beat of the Taylor Swift song that Louisa and I had been dancing to in our living room. The girl posed her question before I fully opened the front door, as if it was automatically triggered by the turning of the doorknob. She was smiling but seemed sheepish as she practiced this new skill of door-to-door solicitation.

I had bought pies and Christmas wreaths from other kids in the neighborhood. I never really wanted what I bought, but I felt like buying them was a gesture of community support and good karma. One day, it might be my kid's turn to raise money for new uniforms or team supplies, and I would appreciate my neighbors returning the favor. On this occasion, the purchase of a cake roll, a decadent swirl of sponge and cream in tube form, helped raise funds for fifth graders in the gifted program at Louisa's school to go on a bus trip to Space Camp in Huntsville, Alabama, at the end of the year. Louisa was in fifth grade now too. She wiggled her way in between me and the front door to see what was going on. The two girls greeted each other warmly. I smiled and waved to the mother who was waiting on the sidewalk. We all just stood there for a few seconds as I felt the situation becoming more awkward.

The choices and circumstances of history can rise up in the present in such extraordinarily mundane ways. To me, the inequities caused by IQ testing were playing out in this otherwise neighborly interaction. On one side of the door, a mother and daughter were asking for support for an opportunity afforded to a child who did well on an IQ test. On the other side, I was being asked to help by buying a dessert that would taste like a cardboard box, even though my daughter wasn't given the same opportunity because she didn't do well on an IQ test. As I stood on my porch, I doubted the girl's mom had any inkling of what I was thinking—that it was more than a little annoying to be asked to support her child's trip when my own daughter wasn't included for reasons beyond her control.

"No thanks. I think we have enough sweets right now," I said, squinting in a fake smile. This was the kindest response I could come up with. This girl wasn't to blame for the frustration I felt about what was going on here, and I wasn't sure the mother was exactly to blame either. If the circumstances were different, would I deny Louisa such an opportunity if it was not given to other children? Why should I expect other parents to take one for the team? It was hard not to think of the trip to Space Camp as some kind of reward, although I was not exactly sure what it was a reward for. For being white and middle-class? For working harder than other kids? Or was it for a fluid ease with learning in school? What was a good reason why some kids got the chance to go on this trip and others didn't? I couldn't help listening to the small voice inside telling me that this trip—and the fact that I was being asked to support it—was complete bullshit.

This wasn't the first time I learned about the Space Camp trip for gifted children. It wasn't flaunted in the faces of those excluded, but it wasn't exactly kept secret either. Because I was growing increasingly attuned to the complicated influences of the IQ test on Louisa's life, and because she was *my* child, how unjust her exclusion was appeared obvious to me. No other parents seemed to be bothered by what I perceived as a pretty solid case of privileging those who happened to do well on an IQ test, but then I brought it up and learned that others were annoyed too.

"So is Caitlyn going on the Space Camp trip?" I asked a mother as we sat on a bench during our daughters' gymnastics lessons. I thought it would be better to err on the side of gifted as I tried to broach the topic, rather than offend by assuming Caitlyn had not made the cut. "No," said Caitlyn's mom. "And I'm not sure how I feel about that." But the clipped, low tone of her voice told me exactly how she felt, and I wondered why we both seemed to give in to a vague pressure not to rock the boat. "I mean, if they're going to organize this big trip, why can't all the kids get the chance to go? Caitlyn loves outer space and science. And she wonders why some of her friends get to go on this trip and she doesn't."

Like Caitlyn, Louisa would have loved to attend Space Camp. She entertains herself for hours on weekend afternoons with her version of science experiments, which involve mixing together any liquids she can get her hands on in our kitchen. She has drawn more pictures of the solar system than I can count. I thought about pushing more. Maybe I should email the teacher in charge of the gifted program, I wondered, and ask him if Louisa might tag along. I fantasized about how this conversation might force the issue, making the teacher name the reason for her exclusion. And maybe if he had to articulate why Louisa was not invited—*because her test scores aren't high enough, because she has a disability*—then he would see that this trip was bullshit too. But I backed off and stewed in my own pot of frustration, not wanting to raise a fuss in a way that might draw Louisa into something that she ultimately didn't seem too upset by.

Perhaps to address the inequity—how it might not seem fair that gifted students got to go on a class trip while everyone else stayed behind—Louisa's fifth-grade teachers organized an overnight trip to an outdoor camping site. Like the Space Camp trip, a fee was required to attend. No saccharine cake rolls were sold for the cause, but there was financial help available and sleeping bags to borrow for those who needed them. Although I don't know for sure, I'd like to think that the teachers realized that the Space Camp trip might lead to some hard conversations about social inequity and what it means to be gifted or not. In the end, Louisa played tug-of-war, slept in a cabin, and searched for fossils with her classmates. I doubt she would have had a better time on a seven-hour bus ride to Alabama. The camping trip tempered the hard truth that gifted programs provide advantages and opportunities for some that would benefit all students.

WHEN I STARTED researching the IQ test, I noticed that books on the founders of IQ testing often mention the precocity of their subjects. Francis Galton's first biographer, for example, claimed that he was an extraordinary childhood genius who could read Latin and do long division by the age of six. From that description, Lewis Terman, who developed the Stanford-Binet IQ test and idolized Galton, estimated that his IQ must have been near 200. Terman's own childhood was reportedly just as portentous. One of his biographers reported that he entered third grade as a six-year-old and exhausted all formal educational opportunities in rural Indiana by the age of twelve. The IQs of Galton, Terman, and other male thinkers works to shore up their authority and the authority of the discipline they created.

In 1926, psychologist Catherine Cox and two assistants scanned over 3,000 biographies in search of descriptions of what dignitaries like Goethe, John Stuart Mill, and Benjamin Franklin were like in childhood. From this information, a group of psychologists estimated the IQ for each historical figure. Lewis Terman, who carried out his own research on gifted children, admitted that "it is easy to scoff at these post-mortem IQs." Never mind that the reliance on biography as an accurate and scientifically valid record makes such studies especially suspect. Terman waves off any concerns and supports Cox's conclusion that "the genius who achieves highest eminence is one whom intelligence tests would have identified as gifted in childhood." Gifted, as diagnosed by the IQ test, was a kind of golden ticket. It could predict which children would go on to achieve the most.

"Gifted" locates a person's IQ score in the realm of nature and assumes its origin is slightly mysterious, outside the realm of precise explanation. A phrase such as "he has a gift for numbers" implies that a facility with mathematics is some sort of endowment from the spiritual rather than a product of his upbringing and environment. In his book *Hereditary Genius* from 1869, Galton used the term "gifted" to mean how someone is uniquely special, as in "a judgeship is a guarantee of its possessor being gifted with exceptional ability" or "If a man is gifted with vast intellectual ability . . . I cannot comprehend how such a man should be repressed." Gifted is part of one's nature. In the age of IQ testing that Galton's statistical methods inaugurated, the notion of gifted became more quantitative and precise. In contrast to the older concept of genius, gifted is not only a term of hyperbole or a description of astonishing creativity. It is shaped by the historically specific ambitions of IQ testing.

TO UNDERSTAND HOW IQ testing shaped the concept of giftedness, it is helpful to return to the bell curve, which encourages us to separate those on either side of its peak. We rarely think that the two sides have much in common, but the bell curve shows us that they do. Each group is defined in relation to normal and in relation to each other. But most importantly, both sides of the bell curve are part of the same system. While the bell curve of IQ testing divides us, each one of us occupying a particular place, it is a system that controls and implicates us all.

The relationship between the two sides of the bell curve preoccupied Terman in his earliest studies. In 1906, he published his doctoral dissertation, *Genius and Stupidity: A Study of Some of the Intellectual Processes of Seven "Bright" and Seven "Dull" Boys*. The study took an approach that he referred to as comparative psychology, something like the field of comparative anatomy, which aimed to classify the physical difference between biological species. Intelligence testing, according to Terman, could be used by psychologists as a tool that would help the burgeoning discipline achieve the same precision and specificity as zoologists had accomplished with the Linnaean system of classification. "In dealing with individual minds we encounter no smaller differences than the zoologist finds in his own field," Terman wrote. In this way, he compared the differences between the gifted and the not-gifted to the differences that zoologists have agreed upon between "the whale and the fish." Like Goddard, Terman wanted a clear and standardized way of measuring and identifying intelligence. His language is particularly chilling, making clear his intentions to use IQ tests as a way to organize humans into a hierarchy of subspecies.

In order to identify and distinguish different levels of intelligence, Terman selected boys who were "among the brightest and most stupid that could be found in the public schools" near Clark University in Worcester, Massachusetts, where Terman earned his doctorate. The names of two dozen boys were put forth by local teachers and principals. These students, all around the age of eleven, were given tests in various skills, including the interpretation of fables and the mastery of chess. Terman then generalized the results to compare their overall mental capacity. This was years before he turned to Binet's example and developed the Stanford-Binet IQ test.

According to Terman, the study demonstrated that these two sets of boys, "the brightest and most stupid," were as different as whales from fish. His conclusions pitted one group against the other and defined intelligence as a marker of human difference. "Group I is superior to group II in all the mental tests," he wrote. He also observed that the ranking of each boy throughout the separate tests was strikingly uniform. According to Terman, the test strengthened his hunch that "endowment" was more important than "training" when determining a child's individual rank among his peers and that IQ scores could be a powerful form of human classification. In this way, the distinction between gifted and stupid was set in stone, each one defined as the opposite of the other.

I haven't found a recent study by an expert in education or psychology that considers a relationship between the gifted and those with intellectual disabilities. One reason for this might be because the way we define intelligence is rarely approached as a system constructed by humans who made culturally and socially influenced choices about what that system looks like. Instead, IQ tests are treated as diagnostic tools. But if the opportunities and limitations faced by many like Louisa are a product of the system of intelligence testing, then the entire shape of the bell curve needs to be scrutinized. One side of the bell curve cannot change without transforming the other. Both are born from particular assumptions about what IQ tests mean and how it assigns people a place in the modern world.

LATER, WHEN TERMAN was a professor at Stanford University, he began a longitudinal study that tracked about 1,000 boys and girls in California public schools who had IQ scores above 140 for over three decades. As something of a child prodigy himself, Terman wanted to debunk the common belief in "early ripe, early rot," that precocious children peak too early and burn out in adulthood. He concluded that tests of "general intelligence, given as early as six, eight, or ten years, tell a great deal about the ability to achieve either presently or thirty years hence." According to Terman, gifted children consistently turn out to be successful and above-average adults.

Terman's studies affirmed his belief that intelligence was biologically and racially determined. His *The Measurement of Intelligence* from 1916 presented a series of case studies of school-aged children, their race, their socioeconomic class, and their IQs. Mirroring the Linnaean system of biological classification, Terman organized his case studies into categories of intelligence: genius or near genius (above 140); very superior intelligence (120–140); superior intelligence (110–120); normal or average intelligence (90–110); dullness (80–90); borderline deficiency (70–80). Terman left the distinctions of feeble-mindedness, an IQ below 70, to his colleague Henry Goddard.

In his case studies, Terman often noted the race of his subjects. Two brothers, M.P. and C.P., were identified as Portuguese and sons of a skilled laborer. They have IQs of 77 and 78, respectively. Terman concluded that no amount of school instruction would ever make them "intelligent voters or capable citizens." He moved on to draw broader conclusions about their race:

> Their dullness seems to be racial, or at least inherent in the family stocks from which they come. The fact that one meets this type with such extra-ordinary frequency among Indians, Mexicans, and negroes suggests quite forcibly that the whole question of racial differences in mental traits will have to be taken up anew. . . . The writer predicts that when this is done there will be discovered enormously significant racial differences in general intelligence, differences which cannot be wiped out by any scheme of mental culture.

I do not know why two boys of Portuguese descent would lead Terman to conclusions about the intelligence of "Indians, Mexicans, and negroes." Fixating on this strange flaw in his logic risks overlooking the horrifying racism of his conclusions that are still with us today. As chairman of the National Education Association in 1922, Terman led a committee that proposed major revisions to elementary education that would reorganize schools into homogenous ability groups based on the classification of IQ scores that he proposed in *The Measurement of Intelligence.* Motivated by a separate-but-equal philosophy, Terman saw such segregation as for everyone's own good and a mark of a true democracy.

"It is a matter of profound significance that nearly 50 percent of these gifted children belong to the professional classes," Terman wrote. He took this statistic to mean that children of the professional classes were naturally smarter, not that white people of privilege were given the opportunities necessary to do their best on the types of questions on an IQ test. He also does not consider how the identification of children as gifted might change their life trajectory. Those labeled as gifted are given opportunities for success that are not afforded to others because they are not labeled as such. I couldn't help but think that the trip to Space Camp seemed like one of those opportunities.

DESPITE TERMAN'S PERSISTENT studies, there was very little national interest in what it meant to be gifted until the 1950s, when the gifted student became a symbol of the United States' international standing. On October 4, 1957, the Soviet Union successfully launched Sputnik, the world's first earth-orbiting satellite. Months later, President Eisenhower signed the National Defense Education Act, which included the first federal support for gifted education. It aimed to improve math, science, and foreign language education, but not for all students. The NDEA committed to fighting the Cold War by providing better instruction in these subjects to gifted students, the nation's best and brightest. And those students were identified through IQ tests, which were already a familiar way of sorting and tracking in America's public schools.

Before the Soviet Union launched Sputnik, Congress was reluctant to provide federal support for education. But the Soviet satellite forced a change in policy. In addition to making low-cost loans available and providing funding to the nation's colleges and universities, the cultivation of America's most intellectually talented children was now a matter of national defense. An article published in the *Boston Globe* in 1959 makes the motivation for a newly found interest in gifted education clear. "If Sputnik did nothing else," it stated, "it awakened the American people to the importance of quality in education." The recent scientific accomplishments of the Soviets were shaking many Americans out of their indifference toward education. "We have become concerned with our own welfare and safety," the article claimed. Defending the nation required embarking on a "treasure hunt" to identify and train gifted students.

I try not to make too much of the connection between the origins of gifted education in the Cold War Space Race and the trip to Space Camp organized at Louisa's school. I doubt our school district is explicitly trying to make gifted children into future astronauts, nor do I believe that the teacher organizing this trip was intentionally prolonging the educational ambitions of the Cold War. But still, I was annoyed that the trip to Space Camp seemed to perpetuate an association of intellectual ability with an interest in science and engineering. *Why not a trip to a Shakespeare festival or an art museum?* this art history professor wondered. Being gifted seemed to mean being good at skills that were associated with a particular vision of progress and innovation in the modern world.

Like intelligence itself, "gifted" is a nebulous and slippery set of characteristics made more concrete by the IQ test. In 1959, James Bryant Conant, a chemist and former president of Harvard University, published *The American High School Today*, a study that recommended reforms to the public school system that favored academically talented students. As policy experts sought to increase gifted programs in public schools, Conant recommended that the cutoff for gifted be moved down to an IQ score of 130, ten points lower than what Terman had established thirty years earlier. He also recalculated the categories on the right half of the bell curve. "Academically talented" students had an IQ of 115 or above. "Superior students" had an IQ higher than 100.

Conant's attempt to develop a precise vocabulary for the deviations above average echoed Goddard's earlier distinctions between idiot, moron, and imbecile. The dream of segregation ordered both sides of the bell curve.

In the early 1960s, experts estimated that there were 600,000 unidentified gifted children in America. How could the country find them? Ordinary citizens were asked to do their part by paying attention to certain signs that someone in their family might be gifted. An article from the *Los Angeles Times* listed twelve signs of a gifted child that parents might notice. If a child showed as many as six, then she was truly exceptional. Such conclusions could then be confirmed by taking an IQ test with a trained expert, the author added. The article also provided consolation for parents who might not have found what they hoped for. "Being normal is still a very good way to be," it reminded parents. "For most of us, that's a lucky thing!" That solace was necessary at all suggested that more was at stake for parents than just the general welfare of their children. Discovering your child was gifted reflected well on the parents, affirming their choices and their status. Normal was only a "very good" way to be.

If a child was truly gifted, there was great danger in leaving him to fester among normal students. In 1958, Barry Wichmann was an eleven-year-old boy growing up in Rockwell City, Iowa. He earned four dollars a week on his paper route and wore dark-framed glasses. He attended sixth grade with children his own age. His father was a piano tuner; his mother a high school graduate who taught music lessons. Barry was primed for a normal American life. But according to *Life* magazine's photo-essay that shared Barry's story with the country, the young boy was in a precarious situation. With an IQ of 162, Barry was isolated by his intelligence. "The Waste of Fine Minds" stated that the odds were against Barry ever reaching his full potential because of a public school system that did not adequately serve his abilities. With his talents wasted, Barry was at risk of potentially doing what would be unthinkable, according to the dramatic tone of the article. "He will end his isolation by becoming an utterly ordinary person."

Articles like the one about young Barry in *Life* introduced giftedness to its readers and garnered support for funding to serve this precarious population of students. *Life* expected its readers to understand IQ as the measurement of an innate ability and to be familiar with IQ tests as a way of identifying differences from normal. It described gifted students as a lost and forgotten group that struggled socially. The article explained that Barry was one of many gifted students who was "isolated by his intelligence, unchallenged at school, unable to even respond much to the loving but uneasy efforts of his parents to guide him." One unnamed expert declared, "The gifted are the most retarded group we have," suggesting a desire to shift the national conversation about intelligence from those who were still being institutionalized and sterilized by eugenics laws toward policies for the gifted, who could potentially "someday pierce labyrinthine complexities and reach profound conclusions."

Published in 1961, Kurt Vonnegut's dystopian short story "Harrison Bergeron" captured the nation's anxieties about intelligence. "The year was 2081, and everybody was finally equal," it begins. "They were equal in every which way. No one was smarter than anyone else." Harrison Bergeron is the teenage son of George and Hazel. Hazel has "average intelligence, which meant she couldn't think about anything except in short bursts." George's intelligence was above normal. He was therefore required by authorities to wear a radio in his ear, which emitted a sharp noise to prevent people like him from gaining an unfair advantage with their brains. Harrison had been arrested for plotting to overthrow the government and for being a genius. But in Vonnegut's dystopian story of a future plagued by an enforced regime of normalcy, George and Hazel don't worry too much about it.

In an age of politicized individualism, the United States' celebration of the self was pitted against the presumed suppression of spirit under communism. Vonnegut's satire plays on national tensions between individual freedom and social responsibility. It stoked fears that treating everyone equally meant turning us all into mindless, oppressively average automatons. It also reflected the way in which IQ testing had brought the nation to a rather reductive form of intelligence, marked by numbers and categories instead of a more complex, ambivalent way of thinking about what the human mind is capable of and what value intelligence has for a society.

Rhetoric about the plight of the gifted student also created a great deal of anxiety about the country's educational system in general. In 1983, the government report *A Nation at Risk* warned of the failure of American students to compete with international counterparts. In one of its most famous passages, the report's authors railed against the system: "The educational foundations of our society are presently being eroded by a rising tide of mediocrity that threatens our very future as a nation and as a people." The report claimed that "the average achievement of high school students on most standardized tests is now lower than twenty-six years ago when Sputnik was launched." In the 1980s, more students graduated from high school and attended college than ever before. But that more populist perspective was not highlighted in the report. *A Nation at Risk* fueled anxiety that the nation was failing its best and brightest, throwing its exceptional self-image into question.

GIFTED IS A concept shaped by history, but the bell curve makes it look much more absolute. A gifted child is one who scores two standard deviations above the mean on an intelligence test or scores in the ninety-fifth percentile on a nationally standardized achievement test. There are a variety of IQ tests that can be approved for gifted assessment, but the WISC and the CogAT are the two most common. The National Association for Gifted Children estimates that the top 10 percent of children in relation to normal IQ test results should be considered gifted. I asked my mom if she remembered when I was tested for the gifted program in third grade. She did not remember. Instead, she assumed that I was in the program like my older sister. I wasn't offended that she didn't remember this detail from my childhood. Her lapsed memory was perhaps because she saw me and my sister as equally capable, equally smart. I was not gifted, but I remember how my dad tried as gently as possible to tell me about the results when they came in the mail. I doubt that my parents were too disappointed, but it still must have been awkward to have to tell your child she is merely normal. Many of my close friends were in the gifted program, and I often wondered what made them different.

I grew up internalizing the distinction between gifted and not. It informed the activities I chose to participate in and the friends I hung around with. As I mentioned, my time on the debate team did not go well. I still got good grades, but I didn't sign up for the Scholar Bowl team or identify as intelligent. That wasn't me, I thought. But when I went off to college, I realized it was me. Moving from Kansas City to New York, where no one knew me, gave me the opportunity to rethink who I was. I realized that whether a test said I was gifted or not didn't have to have any influence on my life at all.

HISTORICALLY, STUDENTS IDENTIFIED as gifted have tended to be affluent and white. Recent evidence shows that students from the wealthiest backgrounds are six times more likely to be identified as gifted than the least affluent students. The Department of Education estimates that 6 percent of public school children are enrolled in gifted programs. But there is no federal mandate to identify gifted students and provide services for their needs. Thirty-five states require their public schools to test and identify students who may be gifted. But schools are not necessarily required to do anything about it. The federal government does not provide funding to local school districts for gifted programs. Those who attend public schools in wealthier communities get the most opportunities. In this way, I guess I should commend our school district for providing a way of raising funds for the trip to Space Camp by selling cake rolls. Otherwise, only parents who could afford it would be able to send their child on the trip.

Here's what gifted education looks like in the twenty-first century: According to the National Center for Education Statistics, 8.1 percent of public school students who identified as white and 12.6 percent of students who identified as Asian were enrolled in gifted programs in the 2017–2018 school year. But only 3.6 percent of Black students, 4.5 percent of Lantinx students, and 4.9 percent of indigenous students were enrolled in gifted programs. *System Failure: Access Denied*, a study published in 2019 by researchers at Purdue and Vanderbilt Universities, found that during the 2015–2016 school year, 3,255,232 students were identified as gifted. But the study determined that, according to the testing standards, about another 3 million students should have been part of gifted programs but were not. Those students attended schools that did not identify gifted students or were part of a racial or ethnic group that was underrepresented in gifted programs.

What are gifted programs for now if the Space Race is over and most of us would resist the idea that public education is a direct form of national defense? In large urban school districts, selection for gifted programs lies in the hands of ambitious, affluent parents, who apply for their child to attend. The application system limits access to those with the time and resources to devote to such a process. Parents submit the results of IQ tests administered by psychologists who they privately hire to ensure that their child is labeled as gifted. Gifted programs and the IQ tests that serve as gatekeepers help maintain the socioeconomic hierarchy. Wealthy, white children get the best education, while others have to settle for less.

"We learned that Liam was gifted in third grade," a father told me. "I'm the parent of a gifted child, but I'm not one myself," a mother pointed out. Parents speak about giftedness as if it is a diagnosis, like finding out a child has a peanut allergy, rather than the outcome of a system of intelligence testing that is set up to reward people of a certain race and socioeconomic class. Parents I interviewed emphasized their concerns about their children getting what they need. "Grace will get bored if she's not in an accelerated class," one father told me. "And then she starts getting distracted and loses focus. She really needs a challenge." Louisa gets bored and distracted, too, and I wondered why my kid's inattention is often read as a character flaw while Grace's boredom is seen as a mandate for more engaging classes. One mother confessed she was grateful for the gifted program because it got her daughters out of the classroom with rowdy boys who were troublemakers. The chaos of a mainstream environment, where some kids get in trouble and disrupt the class, was challenging for her daughters, who like discipline and were intent on doing their best.

I have trouble finding value in these justifications. They seem to perceive gifted education as a way to shield children from the challenges of getting along with others. And while we can't afford to waste the valuable time and patience of gifted kids, it is implied that non-gifted children are less worthy of the best efforts to educate them. We see gifted classrooms as a space that some children are entitled to because they are "good kids" of "good parents." And there is an assumption that gifted kids are obedient rule-followers and the rowdy ones in a classroom can't be gifted too. I thought back to the abuse I witnessed of Amal, who I'm sure wouldn't have been treated with such impatience and disrespect if he were labeled "gifted." Research backs up my impatience with such a rationale. A longitudinal study by the National Center for Education Statistics that took place between 1988 and 2000 asked parents how they thought gifted programs benefited their child. Ninety-eight percent said that they would offer their child greater intellectual stimulation, like the father's concern for his daughter Grace. But there was another popular (84 percent) response in the survey that I doubt many parents would casually fess up to. Gifted programs offered their child the opportunity to associate with other high-ability students, indicating a deep-seated assumption that the best learning happens when students stick with their own kind.

Most of the gifted kids in my public school in the suburbs of Kansas City were upper-middle-class white kids like me. Anecdotally, I am not aware of any distinguished outcomes among my gifted classmates. But in elementary school they had an air of specialness, like suddenly they took a test to discover that they had something the rest of us didn't. By high school, they seemed like everyone else. I assume that now most of them are leading normal lives. A few I know attended public universities and now have middle-class jobs. From my distanced viewpoint, they seem average, a terrible fate according to the *Life* magazine article from 1959.

I went to a decent high school. My parents instilled in me the value of education. I can understand how a parent might feel desperate to find better opportunities for their child if a school is clearly inadequate. But it also seems like a lot of attention is paid to gifted placement when there is no evidence that it makes a clear and consistent difference in the education or future economic prosperity of those who are placed in them. Terman was convinced that gifted children necessarily became successful adults, but there is no conclusive evidence that this is the case. A study from 2021 reported that research on whether gifted programs improve student achievement was surprisingly inconclusive. Because of a dearth of federal oversight of gifted programs, each state and each school district designs their gifted programs in localized ways, which makes the outcomes of gifted education difficult to study. The clearest measurable outcomes of gifted programs seem to be their ability to instill confidence, motivation, and self-awareness, qualities that would certainly benefit all students. Studies also show that low-performing students learn more when they attend classes alongside high-performing students, and a more integrated model has no effect on the test scores of gifted students. More broadly, it just doesn't seem plausible that a single factor in the upbringing of a child, like a gifted program, could be identified as what leads to that child's success or failure in life.

Thanks to the rhetoric of the Cold War, gifted programs have lodged themselves in our educational system as a perceived necessity. The primary argument for gifted programs during the Cold War persists: gifted students are not adequately served in a regular classroom setting and can benefit from an extra challenge. Yet this idea was shaped as much by the national rhetoric and patriotic interests of the Cold War as by scientific evidence. Gary Orfield, co-director of the Civil Rights Project at UCLA, captured the necessary shift in approach to gifted education in 2019: "If you want to do anything except give special advantages to people who already have special advantages, tests aren't the way to do it." Experts like Terman and Conant in the 1950s might have thought, *Yes, of course we want to give special advantages to people who already have special advantages.* The cultivation of those American students with the highest IQs was considered a matter of national security. But Orfield's perspective, and the perspective of many others these days, is entirely different. Our focus should be on democratizing the opportunities and environments that make children learn the most in the first place.

Some are starting to question whether gifted programs are necessary at all. In 2019, a panel appointed by Mayor Bill de Blasio recommended that the New York City Public School District eliminate its gifted programs. The recommendation did not sit well with either the parents of students in the programs or those who wanted access to them. The panel of education experts who recommended the changes argued that gifted programs have become "proxies for separating students who can and should have opportunities to learn together." The *New York Times* reported that, although about 70 percent of students in the New York

City Public Schools are Black and Latino, 75 percent of students in the district's gifted education programs are white or Asian. The inequities and segregation caused by gifted programs in the New York Public School District seemed clear, yet no one really knew how to correct a system based on IQ testing. "I get the burn-it-down, tear-it-down mentality," Marcia Gentry, one of the authors of *System Failure*, said, "but what do we replace it with?"

Despite the ways in which gifted education programs exacerbate racial and economic segregation, the elimination of gifted education is not seen as necessarily the best solution. Rather than dissolving the system, many parents advocated for wider access to it by increasing the number of gifted programs in low-income neighborhoods. In October 2021, just three months before he left office, Mayor de Blasio announced a plan to overhaul gifted education in New York City elementary schools. The new plan included the decision to stop giving a screening test to kindergarten students for which some families paid tutors and bought expensive study materials to prepare. Unlike his predecessor, Mayor Eric Adams committed to keeping gifted programs and added 1,000 seats for students in the city's gifted and talented program shortly after he took office in 2022.

Both sides of the debate want the best educational opportunities for their children. For parents, I imagine it would seem like a risk to give up that privilege for their child. But the problem is that everyone is only thinking about *their* child, a lingering impulse from Cold War individualism that claimed that gifted individuals had to be saved from the masses. IQ testing has turned education into a game of survival of the fittest, making it acceptable to look out for the individual success of your own children without considering how their advantages affect others. Such an individualistic, dog-eat-dog attitude toward education surfaces when educational opportunities aren't equal for everyone. If there were enough funding for all students to get what they needed, no parents would feel as if they had to desperately elbow their way to the front of the line.

The competitive environment of gifted education comes with a high cost to individuals as well as our society as a whole. In 2019, the National Academies of Sciences, Engineering, and Medicine added students who attend "high achieving schools" to a list of at-risk groups that includes kids living in poverty and foster care, recent immigrants, and those with incarcerated parents. All children in this at-risk group are more likely to experience high levels of chronic stress that negatively affect mental health and well-being. Studies have shown that students who attend high-achieving schools can suffer significantly higher rates of depression, substance abuse, and delinquent behaviors than the national average. While articles like the one in *Life* on Barry Wichmann in 1958 instilled a sense of urgency to identify and cultivate gifted students for their own well-being, now it seems like this culture of achievement has only achieved the opposite.

Other large urban school districts have restructured their gifted programs to address segregation and the advantages of students from white, upper-class families. Montgomery County in Maryland no longer allows parents to submit private cognitive evaluations. All third graders—not just those with parents who apply—are considered for spots in the district's top schools. The district also gives less weight to IQ tests in their selection and relies more on performance in a classroom setting. Schools were renamed as "Centers for Enriched Studies," to label the program rather than the students. By avoiding the flawed way in which we diagnose a child as gifted, the change in language seems potentially to be the most profound. So far the district's new approach to gifted education has brought about the intended outcomes. The number of Black and Hispanic students attending Montgomery County's Centers for Enriched Studies increased by 7 percent in one year.

Our school district in rural Ohio couldn't be more different than the New York City Public Schools, the largest and possibly most segregated school system in the country. The tension I feel in our school district is less racial and more socioeconomic. The university where I teach is surrounded by rural farms and trailer parks. The children of relatively affluent families learn alongside children from poorer rural communities. Children of liberal academics learn with kids whose parents wear MAGA hats. It is not without its challenges. But unlike New York City schools that have put children as young as four on a separate educational track, students in the gifted program at Louisa's school meet one hour a day during an intervention period. Other kids might go to a group for non-native English speakers during this time. Some might get extra help in reading. Louisa works with her intervention specialist. No student is put under scrutiny for leaving the room, and hopefully, all students are getting their individual needs met.

I don't think that gifted programs are somehow limiting the funds and resources for Louisa's education. At her school, it doesn't seem like the gifted program and the intervention for students with disabilities have much to do with each other. But maybe that is the problem. The segregation of school programs in terms of intelligence or academic ability reinforces the idea that these types of students shouldn't be part of the same cultural and educational circles. Gifted programs show that an educational system so enamored with the information gleaned from IQ tests leads to segregation. It models specific hierarchies of classism, racism, and ableism to students. It perpetuates a flawed and damaging logic that some opportunities are only available to some kinds of students. We eventually believe that this is inherently true and understand our place in society and the opportunities available to us as inevitable, determined by a test score and its measurement of presumed natural aptitude. The separation for an hour a day at Louisa's school is different than the full segregation in the New York City School District. But we all could use a new approach that prioritizes collaboration and learning together rather than the improvement of test scores.

*   *   *

LOUISA, ANDY, AND I were playing a board game one night. Between rounds, while we were shuffling cards and setting up game pieces, Andy and I talked about how neither of us was gifted and how this now seemed meaningless to us. We talked about the value we see other parents placing on this identity, and how people often talk about gifted programs with us, as if they were something that we would personally see a need for too. "Guys! No one in this house is gifted!" Louisa suddenly intervened. The interruption was necessary. We had lost focus and abandoned the game for adult conversation. I hadn't considered whether she knew what being gifted meant, or if she was aware of which friends were gifted, or if she knew that our world defined gifted as the opposite of what it meant to have an intellectual disability. Clearly, the labels and what they meant were seeping into her consciousness in ways I wasn't fully in control of. But to Louisa, it hardly mattered. She just wanted to play the game.

Does being gifted matter? Yes and no. It matters if you are a person of color whose children never seem to get the educational opportunities they deserve. If you are a white middle-class parent like me, it simply becomes a sign of status. In the end, the separation between those who are gifted and those who are not is largely superficial. It is a difference that was created by the belief that some people deserve more opportunities than others, and the degree to which they deserve more can be measured by an IQ test. But kids are kids, humans are humans. Opportunities to learn from each other are what should matter the most.

High Stakes

I have just returned to my office after teaching a class of 150 students. My stomach is growling because I haven't eaten lunch, but the line of students that starts at my office door is already extending down the hall. They are all silent, leaning against the wall and scrolling on their phones. They took their first midterm last week. I posted the results to the online gradebook right before class, which makes me wonder how all these students have had time to process the results on their own. Maybe this is what they were doing during class. In the next hour, I will talk to at least twenty students about their exams. They will ask me what the average grade was, why b isn't the correct answer on question 12, and how they can study better next time. In the midst of all of these questions, I wish we could talk about what they are learning in this class and whether it impacts the way they think and understand the world around them. But that is not what they want to talk about, or at least it doesn't occur to them to do so.

"What do I need to do to get a C in this class?" one student asks me.

"Well, from a quick look at your exam, it seems like you missed the questions about the primary texts that we studied, like the one about

Michelangelo's sonnets. These texts help us put art in a historical context, so make sure you write down the main points of our discussion about them. Maybe we should talk about this. Where does Michelangelo think creativity comes from?"

"No, I mean what do I need to get on the next exam to get a C in the class."

"Oh," I say, slightly rattled because I don't know the answer, and I wonder if I'm supposed to. "I'm not going to do the math for you, but if you have any questions about studying or the content of the course, I'm happy to help," I reply with a smile. From the quiet rustling sounds in the hall, I try to gauge how many more students are waiting. I have had roughly the same conversation about ten times so far this afternoon. I feel like students value my help in gaming out their grade more than what I can teach them about the history of art.

WHAT MY STUDENTS expect to get out of college and what it is possible for me to deliver are legacies of the IQ test. While I would never say that I give an IQ test to 150 students each semester, the format of the tests I use and the way that it shapes a particularly modern way of learning originates, I have discovered, in the work of psychologist Robert Yerkes. As the United States prepared to enter World War I in 1917, psychologists transformed Binet's intelligence test into a way of identifying which recruits should be officers and which should be soldiers. At first, they proposed to test only recruits suspected of mental incompetence and feeble-mindedness. But Yerkes, president of the American Psychological Association, developed a more ambitious plan. "We should not work primarily for the exclusion of intellectual defectives," Yerkes wrote in 1917, "but rather for the classification of men in order that they may be properly placed in the military service." The sheer numbers of recruits made administering the individualized testing procedures of Binet's intelligence test impossible. So, under Yerkes's leadership, the members of the Committee on the Psychological Examination of Recruits, which included Henry Goddard and Lewis Terman, began meeting at the Vineland Training School during the afternoon of May 28, 1917, to find an alternative. They needed to devise a way to transform test answers from idiosyncratic written responses to correct choices among fixed alternatives that could easily be graded and scored by a team of clerical workers.

The stress of needing to grade quickly and efficiently is not foreign to me. When I see my students lined up at my office door, it is easy to imagine how Yerkes and his team felt when they faced the daunting task of testing almost 2 million Army recruits. As much as I would like to, I cannot have a one-on-one conversation with all of my students to assess what they have learned in my course. So three times a semester my introduction to art history students answer sixty-five multiple choice questions on a bubble sheet to test if they know that Diego Velàzquez painted *Las Meninas* and the Dada art movement was primarily a response to World War I. It is a struggle to draft questions that get beyond testing factual information and evaluate what meaning they find in the history of art. How do Jacques Louis-David's paintings address the volatile politics of the French Revolution? How do Nam June Paik's jury-rigged televisions respond to the spread of media technology in the late twentieth century? I want my students to think about questions like these, and they are not easily answered in multiple choice format. But unless I want to do nothing else except grade essay exams all semester, multiple choice is the best option available. It has the added advantage that it is a format my students are familiar with. For better or worse, multiple choice has become synonymous with American education.

So pervasive is the concept of multiple choice today—including its more recent conversion into drop-down menus on online interfaces—it is hard to believe that there was once a time when no one had yet thought of such a format. In a report published in 1918, Arthur Otis, one of

Yerkes's assistants, described an intelligence test that allowed for answers to be given without writing any words. "The chief object of testing in groups, of course, is economy of time," he wrote. Otis described how his format generated only one correct answer to each question, which could be indicated "merely by making a letter or figure or drawing a line." He studied several earlier experiments in ways to efficiently evaluate reading. For example, the Kansas State Normal School developed a Silent Reading Test in 1915 that presented questions about the comprehension of individual words. "Below are given the names of four animals," one question on the exam asks. "Draw a line around the name of each animal that is useful on the farm: cow; tiger; rat; wolf." The instruction manual reveals that the test was meant to evaluate how well children followed instructions as much as their knowledge about barnyard animals. If a line is drawn under *cow* instead of around it, the answer is wrong. The test required no written answers, only marks, which could be easily and quickly graded.

Otis's group test questions assessed various skills that he believed were good measures of intelligence, including labeling pairs of words as synonyms (*S*) or antonyms (*A*), matching particular proverbs (*make hay while the sun shines*) to the statement that explains its meaning, and a relations test that resembles the analogies students see today on college entrance exams (*hand: arm: foot:* . . .). Yerkes eventually based his Alpha Army Test on these types of questions, as well as arithmetic problems, true-false questions, and lists of words that had to be resequenced to make sentences. One of the subtests claimed to be a test of common sense, although some of the questions seem to assess whether a recruit is brave enough to fight in a war:

> It is better to fight than to run, because
>
> a)   Cowards are shot
> b)   It is more honorable
> c)   If you run you may get shot in the back.

The Beta Army Test, given to recruits who could not read, included picture-completion tasks, tracing the correct path through a maze, and drawing in the missing element in a picture of a common object, like a violin missing its strings. Yerkes and many other psychologists believed that measuring intelligence was different than measuring education. But still, those who took the Beta exam rarely got high marks. One grader noted that, "It was touching to see the intense effort . . . put into answering the questions, often by men who never before had held a pencil in their hands."

At the moment of mass production of the automobile and military equipment, multiple choice brought the evaluation of human intelligence under the logic of the assembly line. Clerical workers used answer keys to grade hundreds of exams within minutes. In May 1918, the monthly testing rate of recruits jumped from 12,000 to 200,000. By the end of the war in November 1918, over 1.7 million men had taken one of Yerkes's tests. The Army was not always willing to comply with the directives of the testing results, and the results did not consistently determine placement as officers or soldiers. Nonetheless, the efforts of Yerkes and his team changed perceptions of IQ tests. No longer were they only given to the feeble-minded to determine genetic deficiency. Now they were legitimate evidence for the aptitude and potential of everyone. The results of Yerkes's Army Exams were widely publicized, setting off debates about the country's national intelligence. But more resonant than the details or accuracy of the results was the fact that Americans had just experienced their first form of high-stakes standardized testing.

AT THE TWENTY-FIFTH anniversary of the founding of the Training School's research laboratory in 1931, Goddard claimed that "the knowledge derived from the testing of the 1,700,000 men in the Army is probably the most valuable piece of information which mankind has ever acquired about itself." In 2012, a group of prominent psychologists published an article that summarized what is known about intelligence. When I read it, I got the sense that psychologists' pride and enthusiasm for IQ tests has hardly waned since the days of Goddard, Terman, and Yerkes. "The measurement of intelligence is one of psychology's greatest achievements and one of its most controversial," the article states. Psychologists still see IQ tests as a triumph, but they are not as adamant about the distinction between intelligence and education. They point out the strong correlation between IQ scores and performance on other standardized tests, such as the SAT. They assert that "the measurement of intelligence—which has been done primarily by IQ tests—has utilitarian value because it is a reasonably good predictor of grades at school, performance at work, and many other aspects of success in life." But this correlation is no coincidence. The IQ test is a reasonably good predictor of success because modern life, including our education system, has been shaped to value qualities measured on an IQ test.

The Yerkes Alpha Army Test constituted a fork in the road for intelligence assessment. The one-on-one tests—like the one I took with Harris or Louisa took with Leila—persist in clinical contexts. But every student who has passed through public education in the last seventy years has been touched by the logic and ambitions of IQ testing. Standardized tests—the SAT, the ACT, the PSAT/NMSQT, the CogAT, the NWEA MAP test, the DAS, the NAEP, the ITBS, PISA, and many others—do the work of IQ tests. Even though psychologists might not consider them valid cognitive assessments and they are not used for clinical diagnosis, they subtly shape future success and prosperity, place a person within a social hierarchy, and translate human experience into statistics.

After World War I, Terman and Yerkes worked with a committee organized by the National Research Council to develop the National Intelligence Tests for grades three to eight. Terman also developed a similar test for high school students, the Terman Group Test of Mental

Ability. Debates about multiple choice testing in the early twentieth century grappled with the same concerns that preoccupy me and other educators today. Critics pointed out that the tests emphasized the memorization of facts and encouraged guessing. Others feared that multiple choice changed the expectations for learning by asking test-takers to respond to information but not to produce it themselves. Nonetheless, these concerns did little to stop the spread of standardized testing, which was increasingly supported by experts.

By the 1920s, some universities allowed prospective students to submit IQ test results as part of their admissions applications. After working with Yerkes during World War I, Carl Brigham took up the position of secretary of the College Entrance Exam Board, where he designed the Scholastic Aptitude Test, or SAT, which was first given to those students seeking entrance into colleges and universities in 1926. Five of its nine subtests were taken from Yerkes's Alpha Army exam.

Soon a fully-fledged testing industry developed around the SAT. Publishers provided test-takers with booklets of multiple choice questions to prepare to strategically make their best guess on the test. After the war, Otis became an editor at the World Book Company, one of the first publishers to recognize the market potential of test prep material. By supervising the publication of study guides to intelligence and achievement tests, Otis not only helped develop the multiple choice exam. He made a living teaching the public how to do well on them. Parents and students alike understood that these tests were more than assessments of a person's natural mental capacity. They were opportunities to get ahead, and those with the most money and privilege paid Otis and others to help them add high test scores to their list of social advantages.

"Teachers must learn to use tests," said Terman in 1919. If they don't, "the universal grading of children according to mental ability must remain a Utopian dream." Within thirty months of the publication of the first group intelligence test, some 4 million children had been tested.

In 1957, Wechsler predicted that by 1960, at least one of every two persons in the United States between the ages of five and fifty will have taken an intelligence test. In this estimate, Wechsler included the several hundred thousand children given IQ tests as part of the adoption process and for admission to private schools. He also included high school students taking college admissions tests like the SAT that he claimed "differ only in part from standard group intelligence tests."

It is fair to say we have learned to use tests. A 1966 study showed that over 90 percent of the nation's pupils had been given at least one intelligence or achievement test during their time in public school. In 1962, most took three to five standardized tests per year, which sounds negligent compared to statistics for students in 2014, when one study found that some eleventh graders spend up to 15 percent of the school year taking national and state standardized assessments, not counting Advanced Placement (AP) or college entrance exams.

STATE AND NATIONAL standardized assessments are particular kinds of tests referred to as high stakes. It is not necessarily the content that makes a test so high stakes, but the decisions that are determined by it. High stakes were born from the strong belief in the prophetic nature of IQ tests and the pressure of that prediction. High stakes are embedded in the purpose of standardized intelligence testing, to determine people's futures in a way that is beyond their immediate will or control. These tests make all of us feel judged, as if we have no power over our future and no ability to change it.

Most high-stakes standardized tests are administered in multiple choice format, which does not tolerate idiosyncrasy or individuality. It also carries the message that the goal of learning is to get the right answer, rather than grapple with ambiguity, become more comfortable with various perspectives on a problem, or make decisions based on complex conditions. It is no wonder it can be so difficult to tease out my students' own ideas about a painting that we study or a text that we read. They have spent their lives seeing the assessment of what they've learned expressed as a test score and worrying whether what they have to say will be the correct answer. My students and I share an understanding that these tests matter. But I have grown to see high-stakes tests as a barrier that prevents my students from telling me what matters to them or how they have found any purpose or meaning in what they have learned.

Since the mid-twentieth century, colleges and universities have perennially used high-stakes exams like the SAT to determine who is offered a seat in an incoming academic class and who is not. But what I continually notice when I talk to students is that, in their minds, the testing and the learning are one and the same. It reminds me of the essay in the *New Republic* from 1923 that declared, "Intelligence as a measurable capacity must at the start be defined as the capacity to do well on an intelligence test." One hundred years later, success is defined as the capacity to do well on standardized tests. They do not just predict a person's academic ability. They define academic ability.

Psychologists like Yerkes, Terman, and Goddard told us that we are unable to change what IQ tests tell us about ourselves and our intelligence. In its history, the IQ test has been used to make high-stakes determinations, such as institutionalization, forced sterilization, and excluding children from attending school. But the impact of high-stakes testing isn't limited to these more extreme outcomes. All kinds of students are suffering from the anxiety of high-stakes testing. While I have plenty of students lined up outside my office door after a test, I worry most about those who do not meet with me. This is the most disturbing and increasingly common way that students are responding to the stress of high-stakes testing. They disengage and isolate themselves to cope with a sense of shame and failure. I worry that they think they don't belong in college. I don't see them. They are on my class roster, but after the first exam or so they disappear. They don't attend class, don't turn in assignments, don't answer emails. I know their names, but I don't know if they are okay.

WHEN I LEARNED how the multiple choice format first developed, I compared it to the ways in which Louisa's reading progress is tracked in school. Her teachers turn to multiple choice tests for the same reasons I do in my college classes and Yerkes did in the Army. There is not enough time or resources to evaluate every student in a more individualized way. Her teachers want to allow their students to make their own choices about what books they read, but they can't possibly know all the books that a student might select. As a solution, Louisa and her classmates take multiple choice exams through a software program that logs a staggeringly comprehensive database of children's literature. When Louisa finishes a book, she answers ten to twenty multiple choice questions that test her comprehension and memory of specific details from the narrative. As Louisa makes her way through elementary school, her progress is tracked in quantifiable levels down to the decimal point. Her reading level is gauged depending on her score on the exams and the degree of difficulty of the book. Katherine Paterson's classic *Bridge to Terabithia* is a 4.6, for example, while Matthew de la Peña's and Christian Robinson's *Last Stop on Market Street* is a 3.3.

One advantage of this system is that it allows students to develop at their own pace. If fourth graders want to read *War and Peace*, then nothing stops them from taking a test on Tolstoy's hefty novel. But it also limits the criteria used to determine an "advanced" reader. The brilliance of *Last Stop on Market Street* is partially based on its pictures by Christian Robinson. The characters of CJ, his Nana, and the bus driver Mr. Dennis are so vividly communicated with few words. But presumably, a deep understanding of the subtle ways in which *Last Stop on Market Street* addresses community, values, and socioeconomic disparities is not valued as much as remembering that Leslie Burke, one of the main characters of *Bridge to Terabithia*, wins a footrace during recess. It turns reading into an isolated practice driven by remembering details from the book's narrative and racking up points, rather than an opportunity for conversation, open-ended questioning, and collaborative learning.

The multiple choice tests that Louisa takes at school do not recognize her scrutinizing response to one of our favorite picture books, Cynthia Rylant's *November* (level 2.6 in case you were wondering). When we first read it, Louisa stopped me when we reached Rylant's magnificent line, "In November, the trees are standing all sticks and bones."

"What? Trees don't have bones!"

"It's a metaphor," I explained. "The author means that the trees look like they have bones." Now Louisa points out metaphors in almost every book we read together. And she uses them, too, as shown by the egg white that she so poetically imagined to be the powdered wig of J. S. Bach. In her own way, Louisa has discovered the wonder of language. She demonstrates a deep engagement that never seems to get acknowledged in the standardized tests she takes at school. But her mastery of the technicalities of metaphor is less important to me than her astonishment at its effects. That one word can draw connections between two things is the magic of language. I have learned that Louisa's curiosity about words and language cannot be measured by the length of the books she reads, or by whether she reads them independently. Just like the multiple choice exams I give my college students, the evaluation of Louisa's reading never seems to get to what matters most.

The multiple choice format persists as Louisa's nemesis. On a recent IEP report, one of her teachers wrote, "A continued theme throughout Louisa's educational career is that formalized testing does not seem to be an indicator of her performance." I am grateful to Louisa's teacher for recognizing this and pointing it out, as if to warn all future teachers to not trust the numbers. Louisa learns, experiences, and is affected by much more than standardized tests give her credit for. But as grateful as I am for the human check, I also wonder how much it matters. If more and more of her time in school is spent taking tests, learning and testing become increasingly synonymous. What does it matter that Louisa knows more than the test shows if learning and testing are considered one and the same?

Andy and I will help Louisa through the testing—figuring out when we care about tests and when we don't, when we want to take their scores seriously and when they deserve to be thrown in the garbage. But metrics shape our realities. Specifically, high-stakes tests have made it nearly impossible for a person with an intellectual disability to even imagine attending college. Such a system was deliberately constructed to keep out those who struggle to do academic work in a prescribed way. Those excluded because of low test scores miss out on benefits of college like career exploration, personal growth, and connections to their peers.

I often participate in events for high school seniors who have been admitted to the university where I teach. They visit campus with their parents in the spring and want to hear from faculty about internship opportunities and the return on investment of the exorbitant cost of tuition. I sit at a table on a stage in front of an audience of a few hundred students and parents. Faculty who teach in other departments—biology, finance, sociology—sit next to me. Parents often ask us, *Would you want your child to go to school here?* I am never eager to be the first to answer this question. Of course, they do not know that I have a daughter with Down syndrome. When it's my turn, I try to answer as truthfully as I can while still being helpful. Yes, I say, I would want my child to go to school here. Faculty get to know their students, and they care about their future. There are lots of opportunities to do research, have an internship, and study abroad. These are true statements, but what I really mean is that I want my daughter to have these opportunities, too, at this university or any other. I do not mention that my daughter has Down syndrome and might not be able to find the support and inclusive practices she needs. I do not mention that I work in a system that I feel increasingly uneasy being part of, one that is inaccessible to the person I love the most.

THE WAYS IN which standardized tests act as gatekeepers to higher education is one of the most startling reasons why we need to rethink their power. But equally concerning is the way in which they have shaped what students see as the meaning or purpose of being in college once they are admitted. The content of the multiple choice exams that my students take and the Alpha Army exam are different, but the formats are about the same. The stakes on an exam in an art history class are lower than the SATs, and presumably lower than those experienced by a young recruit in 1917 taking Yerkes's Alpha or Beta Army Tests. But you wouldn't know this by observing my students. The same intensity prevails. Students are too preoccupied with test scores and grade statistics to pause and consider much else.

In my college students, I see the outcome of an educational system obsessed with the quantification of intelligence through high-stakes tests, so much so that they seem to no longer distinguish between a high-stakes test and other ways of learning. It all seems like a threat, and students seem to exist in a constant state of stress. Research shows that high-stakes tests can have damaging effects on young adults. A 2021 study showed that they spark a number of concerning behaviors in college students—increased anxiety, poor sleep levels, lack of exercise, and increased smoking—that lead to more severe mental health issues. High-stakes tests also lead to lower levels of confidence in students as young as eight years old.

Plenty of recent studies show that high school grades are a better prediction of college success—measured in terms of four-year graduate rate and grade point average—than admissions test scores. Yet I'm not sure how comforting this is, if grades are increasingly the product of multiple choice tests and quantified assessments. Most of my students approach college as a series of test scores to be obtained, which is part of their larger effort to earn the credential of a college degree and to obtain a well-paying job. These are important pursuits. But under those terms, education is all about the numbers. Tasks are completed to get them a score in the gradebook, which then gets them closer to knowing what they need to get on the next task, in order to get the grade that they want, in order to get into the business school, in order to keep their scholarship, in order to please their parents, and on and on. I interact every day with students who make life decisions based on test scores—what classes they take, what they study, whether or not they are willing to take risks and maybe even willing to fail. College barely functions today as an opportunity for personal exploration, for thinking about your place in the world and its history, and deciding what you might want to contribute to make this world a better place.

Under these conditions, *not* going to college may seem like a sensible choice. At a group dinner one night, one of my colleagues mentioned that she tells her daughter, a junior in high school, that she doesn't have to go to college. She told us this with the practiced calm of someone who knows she is saying something provocative, and I wanted to call her bluff. I have a hard time believing that any parent, especially a professor, would so easily let go of the idea of their child attending college. For all its problems, giving up on higher education entirely by shirking its many potential rewards seems risky to the survival of democracy as much as our children's more immediate future. I thought back to my elitist ambitions for Louisa the night before she was born, which were completely unrelated to who she was or would become. Now, attending college seems like a precarious goal for Louisa. If she wants to achieve it, she will have to work harder than most to be admitted to a system that does not value the way she learns. Maybe this colleague had worked through letting go of the necessity of college, but I had a hard time believing that this didn't come without some conflict and struggle. She seemed to dismiss so flippantly something that was socially and economically valuable, yet unattainable, for many.

Sometimes it is hard not to resent my students—and even some of my colleagues—who seem to take for granted the opportunities that college affords them. Louisa will likely struggle to access those opportunities. Recognizing this feels similar to the way I resented the girl trying to sell me a cake roll on my porch. In both circumstances, I feel as if I am asked to nod, smile, and support a system that excludes people like my daughter and uses test scores as an excuse to do so. Unlike most of my friends with kids, I try to stave off the assumption that college is in Louisa's future and approach the possibility that she won't attend with joy. Down syndrome is an exit ramp off the treadmill of achievement and quantified learning on which I see my students struggling to find happiness and purpose. No one expects a person with Down syndrome to do well on the SAT or go to college. Louisa's future doesn't have to be what is normal for most young adults. *Hooray!* I think. *Hooray for not being normal!* The idea that she is not expected to go to college sometimes hits me with great relief. But then I remember that this is a future that she wants.

It is a Tuesday morning, and Louisa does not have school, for no particularly good reason. I recognize that her teachers might think otherwise; in-service workdays are opportunities for training and continuing education. But the spring seems like a particularly treacherous minefield of holidays, snow days, and days when Louisa just simply doesn't have school. These disruptions to our routine might be justified, but Andy and I never seem to be prepared for them. So, on this particular morning, we make contingency plans. Determined that both of us will get some work done today, we take Louisa to campus with us. I take Louisa to my office so I can prepare for my afternoon class, then she will hang out with Andy in the afternoon when I teach. Days like these leave me feeling scattered, at the mercy of forces outside of my control, but there is nothing else to do except sigh, slow down, and enjoy spending a bit more time with my daughter. Louisa doesn't mind this at all, as she is fascinated by college, the students, and the fact that both her parents work in a way that is something like the teachers at her school. As we walk across campus from the parking lot to my office, I ask her, "Do you want to go to college, Louisa?"

"I do," she replies with her typical confidence.

"Okay. There are a lot of colleges to choose from. Do you want to go to a college that is far away from me and Dad, or do you want to go to college here?"

"I want to go here," she says, with unwavering certainty. Her answers to questions about what she wants to be when she grows up vary widely, but her commitment to attending college where her parents teach never falters.

As we walk along the sidewalk, we pass students who smile at the odd sight of a young kid on a college campus on a random Tuesday morning. Louisa refuses to hold my hand. Instead, she mimics the students around her. She straps on her backpack filled with markers, a coloring book, and a new graphic novel, and strides purposefully just ahead of me. She holds an invisible phone in front of her in her left hand. With her right, she scrolls through imaginary posts on social media, until she gets a call and brings the phone to her ear to make plans with her friends for lunch. She hangs up, straightens her knitted hat, and flicks her hair off her shoulder in sorority-girl style. She looks like the students we pass, only younger, but not young enough in my opinion.

As Louisa struts ahead of me, I think about how I am implicated in an educational system that has translated learning and intelligence into a numerical game. I work in a world that provides very few options for success for people with intellectual disabilities like my daughter. I feel a wretched pull, the Janus-faced hypocrisy of it, as we walk and Louisa imagines that she belongs here. The decision about whether and where Louisa goes to college should ultimately be up to her. But I also know that it won't be, at least not entirely. It depends on whether colleges are willing to change to let more people who think in different ways succeed.

I think about what Louisa might not learn about if she doesn't go to college. These are things that will help her make decisions about her future, like learning about climate change—a crisis every person of her generation will have to confront—or studying the disability rights movement of the 1970s. In this way, college seems to potentially offer more to Louisa than just fitting in with a backpack and a phone. College should cultivate empowerment with consequences far beyond grades and test scores. When college is done right, it provides the opportunity to learn about oneself. And this self-knowledge, what is necessary to find one's place in the world, is what people with intellectual disabilities have long been denied.

DURING THE PANDEMIC, many universities took steps to minimize the importance of standardized tests in their admissions process. More than 80 percent of four-year colleges eliminated the requirement to submit standardized test scores as part of admissions applications. These decisions gave me hope that more equitable models of higher education were on the horizon. Such changes would not only support educational opportunities for people with disabilities. Rethinking the role of standardized tests in education would improve learning for all students. But a number of highly selective universities—including Yale, Dartmouth, and MIT—have recently reversed course, citing research studies that show a correspondence between high SAT scores and outcomes like "attending an elite graduate school" and "working at a prestigious firm." The correlation is hardly surprising. But less than 1 percent of college students attend an Ivy League school. Such a focus on the elite doesn't consider how higher education could be accessible to more students by removing unnecessary testing barriers. One reporter recently concluded, "Marinating in admissions anxiety is just part of adolescence." No, it isn't. As the transition away from standardized tests at the beginning of the pandemic demonstrated, it doesn't have to be this way. Change would require that we overcome our obsession with admissions to elite schools. It would mean reenvisioning college as an opportunity for personal growth, knowledge, and community engagement rather than a place of unhealthy competition, anxiety, and entrenched privilege.

When imagining what higher education without standardized tests might look like, we should pay attention to the higher education programs for students with intellectual disabilities in the United States. There are now over 320 of them across 49 states. Almost 200 of these programs are part of four-year colleges and universities. Since the Higher Education Opportunity Act of 2008, which allowed students with intellectual disabilities to be eligible for federal financial aid and provided funding for development, the number of Inclusive Post-Secondary Education (IPSE) programs has almost doubled.

IPSE programs are structured in a variety of ways, but most offer classes alongside peers in all departments and subjects of study, internships and other work-based learning opportunities, and person-centered planning designed for maximum choice. Most offer an alternative admissions process, in which an expressed desire to go to college, live more independently, and pursue professional goals carries a great deal of weight. More flexible courses and GPA requirements give students with intellectual disabilities the leeway to think carefully about what they want to gain from college. Programs also give students access to counselors and peer mentors to succeed on their own terms. Perhaps most importantly, inclusive post-secondary education programs establish expectations for inclusive work. While 18 percent of people with intellectual disabilities are employed, 59 percent of IPSE graduates find competitive integrated employment within one year after completing a program.

In this model, I see a radical and welcome shift to more engagement and purpose—less concern over points on a test and more reflection on how learning affects students' lives. In other words, it is possible that the students who attend these programs are the kinds of students I have wanted in the college courses I teach all along.

I talked with Cate Weir, program director at Think College, a grant-funded project at the Institute for Inclusion at the University of Massachusetts, Boston. Weir supports colleges as they design and implement programs for students with intellectual disabilities. She also advises students and parents about the best programs to meet their needs. I asked her what the biggest barriers have been to people with intellectual disabilities attending college. Weir emphasized that, up until recently, secondary education failed to prepare students with intellectual disabilities for the possibility of college, or really for any future outside of a sheltered workshop. Inclusive learning experiences in high school used to be rare, she reminded me. Children might have been included until second or third grade, then they gradually spent more of their time in functional classrooms, which did nothing to prepare students for an inclusive life, much less college.

Weir also explained that a rigid understanding of college learning based on standardized testing created roadblocks. In the early 2000s, she worked as a faculty member and disability services coordinator at a community college with an open admissions policy. "The biggest barriers were placement tests," she told me. Students with intellectual disabilities were placed in pre-college classes in math and English and had to test out of those classes to enroll in what Weir described as "other classes that we knew they would be really good at, like hands-on learning and things they were passionate about. But they were stuck in this remedial place where they had probably already been remediated for fourteen to sixteen years." To test out of the English class, for example, students had to pass the Nelson-Denny Reading Test, which measures a student's reading rate in words-per-minute and evaluates vocabulary and reading comprehension through multiple choice questions. With this situation in mind, it is easy to see what the barriers would be at more competitive institutions of higher education. "These students often didn't have regular high school diplomas. They didn't have transcripts with any academic preparation. Their high schools just didn't prepare them in any way for college." But eventually more students with intellectual disabilities were included in regular classrooms in high school, and what they demanded of their education began to change.

Those who wanted to attend college had to fight hard for their right to do so. Micah Fialka-Feldman is now an outreach coordinator in the Taishoff Center for Inclusive Higher Education at Syracuse University. I met Micah when he visited the university where I teach to talk about his self-advocacy as a person with an intellectual disability. I called Micah a few months after his visit to find out more about his views on IQ tests. "I was tested when I was eleven, but my parents never told me," Micah explained to me when we talked on the phone. He came across his test results when he was moving to Syracuse from Michigan, where he grew up. He needed to apply for services to help him live independently. "I did some research. It's just a number. I can do more than the test shows," he told me with unwavering confidence, as if he had made this case his entire life.

The test did not predict that Micah would have the determination and persistence to win a federal lawsuit to live in the dorms while he was a student at Oakland University in Michigan. The school's administration denied his application for housing while enrolled in a certificate program for adults with intellectual disabilities. Micah sued Oakland University for violating his rights to attend on an equal footing with his peers. "During the case I was questioned in a room," Micah said. "They asked me, 'How do you leave during a fire drill?' I said, 'You go outside.' Then the other question was 'How do you wake up in the morning?' I told them 'I set an alarm clock.'" I have college students in my classes who do not seem aware of how useful setting an alarm could be. Yet their right to live among their peers in dorms is never scrutinized.

The questions suggest doubt about Micah's ability to handle certain situations that might arise when living independently. More subtly, that doubt is expressed through the language of intelligence testing, gauging logic, reasoning, and decision-making skills. I couldn't ignore the similarity in questions. "How do you leave during a fire drill?" seemed to be a test of logic and problem-solving abilities, just like Binet's question for ten-year-olds, "What ought one to do when one has missed the train?" The questions also reminded me of the endless forms I had filled out for Louisa that asked me to rate how often she puts her toys away or how often she follows household rules. All of these questions were underscored with ableism and judgment. And just as Goddard used similar questions to determine who should be excluded from schools and communities, the questions Micah faced were meant to exclude him. Oakland University adopted the language and purpose of IQ tests, in which inclusion and opportunity depended on his answers.

Given the ways in which people with intellectual disabilities historically have been shut out of educational opportunities in this country, that there are now over 320 higher education programs is an astounding sign of improvement. Yet the history of IQ tests and how they shape the definition of intellectual disability still plays a complicated role. Most IPSE programs require students to have a documented intellectual disability. But Weir informed me that there is not always consensus about what this means.

"I spent most of my career dismissing IQ as a construct," Weir told me. I couldn't help but grin with satisfaction. "But now I find myself in a strange position. These programs are designed for people with intellectual disabilities. And how do we define that?" The Higher Education Opportunities Act of 2008 references the AAIDD definition of intellectual disability, which uses an IQ of 70 or below as one of three criteria for diagnosis. Weir described to me how she constantly tries to thread a needle, advising university program coordinators on how they might demonstrate that a student has an intellectual disability even if he or she has chosen not to take an IQ test. Such a resistance stems from the same concerns that I have about Louisa's diagnosis—since their invention, IQ tests have so often been used to limit a person's opportunities. If students and their parents resist the label of intellectual disability from kindergarten through twelfth grade because of the biases and threat of segregation that comes with it, there is no documentation of those students having an intellectual disability. But in a painfully ironic turn, the label is what students need for inclusion and access to college. "Suddenly this number becomes paramount, but for the opposite reason than how we used to worry about it," Weir told me. Students who might have benefited from these programs have been turned away because they haven't taken an IQ test and do not have an official diagnosis of intellectual disability.

Those who struggle the most shoulder the consequences of the bind that Weir described to me. On one hand, I understand the need to stay true to the definition of intellectual disability in order to serve those who have previously been excluded, segregated, and devalued by this label. But on the other hand, these programs could provide opportunities to people who—for a variety of reasons—might have not been labeled with an intellectual disability but have struggled just as much to find where they belong. IPSE programs provide accommodations, modifications, and flexible admissions criteria (except for the IQ score) that could provide opportunities for so many.

In a twisted way, this complication reveals how IQ tests, at their core, exclude some and privilege others. It also demonstrates how arbitrary the decisions are that are determined by high-stakes testing. Is someone with an IQ of 80 really less in need of opportunity than someone with an IQ of 70? And, alternatively, does a student with an IQ of 127 or 125 or 110 instead of 130 not deserve the privileges of gifted programs? Thinking about these questions, I could only feel certain about the exclusionary motivations of IQ tests and the other high-stakes forms of tests they spawned. After I talked with Weir, I was also left with a great sense of fear. Louisa might be one of the kids who find themselves in this "no-man's-land." Her IQ score might be too high to officially qualify her for enrollment in an IPSE program, but too low to experience college in any other way.

THE UNIVERSITY WHERE I teach does not have an IPSE program, but that might change. A few summers ago I attended the Inclusive University Program, a one-week residential college experience for students with intellectual disabilities on campus. Students in the program and undergraduate volunteers live together in the dorms for the entire week. I met them every morning in a classroom to learn from a talented colleague about inclusion and the history of disability studies. To some degree, I was an outsider during the week. I did not bond over meals, share dorm rooms, or attend late-night dance parties like the students did. But what a pleasure it was to learn alongside them. I was greeted with enthusiasm and sincerity every morning when I walked into class. Students listened to each other and supported one another. I got used to being in a classroom with people who learn and process in diverse ways, which can often look and sound unpredictable. I wonder how these students would do in a less familiar academic environment, where comfort and acceptance were not ensured. But such challenges should not deter from the overall lesson. As the professor instilled in countlessly creative ways, students with intellectual disabilities can benefit from and contribute to higher education. The burden is on laws, language, and the educational system to make this world more accessible. It is a powerful and complex shift in thought, a basic principle of disability rights that has not yet been fully implemented in higher education.

The Inclusive University Program seemed like a foil to all the things that the traditional university system gets wrong. It prioritized community building and the inclusion of a variety of experiences. By writing papers, making videos, or drawing pictures, students expressed their ideas about disability in multiple ways. But what I appreciated the most was the collaborative spirit of the classroom. It felt like we were all working and building something together. I thought about how my own classes were embarrassingly bland in comparison. My students seemed to be focused on solitary pursuits—earning a good grade—while students in this program were models of collaborative inquiry. I began asking myself what I could do to make my classes feel like a community and how I could encourage more personally meaningful responses to what I teach.

Perhaps most importantly, students of all abilities had the opportunity to live and learn in a single environment together. At the end of the week, the students presented their plan for a two-year inclusive program to a group of invited faculty and staff. One of my favorite tenets addressed how students with intellectual disabilities would be enrolled in the first-year orientation course for all university students. After taking the course, students would be eligible to co-teach the course in the following semester with a professor. I can't imagine a more powerful statement about the place of people with intellectual disabilities in higher education. While the benefits of college to these students are clear, how college can be improved by inclusion and access is an equally exciting question to consider.

College should be a goal for Louisa, if she continues to want it to be. It is an increasingly realistic goal, thanks to programs for people with intellectual disabilities that have flourished in the past ten years. Yet I still wonder if higher education is a system far too embedded in the quantification of intelligence and standardized tests to reconsider its purpose. In other words, I wonder whether higher education is worthy of her.

Paradigm Shift

L ouisa's second round of IQ testing did not occur in the spring of
2020 as planned, due to the coronavirus pandemic. I met with Brian,
the school psychologist, in February, when he explained to me about the
"strange no-man's-land" that Louisa occupied and I stared at the Charlie
Brown poster on his office wall. In March, Louisa's school closed and
all interaction with her classmates and her teachers migrated to a tiny
computer screen. For the rest of the spring, online learning seemed like
barely a solution to an impossible situation. But the school did its best to
offer some kind of instruction. Louisa's teacher sent DIY videos about
subtracting double-digit numbers. I filmed Louisa performing an inter-
pretive dance of the weather cycle—acting out the stages of evaporation,
precipitation, and condensation through waving arms and deep knee
bends—and sent it to her teacher. We made the most of it.

When all hope of returning to the classroom faded, the school
arranged a time for families to pick up the desk supplies and art projects
that students had left behind. Louisa's brightly colored scissors, folders,
and crayons were packed tightly in a plastic bag like evidence from a
crime scene. While navigating our own transitions to teaching online,

Andy and I flailed, trying to establish new routines for working, learning, and living under the same roof. I tried to stay connected to my own students, but I was preoccupied with Louisa and how the world seemed to be failing her. Despite the world's hideous state, I was determined to nurture her through it. We would read and subtract and creatively interpret scientific principles until the world we had fallen into, a place of crushing disappointment, righted itself.

Like so many other things, the decision about whether Louisa would go through another round of IQ testing was put on hold. Instead, I learned that a number of states had medical contingency plans in place that addressed whether to provide lifesaving equipment to people with intellectual disabilities should equipment become scarce. Suddenly, the relevance of the history I was then only starting to research—Goddard's identification of the "feeble-minded," Holmes's ruling on eugenics— locked into a horrifying immediacy. Alabama's contingency plan provided the most explicit discrimination, stating that "persons with severe mental retardation, advanced dementia, or severe traumatic brain injury may be poor candidates for ventilator support." Arizona's guidance was vaguer—at least refraining from using the outdated term "mental retardation." But the suggested action was nonetheless clear. Arizona doctors must "allocate resources to patients whose need is greater or whose prognosis is more likely to result in a positive outcome with limited resources." Several disability advocacy organizations questioned what Arizona's plan meant by "positive outcomes," and argued that the phrase put people with intellectual disabilities in a vulnerable position. In this bleak scenario, the IQ test contributed to a rating of the value of life, making life-or-death decisions much easier than they ought to be. These states eventually revised their plans, yet I realized that Louisa and others with intellectual disabilities might be easy victims of the pandemic, not just because of concurrent medical conditions (although those increased risk too), but because of dire social conditions and low expectations.

In the fall, the school year started off as a series of Zoom meetings. The background noise of unmuted students made it difficult for Louisa to concentrate. She also couldn't contribute to discussions fast enough. Her teacher made an effort to engage students in conversation and connect them to this strange, new classroom space. But before Louisa was able to get her teacher's attention, the relevant conversation had often passed her by. Louisa worked through some significant speech challenges to be understood. When the teacher invited students to share something about themselves to the group, Louisa raised her virtual hand. When called on, she shouted, "I have Down syndrome!" "You have what?" her teacher asked. "Down syndrome!" Not understanding what she was saying, her teacher offered a generic "Okay! Great!" and moved on. Thrilled to have shared something about herself, Louisa moved on, too, yet the opportunity for her peers to know the term *Down syndrome* and to discuss how people with disabilities are a unique and respected part of their community was lost.

Louisa sat at our kitchen table, slogging through her online writing and math assignments with me, who failed to explain anything with clarity. I was unreasonable in my ambitions as a parent-teacher. I convinced myself she wasn't learning enough and somehow believed that this would be the perfect time to teach Louisa to count to twenty in Italian and read at a faster pace. I should have known that unreasonable expectations lead to friction and disappointment. I was trying to convince myself and others that we were fine—that I could, in fact, homeschool my daughter while working and never leaving the house. All we had to do was work a little harder. Andy did better, helping Louisa move through her required work for school and then leaving her to draw, sing, or do something else that made her happy.

While I worried about how to keep Louisa on track, the Zoom classroom and the headlines about state contingency plans showed me how alarmingly easy it was to overlook the inclusion of people with intellectual disabilities in our communities and our schools. I read countless news stories that stoked anxieties about student test scores: "The Pandemic Erased Two Decades of Progress in Math and Reading," "Test Scores Dropped to Lowest Levels in Decades." These stories echoed the ways that IQ tests foster anxieties about intelligence and education. Would kids *fall behind* during the pandemic? Would they be able to *catch up* when they returned to the classroom? I worried about Louisa's ability to learn online, but it was the lost experience of learning with her peers that troubled me the most. The inclusive communities that schools could provide seemed to be less important than maintaining test scores and achieving good grades. Persistent conversations about test scores seemed like a misguided attempt to cling to normal in a decidedly abnormal time, despite everything going on outside the Zoom classroom.

I now think about the earliest moments of the pandemic, before everyone figured out how to carry on online and states had developed medical contingency plans, as fleeting glints of hope. We might have affirmed the value of all lives, those with disabilities or otherwise. We might have reimagined what we value about education and what we think we learn from standardized test scores. We could have valued community over individual achievement. But meaningful change never really occurred. We turned our attention to studies showing that students lost the equivalent of one-third of a year of learning to the pandemic. Unsurprisingly, those losses were most severe among students from low-income backgrounds. There is serious concern that those losses will exacerbate economic disparities, following these students for the rest of their education and into the workforce. Indeed, a great deal was lost.

What children learn, and how much they learn, matters. But as I watched the grid of squirmy kids and one unfathomably patient teacher on Louisa's computer screen, I realized that far more important is *how* we learn. The face-to-face classroom, at its inclusive best, teaches children how to help each other. It models how to live and work in a community. Kids learn to communicate their thoughts and to respond patiently, listening while others do the same. In my mind, efforts to quantify what was lost in the pandemic double down on the tenuous value of what test scores can tell us. Statistics and standardized tests can never really address the community building, the mutual support, the accountability, and the other unquantifiable parts of school. Depending on statistics to measure that loss does not acknowledge the trauma of the spring and fall of 2020. In the frenzy to catch up, we risk forgetting what happened. In our desperation to return to normal, we overlooked opportunities to change the aspects of normal that never really worked well in the first place. And still we rely on standardized tests to tell us things, all for the sake of maintaining normalcy.

THE PANDEMIC SERVED as a reminder of how entrenched our world is in a particular understanding of intelligence and how we value some lives over others. But the pandemic also clarified what changes need to happen to provide more equity for those with intellectual disabilities. To begin, we need psychologists, school systems, social workers, and policymakers to place less emphasis on the IQ score when charting out plans for support and care. And there are ways in which the approach to IQ testing is moving in this direction. During the pandemic, I talked over Zoom with Julie Rubin, a psychologist with over thirty years of experience teaching psychological assessment to graduate students and administering IQ tests in public schools. I asked her what she thought IQ tests test. "I don't really know what intelligence is. I'm not sure exactly of what I'm testing." Her response left me breathless. How could someone who has administered IQ tests for over thirty years not know exactly what she is testing? Eventually, her response also led me to imagine a way in which intelligence testing might overcome its pernicious past.

For many clinicians today, including Rubin, an IQ score can roughly indicate a rate of learning. Based on the definition of IQ established long ago, this means that if a child has an IQ of 50, for example, this would indicate that she is developing at approximately half the typical rate of a child her age. From this perspective, the number can help create a successful school experience by designing an individualized curriculum. Rubin emphasized the importance of this to a child's self-esteem—that learning is designed in a way that is appropriate to a specific person, not what a first or second grader should be capable of.

Rubin believes that IQ tests are valuable tools. "I can't envision not being able to use an IQ test," she told me. Without being certain what an IQ test measures, she believes there is value in its standardization and comparison. The IQ test is a vital part of her practice, not because it tests something physiological, but because so many others have taken the test. It serves as a way to measure one child's development against the thousands whose scores were part of the data used to norm a particular IQ test. Her approach is not motivated from a preoccupation with innate intelligence, and not knowing precisely what IQ is doesn't prevent Rubin from helping the children she works with.

Rubin described to me what psychologists call an ecological perspective, which takes into account the many influences that impact a child's behavior and learning. In our conversations, Rubin asserted over and over that cognitive tests are just *one* of several ways she assesses the needs of children. Judgments and predictions made from IQ tests alone—the typical approach in the early twentieth century—are not part of her practice. Competent cognitive assessment is done from an ecological point of view, which gathers information from multiple sources, including IQ tests, but also interviews, behavioral observations, and the awareness of a person's cultural perspective. Rubin trains other psychologists to be more aware of the cultural biases of intelligence testing and to consider the language in which tests are administered. These may seem like obvious considerations for a responsible psychology practice in the twenty-first century. But given the history of intelligence testing, the cultural sensitivity expressed by Rubin is remarkable.

Psychologists like Rubin, who are concerned with how the lives of people with intellectual differences can be improved, minimize the importance of the overall IQ score. What matters most is the information gleaned from the individual subtests. What are the specific kinds of tasks that this person struggles with the most? What could we change about this person's environment in order to minimize that struggle? What are this person's relative strengths? Rubin made clear to me that the way forward is to see the IQ test as a measure of how well a person is functioning within an environment rather than a measure of a person's innate abilities. We must move toward an approach to intelligence testing that respects the rights of individuals to be different and idiosyncratic. This would place the burden on the school or community to change, not the person.

Psychologists have even suggested a change in terms, from intelligence, a concept about individual performance, to intellectual functioning, which emphasizes the relationship between people and their environment. According to many psychologists I've talked to, intellectual functioning is a kind of back-and-forth between a person and her surroundings. In other words, intelligence can be perceived as how well a person is getting her needs met in a certain context. Psychologists measure intellectual functioning through real-life observations and questionnaires about behavior and daily living circumstances collected from teachers, caregivers, and the person being evaluated. The process is quite different from what I experienced taking an IQ test with Harris, when I was assessed in an isolated room, as if my intelligence could be most accurately measured when I was separated from my everyday routine.

While intelligence implies a competitive sense of superiority, independence, and self-sufficiency, intellectual functioning values dependence and social connections. I thought about Micah Fialka-Feldman and how he had to prove that he deserved to live in the dorms at Oakland University. Rather than putting the burden on Micah, Oakland University might have asked what support they could provide him to study and live among his peers. In Louisa's case, the black-and-white cards, the music, the well-curated toy collection, and the shelves of books might not have changed Louisa's IQ, but they were part of an environment of intellectual functioning, designed to help and nurture her the best we could.

My conversations with Rubin also clarified for me a difference between researchers and clinicians. Research psychologists are interested in procuring meaning from a massive amount of statistical data. They focus on the aggregate, and the needs of an individual person from that broad perspective can be easily overlooked. Research psychologists also use data to predict things, like assuming that a child with a certain IQ will or will not be able to go to college or have a particular job in the future.

But plenty of researchers are rethinking assumptions about the psychological or neural basis of intelligence. In 2019, psychologists Kristof Kovacs and Andrew Conway published an article that was one of the most assertive challenges to date. "Positing a general factor [of intelligence] gives the false impression that there is a psychological explanation, whereas the actual explanation is purely statistical," they wrote. A psychological explanation, according to them, would point to "actual processes and mechanisms" that create intelligence. But such an explanation has not emerged. Their challenge to the concept of general intelligence proposes that it might be better to focus on information obtained about specific cognitive abilities through subtests, rather than assuming that there is one entity called intelligence that can be tested in multiple ways. It makes space for the idea that IQ tests are a product of a certain historically and culturally specific way of thinking about intelligence rather than a way to discover something physiological, like a heartbeat or blood pressure.

If more psychologists begin to see intelligence as a product of a statistical calculation, then I can imagine ways of measuring and assessing that open up a different future for Louisa. What if, for example, intelligence testing did not measure human worth, but how well we take care of one another? How well someone is being supported by their family, their school, and their community?

Research psychologists hold onto the idea of general intelligence because it can predict things. But it turns out that IQ tests are pretty fallible predictors of individual academic ability. A study from 2004 found that half of students with IQs between 70 and 80 academically achieved substantially more than predicted. Given the multitude of other factors that impact learning—parental involvement, home environment, quality of instruction, and other idiosyncrasies about a human life that can't be quantified—IQ scores alone cannot predict achievement for any individual student. The study admits that IQ tests are one of the flagship developments in the history of psychology, but it also asserts that they are not sufficient ways of making any predictions about a child's academic success.

The study's results seemed like a groundbreaking admission to me, and I felt a deep sense of satisfaction when I read its conclusions. Academic success depends a great deal on how well a person's environment supports her academic success. But there's another way of looking at the study that suggests the damage done by IQ tests in the past. It notes that IQ tests have become a self-fulfilling prophecy. As IQ tests gained credibility in educational contexts, they solidified low academic expectations for students who did poorly on them. There is ample evidence that students with disabilities—and not just intellectual disabilities—have been academically affected by low expectations. Given the deterministic meaning that IQ has been given for most of its history, such findings suggest that generations of children have been denied the right to an environment of rich academic support due to implicit bias and what people *think* an IQ score means. Looking toward the future, such studies make the case for devaluing IQ tests and other standardized testing formats.

Louisa started sixth grade last fall and moved from the familiar halls of her elementary school to a completely different routine. On Louisa's most recent IEP, the one that accompanied her as she made the transition from elementary to middle school, her intervention specialist wrote, "Any sort of formalized testing has proven to give inaccurate reports when reflecting on her ability and performance in class on a regular basis." This IEP was particularly important to me. It introduced Louisa to a whole new group of educators who didn't know her but might have a whole range of preconceptions about what an eleven-year-old with Down syndrome might be like. It also marked the beginning of middle school, and who doesn't associate social awkwardness and traumatic changes with those years? It can be the time in a young person's life when it becomes hardest to find where and with whom to belong.

I read the report as a wholehearted attempt to bridge a gap. Louisa's intervention specialist—an amazing educator who I grew to trust deeply—knew she needed to speak across the time and distance between Louisa's old and new schools. She tried to facilitate the process of getting to know a new kid. The report explains that Louisa's test scores are low; they often fall below the first percentile. But it also counters this by describing how much Louisa can do in a classroom setting when she interacts with her teachers and peers.

I cried when I read it. It wasn't the first time that tears blurred the administrative language on Louisa's IEP, but they have usually been caused by frustration and sadness. This statement made me feel that my girl was supported, that her teachers were doing the best they could to communicate Louisa's potential while working under the constraints of a deeply flawed system. *We are trained to think that test results mean something*, it seemed to say to me, *but don't be fooled. Louisa is a bright student who learns best through human interaction and meaningful relationships. Screw the tests*, is what I read, and what I hope her new middle school teachers understand. *Get to know Louisa.*

My worst nightmare would be for a teacher to give up on Louisa, to decide she is not capable of learning a particular lesson or skill because she has Down syndrome. But at the same time, I try to let go of the alternative, that Louisa is constantly measured against her peers and valued for her academic achievement and test scores. Will Louisa ever learn calculus or write a twenty-page research paper? Maybe, maybe not. But perhaps the standards of success should shift away from being normal to being herself. I want her to learn as much as possible, but I want that learning to manifest itself in individualized, immeasurable ways that are part of the rich complexity of being human. It is a radically unscientific approach, but we must turn away from the comparison to normal and toward the fulfillment of a person-centered pursuit of success and happiness. I don't know what my role as Louisa's mother is if it is not to advocate for this kind of approach.

OTHER PSYCHOLOGISTS ARE drawing attention to how little IQ tests actually tell us about people who need the most support. At Cincinnati Children's Hospital and Medical Center, psychologist Anna Esbensen and her team have published several studies on certain parts of IQ tests that assess working memory and cognitive flexibility, the ability to switch between different mental tasks or strategies. Louisa was part of these studies; her sessions with Leila contributed to this scientific data.

But the study was not testing Louisa. Esbensen's work scrutinizes how well IQ tests can provide useful information about people with Down syndrome.

Psychologists depend on IQ tests to accurately measure what they claim to. They also expect scores to remain consistent throughout repeated testing attempts. But Esbensen's work suggests that the reliability and accuracy of some sections of IQ tests are weaker for individuals with intellectual disabilities, especially people with Down syndrome. IQ tests seem to do a better job at reinforcing qualities associated with normal than providing real care and support for those who fall outside of that category. This conforms to the original purpose of IQ tests at the hands of psychologists like Goddard and Terman, who did not prioritize the help or care for those with intellectual disabilities. Rather, they focused on identifying and segregating those with differences from the rest of normal society. Esbensen and I talked about what IQ tests measure and how they might be improved to better care for people with intellectual disabilities.

"Psychologists hold on to IQ tests because they provide good information about cognitive strengths and weaknesses," Esbensen told me. "A psychologist would never say 'I'm going to stamp your child with a 70.' I don't care about the overall score. I care about what the strengths and weaknesses are for a particular kid and what we can do to support them." She expressed frustration with the way in which some schools and other public services employ the IQ score. It reminded me of my conversation with Cate Weir at Think College, when she told me about the tendency to use the IQ score as a strict cutoff for inclusion in higher education programs. Esbensen pointed out that IQ scores are used by non-psychologists "without any understanding of confidence intervals or that there are strength and weakness profiles throughout." To talk about a person's strengths and weaknesses implies that a person has both, and this alone is a remarkable difference in perspective from those who have used the IQ score as shorthand evidence of where people belong and what their life potential is. In all of Goddard's and Terman's case profiles that I read through, I never encountered either of them talking about the strengths of a "feeble-minded" child.

Esbensen also recognizes that there are subtests on the Stanford-Binet and other IQ exams that do not provide accurate information about the abilities of people in the bottom 1 to 2 percent of scores. On most IQ tests, if a person scores below a particular threshold, for example an IQ score of 40, the assessment loses nuance, and the potential for error is huge. Two kids who have very different strengths and weaknesses could have the same low IQ score. But that number would indicate very little about individual needs. At the same time, the bell curve is set up to provide a great deal of information about the difference between a score of 100 and 120. This has led to a lack of reliable and valid cognitive assessments for people with intellectual disabilities like Down syndrome, arguably those who need them the most.

I find it helpful to think about how this information bias also informs the typical grading scale in school. There is quite a bit of nuance provided between an A and A– or a C+ and C, but very little about anything below an F, usually a score of 60 percent or below. I would want to know and celebrate if Louisa improved her score from a 30 percent to a 55 percent, but usually we don't see that kind of improvement as being particularly important. It is all designated as failure.

I asked Esbensen why people with Down syndrome are not included in standard norming procedures. In other words, why isn't the scoring of IQ testing designed to tell us information about those who need help the most? I felt like I knew the answer to my question before I finished asking it. "It's the fault of the bell curve, really," Esbensen answered. "There are fewer people in the overall population that have an intellectual disability than do not. And so, in this logic, it follows that psychologists would know less about people with low IQ scores. The bias is built into the science of scale development."

I understand that, to many, this might not seem like a bias at all. The system is doing what it should, focusing on the majority and allocating resources to the most people. That is one way of looking at it. For more than a century, the bell curve has told us who is in and who is out, who matters and who doesn't, who belongs and who has to go it alone. But there are other ways of considering what we owe each other, especially people who are not part of the bell curve's crest. To start, it would involve letting go of a belief in fixed hierarchies and stable definitions of people's worth. We would need to turn to structures that value connections over categories. Rather than identifying her as part of a small, insignificant percentage, I would like a world that sees Louisa as one of its valued members and welcomes the unique contributions she can make. I would like a world that sees the support and extra help that Louisa needs as a chance to provide access to someone who deserves it, rather than as an inconvenience, time taken away from faster lesson plans and a more efficient classroom. It may not be easier, as it is certainly more convenient to just forget about those in the minority. But as my experience with college students constantly reminds me, those in the majority aren't well-served by our current ways of understanding intelligence and success either. We would all benefit if we looked for new ways to recognize how much a person brings to the world.

Historically, psychologists focused on diagnosis. If a child's IQ was below 70, then that was all they needed to know. But now, more tests are providing extended scoring to recognize the unique cognitive profiles of those with low IQ scores. Through her research on the accuracy of certain cognitive tests, Esbensen is pushing for more. Before strengths and weaknesses are assessed, she wants to be sure that people who score lowest on an IQ test can engage with the tasks they are asked to do in the first place. Can a list of fifteen words to remember be shortened to seven? Will kids wear out because of attention span? Are test-takers even attempting to complete what is asked of them? At this point in our conversation, I remembered watching Louisa squirm at the end of her tests with Leila. Louisa was focused on her snack and no longer interested in answering questions or moving shapes into a pattern. I misread this as Louisa not being interested in cooperating, but the truth was her attention span was simply exhausted. And who among us is at their best when tired and hungry?

Esbensen is also looking at changes in scoring of particular subtests. For example, in the Stanford-Binet, a working memory assessment asks test-takers to repeat sentences that have been recited to them by the test administrator. If test-takers get two or more words wrong, they receive zero points. So a person could remember no words or four words of a six-word sentence and still receive the same score. Esbensen proposes counting the number of words that are correct, which would allow for a wider range of scores and abilities to be assessed.

To further complicate what IQ tests can tell us, studies have shown that the cognitive processes underlying the performance of a task on an IQ test for one person may differ from those used by another person to perform the same task. In other words, subtests do not always accurately and consistently assess the same skills for all people. When test structures are created for the general population, they may be misleading when applied to individuals who fall outside of that category on an IQ test. Historically, IQ tests like the Stanford-Binet struggled to capture and acknowledge the full range of cognitive abilities. But psychologists have recently worked with the authors of the fifth edition of the Stanford-Binet test to develop extended scoring below 40. There is hope that test developers are interested in making their score more accurate in the future.

I started to wonder whether IQ tests could ever be fully separated from their purpose and bias at the hands of psychologists in the early twentieth century. Would it ever be possible to employ IQ tests in ways that improve the lives of those who need the most support? I am hopeful that Esbensen's research might help us overcome the bias that seems to be at the core of the content and scoring of IQ tests. Maybe this is our best chance, as I'm not naive enough to think that IQ tests are going away.

WHEN PSYCHOLOGIST ROBERT Schalock attended college in the sixties, he volunteered at an institution called Lakeland Village near Spokane, Washington, and interacted as a volunteer with the people who lived on the ward for those who were then labeled "profoundly retarded." He spent significant time with a man in his early twenties named David, whose IQ score was considered low, but who was also remarkably creative in terms of practical and social skills.

Schalock spent time with David for several years. "Hey, David, can you make me a giraffe?" Schalock often asked him. Happy to oblige, David looked around for a piece of paper. He would glance at Schalock, mumble a bit, and then produce a highly detailed and accurate picture of a giraffe. Doctors, nurses, and visitors asked David to draw other animals. They were always perfect depictions. Schalock began to wonder, *How could this person who has a diagnosis of "profound mental retardation" do something so sophisticated?* Schalock began to realize that something was wrong with what psychologists thought an IQ score reflected about a person's potential.

When Schalock was in graduate school a few years later, he spent time at the Rainier School, an institution like Lakeland Village or Goddard's Vineland Training School. He observed people with phenylketonuria (PKU), a rare genetic condition that causes significant cognitive deficits if left untreated. "It's one of those indelible memories," Schalock told me. "I walked into the ward and it turned out to be a cage. It was a wire cage where people were placed. Instead of a shower, they got a hose. This was in 1965. This was the situation that forced me to rethink how people with intellectual and developmental disabilities should be treated." Eventually, he spent his career as a psychologist questioning the definition and values our world places on intelligence and its measurement.

When we spoke, Schalock's discomfort with the understanding and treatment of people with intellectual disabilities in the history of psychology was clear to me. But he is no outsider. Schalock, along with a team of professionals and self-advocates, was involved in developing the eleventh and twelfth editions of the AAIDD's definition and classification manuals, which brought about meaningful change in the practices and policies regarding people with intellectual disabilities. With his colleagues Marc Tassé and Ruth Luckasson, Schalock argued that the initial edition of the DSM-5 inaccurately described the relationship between intelligence and adaptive behavior. When Binet, Goddard, Terman, and others developed a way for intelligence to be formally addressed, the IQ score became the linchpin of diagnosis. Even though the first version of the DSM-5 listed other factors—adaptive behavior and age of onset—as criteria for the diagnosis of intellectual disability, an IQ score was still considered the most important factor. But now, as reflected in the revised version of the DSM-5, adaptive behavior—the conceptual, social, and practical skills that a person learns and uses in everyday life—is considered an equally important consideration. According to Schalock, there has been an overreliance on IQ scores in the diagnostic process and an error in assuming a causative relationship between IQ score and adaptive behavior. Not only would this causative relationship be impossible to prove, Schalock claims, it is not supported by evidence. There is a strong correlation between intelligence and adaptive behavior, as Edgar Doll established in 1936, but there is no evidence that the relationship is causal. By making this distinction, Schalock asserts that an IQ score and the assessment of adaptive behavior should have equal weight in diagnosis. And, perhaps more significantly, it establishes that classification based on an IQ score does not determine a person's ability to have a full and rich life. As Schalock witnessed early in his career, that ability is often dependent on environment, including the prejudice and biases that shape it.

But changing diagnostic practices isn't enough. More tenets of our society need to be involved to enhance the equity, autonomy, and inclusion of people with intellectual disabilities. Schalock and his colleagues have called for a new paradigm of shared citizenship to guide the policies and practices related to people with intellectual disabilities. The purpose of support and intervention needs to change, they argue, from a focus on segregation and medical diagnostics to a perspective that primarily considers what supports a person needs in order to best contribute to a community. The shared citizenship paradigm envisions the engagement and full participation of people with intellectual disabilities as equal, respected, and contributing members of every aspect of society. Citizenship, in the way that Schalock imagines it, refers to a state of belonging in one's community, country, or society. But it also suggests an active role in that community, one in which a person is involved in making decisions and contributing to its well-being. This would require a concerted effort, not just by psychologists, but by educators, physicians, policymakers, and service and support providers to rethink the role of people with intellectual disabilities in their communities.

The approach to intelligence and IQ tests is changing. But as this book has attempted to show, there are many ways in which its logic has been embedded in the structure of our everyday world. It guides how we understand the value of education, parenting, and employment. Changing these structures would involve more than just depending on new ways of thinking about the purpose and diagnosis of intellectual assessment. After all, psychologists are only involved in a person's life up to a point.

In her book *The Invisible Kingdom*, Meghan O'Rourke draws attention to how American medicine is set up to be hyperspecialized. This leads to a system in which professionals don't speak to each other, and this kind of structure is one of the barriers that stand in the way of patients getting the care that they need. I see a similarly flawed structure in the care of people with intellectual disabilities. Psychologists rarely talk to a child's teachers directly; parents are expected to fill the intermediary role. And even within the same school, it can be difficult for teachers and school psychologists to find the time to collaboratively discuss the needs of a particular student. The annual IEP meeting is the only time in which this happens with any systematic coordination. Once a year, we meet in a conference room to discuss a document that Louisa's teachers, intervention specialists, school psychologist, and Andy and I have contributed to in our separate ways. The meeting usually lasts around ninety minutes. That's it. Ninety minutes of collaborative discussion for a year's worth of development and learning. For the rest of the year, I often wonder if teachers refer to the IEP document at all, or if they ever find the time among their countless other responsibilities to compare how Louisa is doing in their classes. I wonder if the psychologists we see pay attention to the forms that the teachers fill out for behavioral assessment, or if the teachers see the cognitive assessment that the psychologists drafted. The siloing of psychologists and educators into isolated resources hinders a more holistic, community-based approach to support.

In order for a broader paradigm shift to occur, we would have to value the people who work in disability care professions and pay them more so that there is consistency and experience in these positions. We would need to train educators—from kindergarten teachers to college professors—to teach all types of learners. Employers would need to value community investment and inclusive workplaces over efficiency, speed, and the size of their profit. Doctors would need to listen to patients with disabilities, involve them in medical decisions, and see that life with a disability does not make it less valuable. It would involve taking this new logic beyond the field of psychology and considering how it might inspire a shift in the way we think about our priorities. It would require us to move away from high-stakes testing and reevaluate what we think those tests are telling us. In other words, it would involve rethinking the relationship between intelligence and care.

Like Rubin and Esbensen, Schalock advocates for minimizing the weight of IQ tests in diagnosis and plans for community living and shared citizenship. Regarding an IQ score, Schalock told me, "It doesn't have a lot to do with preparing a meal." In other words, if a team of caregivers is trying to help someone accomplish a particular task in daily life like cooking, assessing that person's environmental circumstances—access to a grocery store, clearly written instructions in recipes, the right tools and equipment—will be much more helpful than knowing that person's IQ. Focusing on adaptive behavior implies that a person is inherently capable, and the right circumstances for accomplishing a goal need to be found. Focusing on a person's IQ implies a different approach—judging whether a person is capable at all. But life skills can be mastered to a degree that far surpasses what might be predicted by an IQ score. Schalock explained that when a diagnosis was based on intelligence tests alone, "It was a death diagnosis in terms of potential. Intelligence doesn't fluctuate but adaptive behavior does." I can't help but think that this is essentially what happened to David, the young man that Schalock visited at Lakeland Village. In the 1960s, a low IQ score sentenced him to life in an institution. But Schalock glimpsed his potential, what might have been possible for David if his social and practical skills were valued. By minimizing the role of IQ tests in the diagnosis of intellectual disability, Schalock and other psychologists are addressing what can change, rather than focusing on the fixed meaning of an IQ score.

The shared citizenship paradigm involves an implicit admission that we have constructed a society and culture that make it extremely difficult for some people to successfully navigate the world. Seeing the problem this way requires a paradigm shift—to believe that there is nothing wrong or burdensome about a person, and to place the responsibility on a person's environment to change.

Although I am hopeful about the ways in which the psychologists I talked to make use of the IQ test, I can't help but wonder about the strange paradox of it all. The IQ test shaped the biases faced by those with intellectual disabilities in the contexts of education, employment, and so many other aspects of their lives. It seems strange to me now that IQ tests could have a role to play in efforts to confront and remove those biases. It would require finding a way to save what meaningful information can be gleaned from IQ tests and rejecting the deterministic approaches of the past.

When we spoke, Schalock was warm and generous. I felt like I was talking with a mentor I had known for years. I tried to tell him about Louisa, how amazing she was, but I didn't know where to start. And soon there was a lump in my throat and I couldn't get the words out. So, instead, I asked Schalock why IQ tests couldn't be jettisoned from the practice of diagnosis and care entirely. "It would be chaos," he responded. There are simply too many laws, rules, and regulations in our society now that are diagnostic based and depend on the IQ test. "So we can live with IQ, but it is not the only factor." Practically, we may not be able to get rid of IQ tests, but we can minimize the impact of the score. "Whatever intelligence is, it is a reality," Schalock told me. After years of research and parenting, I now agree. IQ is a reality, in the sense that it is a social structure shaped by beliefs and biases that we take for granted. But beliefs and structures can change. And as the pandemic taught us, it is possible to adapt to a new normal. In the meantime, those with intellectual disabilities and the ones who love them must demand a better future while living with a reality that is shaped by the past.

This might be one way in which I reckon with the history of IQ tests and move forward. To reckon means to consider, but also to settle accounts. It means deciding what I can and cannot control, what I can change and what I'm going to have to accept as one individual mother. It is a calculation of how much this history is still with us in the present, and how we might move past it in the future.

Narratives

Louisa is now eleven, and we are reading a children's book about Ruth Bader Ginsburg that compels her to ask me about the Supreme Court. I say that the Supreme Court tries to make sure that we have good laws. They decide when rules are bad and aren't working very well. They make sure that the laws don't exclude people. I tell her that there used to be laws that were unfair to people with Down syndrome. I do not mention that there are still laws that are unfair to people with Down syndrome, like laws that allow people with Down syndrome to be paid less than minimum wage for work, or policies that make it difficult for people with Down syndrome to receive organ transplants, or rules about what social support she can receive if she ever wants to get married.

"Do you have Down syndrome, Mama?" Louisa asks me. "No, I don't," I say. "It's something that makes you unique and special." Andy and I have talked to Louisa about Down syndrome in all the ways that parents are supposed to. I have told her that it is something she was born with and she seems to understand that it is an important part of her. When she introduces herself to someone, sometimes she says, "I am Louisa and I have Down syndrome." She is proud and confident, as Andy and I have taught her to be. But there are two ways I can think of to tell Louisa about Down syndrome. The first is to explain what a chromosome is and say that Down syndrome is one of the many traits that make up who she is. The second is to explain what our society perceives Down syndrome to be. The latter is the more complex narrative, riddled with the values of intelligence testing. It is this story that I find so necessary to tell to her, but also too unbearably devastating to do so. How, for example, will I ever explain to her that if she was born fifty years earlier, she might not have been able to go to a school with her friends? How will I explain to her that some laws that are unfair to people with Down syndrome are remnants of the ideas of eugenicists like Goddard? How will I manage to help her see that this is not her story, but that it nonetheless informs the way that people see her?

For more than 100 years, IQ tests have shaped a particularly persuasive and entrenched narrative about human value and belonging. This narrative tells us that high test scores equal success, prosperity, and happiness, and that our ability to achieve that success is also a measure of our worth. It took Louisa to show me how this narrative benefits some and disadvantages others. But I have also learned that the narrative can change, that we can value different aspects of intelligence and education, which would lead to a more equitable world that affirms a diversity of ways of being in it.

It is often assumed that IQ testing, if it is pernicious at all, only affects a small percentage of the population, the 2 percent or so with intellectual disabilities. But the logic of IQ tests has embedded itself in our culture in powerful ways that impact all of us. For a long time, psychologists were convinced that our IQ predetermined our narrative, our life path. This belief persists today and muddles each individual's ability to define her own identity. If you constantly receive messages from parents, teachers, and culture more broadly that high test scores matter above all else, you will believe it. Whether your test scores are high or not, this is an artificial and exhausting narrative to follow. I grew more sensitive to this as a teacher when I became Louisa's mother. I began to worry that I was part of a narrative that was harmful, not only to my daughter, but to my students as well.

I witness my students searching for the fulfillment promised to them by our culture of testing and intelligence. They face deep, personal struggles when they cannot find it. But some of my students are starting to search for new narratives, alternative paths to the one they have been told they should follow. Once, after giving a final exam, I reminded one of my bleary-eyed students that she hadn't turned in her writing assignment that was due a week before. Her final grade in the course was going to take a hit. "I know. I'm good," she told me. She explained that she really loved the class but was struggling and choosing to prioritize her health over her grades. "Cool," I said and wished her a restful break. I admit that there was a time when I might have seen this student as a failure. I might have even chided her for not completing her work. But now I think about how that student was taking control of her narrative and making a decision that was actually . . . smart.

NARRATIVES AND HISTORY tell us who we are and what we believe. Tales from the medical community about intelligence often focus on genetically determined deficiency. Descriptions of Down syndrome, like one found in Siddhartha Mukherjee's acclaimed book *The Gene: An Intimate History*, provide a long list of cognitive impairments people with Down syndrome may experience. Mukherjee writes, "Many children die in infancy or childhood and only a few survive to late adulthood." Beyond this factual inaccuracy—the life expectancy of people with Down syndrome has actually increased dramatically in recent decades, from twenty-five in the 1980s to more than sixty today—the statement makes clear that Mukherjee and other medical professionals cast Down syndrome as a genetic defect, implying that it is an unfortunate aberration from health that needs to be pitied or cured. Mukherjee's words reminded me of Bernard Bard and his son Philip. Bard trusted the narrative that doctors gave him, sealing the fate of his son before his story ever even had a chance to unfold.

Such narratives are typical of what new parents still encounter the first time they do an internet search for Down syndrome. The website of the Centers for Disease Control classifies Down syndrome as a birth defect and emphasizes developmental delays and cognitive abnormalities. Given the narratives of Down syndrome provided by medical sources, there is still a need to write alternative stories that emphasize the things kids like Louisa can do, instead of assuming that there are many things they can't.

I searched for more complex narratives that respected Down syndrome and other intellectual disabilities as part of the human condition. They were hard to find. Stories I heard on the news about a young woman included on the high school cheerleading squad or the student awarded homecoming king by his peers only reminded me of how problematic it was that these stories were newsworthy in the first place and how hard they tried to make me feel good that people with Down syndrome were allowed these token moments of inclusion. These tales don't change the narrative. They only provide fleeting opportunities for people with Down syndrome to be part of old stories. Other stories I read seemed deeply untrue—that Down syndrome ruins the lives of parents, causes financial ruin, and leads to social isolation. And there are only a few memoirs written by people with Down syndrome who share their own story.

Given the deep bond between parent and child, I assumed that memoirs of parents might provide a fuller and more complex picture of humanity. But to counter narratives of medical deficiency, some parents have developed plots of spiritual awakening, in which they are taken from despair to enlightenment by the growth of their child. By following a plot trajectory that is defined by grief, memoirs often suggest that the child's main function in the world is to provide a lesson to the parent. Such lessons extend into the religious realm; children with Down syndrome are described as special gifts from God. Some parents assert a kind of clairvoyancy for their children, compensating for the dehumanization of medical narratives with claims to superhuman powers. I can relate to one of the conclusions that parents make: what you see is not always what is happening. Yet this doesn't mean that Louisa has supernatural powers. Such a claim would deny her humanity as much as the diagnostic narrative of Mukherjee. It also narrowly portrays a child through the single lens of the spiritual needs of the parent. I sought something more honest, not wrapped up in simplified messages of God's plan.

I came to realize that my experience of motherhood did not fit the plot of maternal awakening and certainly didn't fit the plot of a tragedy. These stories would cast my daughter in the role of someone to be pitied or an angel from heaven. She is neither; both narratives deny her the dignity of human complexity. Eventually I tossed out the old narratives and realized that my daughter deserves a new one. The ultimate act of empathy would be to make a space for the voices of those with intellectual differences, providing ways for those like my daughter to tell her own story.

And so there will be no moment of redemption, no moment in which Louisa will overcome what makes her unique and prove that she is just like everyone else. Such a moment would only affirm the barriers in place, that they don't really need to change. Limitations can be overcome if we work hard enough to do so, many narratives of struggle tell us. We will continue to encourage Louisa to work hard and to do her best. But, in fact, Louisa is extraordinary just the way she is, and there is nothing she needs to be or overcome in order to prove that.

Our understanding of intelligence, its values and purpose in our world, needs to change. Not Louisa. Until we reckon with the history of

IQ tests and see their impact on our world, we should not feel too proud of fleeting moments of inclusion that ultimately reinforce the belief that our values of intelligence are just fine the way they are.

But new narratives can't escape the influence of old ones. Andy and I continue to allow psychologists and school administrators to give Louisa an IQ test every three years. For me, the uncertainties of living off the intelligence grid, so to speak, are too vast. A truth I discovered early on in this journey persists—not taking an IQ test would risk denying Louisa care and support that she might need. I still resent that Louisa has to endure more tests than most kids, who already take so many that the distinction between learning and testing seems to have all but disappeared. I still fear that someone will judge her unfairly. But that does not mean I can't demand that the evaluation for care and support is better and more humane than it has historically been. New narratives have to reckon with history, and I can still demand that our world starts to see beyond the IQ score. And if Louisa wants to stop taking so many tests in the future, then we will support that decision.

WHEN LOUISA STARTED middle school, I figured that was as good a reason as any to address the boxes upon boxes of toys in our basement and decide what to do with them. But actually I knew what was to be done with them, as we can't store them forever. The idea of still holding on to her baby toys as Louisa enters middle school seemed ridiculous and a great motivation to clean our basement. But it was equally difficult to imagine giving them away. There were sets of colorful wooden beads that Louisa manipulated with her chubby baby fingers to string them onto a shoelace. There were puzzles with simple geometric shapes that now looked to me like distant relatives of the form board test that Goddard relied on. I packed make-believe food into paper sacks—wooden shapes painted and velcroed together to look like cucumbers and hamburgers, plastic teapots, a pretend mixer. Going through these toys seemed like a cruel form of self-inflicted grief. I could linger in these memories of the early days of babyhood, but never return to them.

I repeated to Andy over and over as we taped boxes, *Keeping these toys won't make time stop; keeping them won't stop her from growing up.* I needed to remind myself of this. There was an irrational part of me that thought that by giving all of these toys away, Louisa would lose what she had gained from having them. Would her fine motor skills suffer if I gave away the toy pig and its plastic coins that she grabbed and dropped into the slot on its back? Or, even worse, would she forget all the time we spent reading books and playing on the polka-dot rug in her bedroom if the books and toys were no longer in our house? I still can't quantify how much all these things helped Louisa, but I know that it was the time we spent together playing, laughing, and learning that matters most.

In a way, I am back at the beginning, uncertain what the precise purpose of all these toys and activities are, but also completely unable to give them up. I've realized that the resolution, the reckoning that needs to be done, is about learning to sit with the uncertainty and the lack of explanation for how I can help Louisa be her best self. Despite my efforts, I am not entirely responsible for who Louisa is, and that lack of control is one of the hardest things to reckon with.

Sometimes I look at Louisa and I can't believe that she is here and I am lucky enough to be her mother. I feel this as I watch her twirl around in our backyard from the deck at the back of our house, the same spot where Andy and I ate fish tacos the night before she was born. Her arms are stretched out to the sides and she is singing at the top of her lungs. She is lost in an imaginary world of play as the yellow and red leaves fall from towering trees and dance around her. I feel a deep gratitude when her small body curls into mine just before she falls asleep, her breath gradually falling into an even rhythm and her fingers becoming perfectly still.

I wish I could offer the pat resolution that we cracked the code and Louisa is now sailing through school without frustration, lost assignments, and long hours of homework to keep her on track. But middle school brought new routines, higher expectations, and skills to be mastered. Louisa memorized her locker combination but can't get the spinning and sequencing of numbers quite right. The locker jams and I worry that her teachers are getting tired of helping her. There is more work, and the faster pace is exhausting. There is so little time to slow down and rest. The routine is teaching me more about why my college students are so grade obsessed. It starts in middle school, with the online gradebooks and the relentless demands to learn, test, repeat.

But there have been some bright spots too. A few weeks after Louisa started sixth grade, her social studies teacher emailed me to share how proud she was of her. Louisa was one of the few students who knew the names of all twenty-five kids in the class. Two-thirds had gone to other elementary schools, and Louisa had met them only weeks before. But the memory skills weren't really what her teacher wanted to celebrate. Louisa knew those names because she values every one of her classmates. People matter to her more than anyone I know. What if we all valued community like this? What if we valued our connection to each other, our ability to care for one another and support one another, as much as Louisa? Such a world is possible. We only have to be open to pursuing it. This better world is free from the established narratives about intelligence that the adult world creates and enforces.

During a social studies unit on identity, Louisa's teacher asked if she would like to do a presentation to the class on Down syndrome. I remembered Louisa's failed attempt in third grade to share with her peers, shouting into a Zoom class on her computer screen and barely being understood. But this time, Louisa stood proudly at the front of the room speaking to them about this important part of her. Her classmates asked her questions about when she was a baby and how to be a good friend to her. They talked about other people they knew, friends and loved ones who had Down syndrome. The students, her teacher told me, were enthralled. There aren't many eleven-year-olds who want to stand in front of the class and talk, but Louisa did it with confidence and pride. Most importantly, she showed them what she is capable of. She told her own narrative, and she told them she belongs.

Acknowledgments

Two amazing people found promise and purpose in this book at an early stage and saw it through to the finish line. Thank you, Heather Carr, my steady and true literary agent, who took this project up and dedicated herself to finding it the right home. That home was with Elizabeth Gassman at Diversion Books. Liz's editorial dedication to this book was galvanizing. Her patience, insights, and challenging questions continually made this a better book. Thank you, Heather and Liz, for believing in me. And thanks to the entire team of book wizards at Diversion Books.

Thanks to the many friends and colleagues who supported my work, let me talk through my growing understanding of IQ testing, shared their experiences with me, and read drafts from this book in earlier stages, particularly Elise Clerkin, Katie Day Good, Annie Dell'Aria, Christopher Feliciano Arnold, Jordan Fenton, Micah Fialka-Feldman, Laura Gaddis, Leigh Grossman, Michael Hatch, Ashley Johnson, Kate Kuvalanka, Lauren Markham, Tim Melley, Ricki Sabia, Bill Stumpf, and Kyle Stumpf. My dear friend TaraShea Nesbit encouraged me to write about what I couldn't stop thinking about, and then to keep writing at every step. Thanks to Viet Thanh Nguyen for a conversation in a car ride to Cincinnati I'm sure he does not remember. It made me believe that I might be able to write this book. Thanks to everyone who participated in the Inclusive University Program at Miami University in the summer of 2019 who taught me what college could be like.

I am grateful to the psychologists and scholars who generously answered my questions and provided opportunities for me to learn more about their work, including David Annable, Anna Esbensen, Jennifer Green, Aaron Luebbe, Vaishali Raval, Robert Schalock, Kellie Voth, and Seth Wilensky. Julie Rubin was an especially important interlocutor and resource. I am truly grateful for her time and generosity. Thanks to Cate Weir at Think College and the entire organization for their incredible work. Thanks to the Cummings Center for the History of Psychology, especially Lizette Royer Barton, for making their research materials available to me.

I could never say enough to express my deep gratitude to the teachers who have nurtured Louisa and, in turn, taught me so much. I am in awe of grade school teachers. Their hard work is what keeps the world running. So many make a difference on a daily basis and help children become their best selves. From preschool to sixth grade, Louisa had some of the best. Thank you.

Thanks to my husband, collaborator, and true life-partner, Andrew Casper. And thanks, of course, to Louisa, who permitted me to share some things about her life in this book, and whose brilliant spirit pushes me to imagine a better world.

Notes

What the Test Tests

2 **"not great mental development"**: Bard and Fletcher, "The Right to Die," 59–64.

6 **Ethan Saylor:** Ethan Saylor died on January 12, 2013, in Frederick County, Maryland. Three off-duty deputies tried to forcibly remove him from a movie theater when he failed to buy a ticket. Witnesses heard Saylor being put into handcuffs and crying out. He was twenty-six years old.

9 **do not include a word for disability:** Nielsen, 2–3.

11 **eating fish:** Liu, Cui, Li, et al.

12 **"it would smell bad":** Binet, "Children's Perceptions," in Pollack, Brenner, eds., 107.

12 **"activities of intelligence":** Binet, "New Methods for the Diagnosis of Intellectual Level of Subnormals," in *The Development of Intelligence in Children.*

12 **fueled proficiency in all mental functions and tasks:** Spearman, *The Nature of "Intelligence" and the Principles of Cognition*, 6.

13 **"the capacity to do well on an intelligence test":** Boring, 37.

13 **inaccurate but overwhelming force:** The subtests are usually described as a battery, a term that suggests the similar approaches of IQ testing and combat. A battery was originally a military term used to describe a unit of artillery consisting of six of more guns. The Oxford English Dictionary defines it as "a number of pieces of artillery placed in juxtaposition for combined

action." The idea was to compensate for the inaccuracy or failure of any one form of artillery to hit its target by compounding weapons.

13 **"so long as they are numerous"**: Binet, "Nouvelles Recherches sur la Mésure du Niveau Intellectuel chez des Enfants d'École."

14 **"classifying a group of people"**: Lippmann, "The Mystery of the 'A' Men," 247.

14 **attention to visual stimuli:** Wahlstrom, et al, 249–250.

15 **1 percent of possible variance:** Butcher, Davis, Craig, Plomin, "Genome-wide Quantitative Trait Locus Association Scan of General Cognitive Ability Using Pooled DNS and 500K Single Nucleotide Polymorphism Microarrays." This study is referenced in Nisbett, "Intelligence: New Findings and Theoretical Developments," 135.

15 **The idea of normal developed:** Davis, "Introduction: Disability, Normality, and Power," 3.

16 **between 1860 and 1920:** According to a Google Ngram search.

16 **"constitute Monstrosity"**: Quetelet, 96.

17 **"inner to outer relations"**: Spencer, 486.

19 **"except Aristotle"**: Quoted in Diamond, "Buckle, Wundt, and Psychology's Use of History," 143–152.

THE DSM

24 **"occupational functioning"**: DSM-V, 31.

24 **DSM-5:** My research on the DSM began in 2020, before the publication of the DSM 5-TR, which made important revisions to the diagnosis of intellectual disability, as I discuss in "Paradigm Shift." To accurately recount the development of my research, I refer here to the DSM 5, but in the later chapter I refer to the DSM 5-TR.

28 **"to be called Asperger's"**: Quoted in Parsloe and Babrow, 488.

33 **"cannot be observed in practice"**: Quoted in Grob, 422.

35 **part of the diagnosis:** The DSM 5-TR (text revision), published online in March 2022, states, "IQ test scores are approximations of conceptual functioning but may be insufficient to assess reasoning in real-life situations and mastery of practical tasks."

35 **"is essential to any good scientific definition"**: Detterman, 540.

Mind Games

41 **within his social and economic environment:** Boake, 394.

41 **"cope with its challenges":** Wechsler, "Intelligence Defined and Undefined: A Relativistic Appraisal," 139.

42 **"ability to do things":** Wechsler, *The Measurement of Adult Intelligence*, 138.

49 **"familiar to the Western middle class":** Ogbu, "Cultural Amplifiers of Intelligence: IQ and Minority Status in Cross-Cultural Perspective," 248, in Fish, ed.

50 **"extremely culture-specific":** Greenfield, 81–122.

A Laboratory and a Garden

57 **"mechanism which is inborn":** Goddard. *Human Efficiency and Levels of Intelligence*, 1.

58 **"the most ignorant shall teach us the most":** Byers, 41.

59 **"only the worst cases are sent to institutions":** Quoted in Fancher, 107.

60 **no higher intelligence than a two-year-old:** Goddard, "A Measuring Scale for Intelligence," 41–46.

60 **proximates:** Goddard, "Four Hundred Feeble-Minded Children Classified by the Binet Method," 395.

60 **"normal people out of them":** Goddard, "Four Hundred Feeble-Minded Children Classified by the Binet Method," 395.

60 **"at five about half":** Goddard, "A Measuring Scale for Intelligence," 148.

61 **"beyond his grade of intelligence":** Goddard, "Two Thousand Normal Children Measured by the Binet Measuring Scale of Intelligence," 233.

62 **"special class for defectives is probably the wisest solution":** Goddard, "Two Thousand Normal Children Measured by the Binet Measuring Scale of Intelligence," 237.

62 **New Jersey legislature:** Chapter 234 of New Jersey Public Law of 1911. See Zenderland, 124.

62 **"with the Binet scale it was possible to get ninety percent":** Goddard, "The Binet Tests in Relation to Immigration," 106.

63 **"immigrants were of surprisingly low intelligence":** Goddard, "Mental Tests and the Immigrant," 251.

63 **"to investigate them with scientific thoroughness"**: Wallin, "The Problem of the Feeble-Minded in its Educational and Social Bearings," 116–117.

63 **"obstinate, and stealthy"**: Goddard, "The Story of Abbie," 182.

65 **an overrepresentation of about 13 percentage points**: Government Accountability Office.

68 **1,591,473 removals**: Williams, "Discipline Discussions: Our Discipline Policies Reflect Our Priorities."

69 **"for several generations"**: Baldwin, 84.

70 **Deborah Kallikak**: Deborah Kallikak was not the girl's true name. Goddard derived the pseudonym *Kallikak* from the Greek words *Kallos*, meaning "beauty," and *Kakos*, meaning "bad" or "evil." The juxtaposition emphasized the struggle between opposed, inherited traits. Smith and Wehmeyer, "Who Was Deborah Kallikak?" 169–178.

70 **"sexually and otherwise"**: Goddard, *The Kallikak Family*, 11–12.

70 **"Bad stock"**: Goddard, *The Kallikak Family*, 12.

71 **"Martin was feeble-minded?"**: Goddard, *Feeble-Mindedness: Its Causes and Consequences*, 28–29.

71 **Deborah's ancestry**: See Smith and Wehmeyer, "Who Was Deborah Kallikak?"

72 **"not much more serious"**: Goddard, *The Kallikak Family*, 108.

72 **three-to-one ratio**: See US Commission on Civil Rights.

72 **specific learning disability**: National Center for Educational Statistics, https://nces.ed.gov/programs/coe/indicator/cgg/students-with-disabilities.

73 **"fetish to be worshipped"**: Haskell, 114.

73 **"inborn intelligence of all people"**: Lippmann, "The Mental Age of Americans," 213.

74 **"Sunday newspaper puzzles"**: Lippmann, "The Reliability of Intelligence Tests," 276.

74 **a group of Iowa farmers**: Wallin, "Who Is Feeble-Minded?" 706–716.

75 **Law for the Prevention of Offspring with Hereditary Defects Act**: See Whitman.

76 **Clarence becomes the laboratory experiment**: Goddard, "A Suggested Definition of Intelligence," 245–250.

76 **the practice continues in other countries around the world**: See Hurtes.

Functioning

82   **"high-grade feeble-minded child"**: Goddard, "What Can Public Schools Do for Subnormal Children?" 37.

83   **"normal subjects of low intelligence"**: Doll, 288.

84   **"the geneticist will find correspondingly much satisfaction"**: Doll, 291.

85   **"meeting cultural expectations"**: Dictionary of Psychology, American Psychological Association. Online.

86   **"can't fight the system anymore"**: National Council on Disabilities, 25.

88   **are educated in inclusive classrooms**: *44th Annual Report to Congress on the Implementation of the Individuals with Disabilities Education Act, 2022*, 58. While the total percentage of students with disabilities included for 80 percent or more of their time in general education settings has risen steadily in the past twenty years, the percentage of students with intellectual disabilities has remained stagnant for decades. In a 2018 study, the National Council on Disabilities reported 16.6 percent in 2015–2016, 13.9 percent in 2005–2006, National Council on Disabilities, 38. The percentage of students with the most significant cognitive disabilities, who take alternative learning assessments with different expectations for achievement on content standards and who are the least included in a general classroom, is around 3 percent. See "Taking the Alternate Assessment Does NOT Mean Education in a Separate Setting!" TIES Center Brief #2, May 2019. https://files.tiescenter.org/files/Mdg9JhH6n-/ties-brief-2.

88   **study that tracked 11,000 students**: Wagner, et al.

89   **educating students with and without disabilities in the same classroom**: Hollowood, et al.

89   **less fear of human differences**: Staub and Peck.

89   **no research conducted in the last fifty years that supports**: National Council on Disabilities.

91   **"individual blaming him or herself"**: Schalock, et al, *Intellectual Disability: Definition, Classification, and Systems of Supports*, 11th edition, 153.

92   **80 percent may experience dementia by age sixty-five**: Hithersay.

96   **"support these companies"**: Transcribed remarks of Kansas State representative Sean Tarwater on February 14, 2023.

97   **ABLE account**: Achieving a Better Life Experience accounts aim to ease financial strain by providing a tax-free way for people with disabilities to save and cover qualified disability expenses.

NATURE NURTURE

103 **in an 1875 essay about twins:** Galton, "The History of Twins, as a Criterion of the Relative Powers of Nature and Nurture," 566–576.

105 **"educational capacity permits":** Burt.

106 **"always feeble-minded":** Terman, "Were We Born This Way?" 659.

112 **"somewhat like the distribution of blood types":** Jensen.

114 **disparity in IQ scores among racial groups:** Nisbett, et al, "Intelligence: New Findings and Theoretical Developments," 146.

115 **Head Start:** Schanzenbach and Bauer.

118 **boost brain function:** See Plomin, Von Stumm; Zabaneh, et al.

TESTING MOMS

121 **eBay:** Roberts.

122 **Accessing IQ tests:** The American Psychological Association maintains a "Statement on Third Party Observers in Psychological Testing and Assessment; A Framework for Decision Making," which describes reasons for why test materials should not become "retrievable records."

122 **"large department stores":** Kohs.

122 **blocks at home:** See Arthur, *A Point Scale of Performance Tests.*

123 **It is a big business:** Pearson, the company that publishes the WISC and WAIS tests, reported $1.77 billion in revenue from assessments and qualification exams in 2022. Revenue from the WISC and WAIS exams is a fraction of that total. Pearson Annual Report and Accounts, 2022, https://plc.pearson.com/sites/pearson-corp/files/pearson/annual-report-2022/pearson-2022-annual-report.pdf.

124 **"waiting patiently for their turn":** Galton, "On the Anthropometric Laboratory at the Late International Health Exhibition," 206.

124 **paying Galton for data:** Sokal, "James McKeen Cattell and the Failure of Anthropometric Mental Testing, 1890–1901," in Woodward and Ash, eds., 330.

124 **World's Fair in Chicago in 1893:** *World Columbian Exposition, Official Directory* (Chicago: 1893).

125 **"intelligence tests are dangerous tools":** Hines, 70.

126 **"parents ask when they come to us":** Goddard, "Four Hundred Feeble-Minded Children," 396.

126 **Goddard was receiving a steady diet of letters from parents:** Henry Goddard Papers, Cummings Center for the History of Psychology, M215, folder 1.

127 **before they are born:** See Raposo.

131 **"not as individuals":** Engler, 11.

131 **"intellectual sphere":** "Adults Urged to Aid Child for I.Q.," the *New York Times*, January 20, 1959, 41.

GIFTED

143 **IQ must have been near 200:** Terman, "The Intelligence Quotient of Francis Galton in Childhood," 209–215.

143 **One of his biographers reported:** Fancher, 132–133.

145 **"the whale and the fish":** Terman, *Genius and Stupidity: A Study of Some of the Intellectual Processes of Seven "Bright" and Seven "Dull" Boys*, 6.

146 **"thirty years hence":** Terman, "The Discovery and Encouragement of Exceptional Talent," 224.

147 **"by any scheme of mental culture":** Terman, *The Measurement of Intelligence*, 90.

148 **a mark of a true democracy:** Terman, et al, *Intelligence Tests and School Reorganization*.

148 **"belong to the professional classes":** Terman, "Were We Born That Way?" 658.

149 **"treasure hunt":** Fine, A12.

150 **signs of a gifted child:** Abraham, C12.

151 **"reach profound conclusions":** "Crisis in Education, Part III: The Waste of Fine Minds," *Life* 44 (April 7, 1958): 89–97.

153 **least affluent students:** Grissom.

154 **National Center for Education Statistics:** Digest of Education Statistics, Table 204.90, https://nces.ed.gov/programs/digest/d21/tables/dt21_204.90.asp.

154 **underrepresented in gifted programs:** Gentry, et al, *System Failure*, 4.

155 **longitudinal study by the National Center for Education Statistics:** Bhatt, 573.

156 **study from 2021:** Redding and Grissom.

157 **"tests aren't the way to do it":** Quoted in Shapiro.

158 **"what do we replace it with?":** Calvan.

159 **added students who attend "high achieving schools" to a list of at-risk groups:** Jennifer Breheny Wallace, "Students in High-Achieving Schools Are Now Named an 'At-Risk' Group, Study Says," *Washington Post*, September 26, 2019. https://www.washingtonpost.com/lifestyle/2019/09/26/students-high-achieving-schools-are-now-named-an-at-risk-group/.

159 **Centers for Enriched Studies:** Dana Goldstein, "Rethinking What Gifted Education Means, and Whom It Should Serve," *New York Times*, September 13, 2018, https://www.nytimes.com/2018/09/13/us/education-gifted-students.html?searchResultPosition=3.

HIGH STAKES

163 **"military service":** Robert M. Yerkes to Bird T. Baldwin, May 4, 1917, Psychology Committee of the National Research Council Papers (National Research Council, Washington, DC). Quoted in Kevles, "Testing the Army's Intelligence: Psychologists and the Military in World War I," 567.

164 **The committee on the Psychological Examination of Recruits:** the committee was composed of Robert Yerkes (chair), W. B. Bingham (secretary), Henry Goddard, T. H. Haines, Lewis Terman, F. L. Wells, and G. M. Whipple.

164 **Arthur Otis:** Yerkes acknowledges Otis's significant contribution to the multiple choice IQ exam in *Psychological Examining in the United States Army*. He writes, "The Otis test embodied certain ingenious devices which permitted responses to be given without writing, and made possible objectivity in scoring," 299.

165 **"drawing a line":** Otis, "An Absolute Point Scale for the Group Measurement of Intelligence," 240.

165 **It is better to fight than to run:** Yerkes, *The Army Examination Alpha Practical Judgement Test* (1921). Soldiers were allowed ninety seconds for sixteen questions.

166 **"held a pencil in their hands":** Quoted in Kevles, 576.

166 **monthly testing rate:** Kevles, 572.

167 **"ever acquired about itself":** Byers, 70.

167 **"success in life":** Nisbett, Aronson, Blair, Dickens, Flynn, Halpern, Turkheimer, 131.

168 **where he designed the Scholastic Aptitude Test, or SAT:** See Lemann, 30–31.

168 **some 4 million children had been tested:** Cronbach, 1.

168 **"group intelligence tests"**: Wechsler, "Measuring the IQ Test," 197.

168 **college entrance exams**: Hefling.

170 **"capacity to do well on an intelligence test"**: Boring, 35.

174 **high-stakes tests can have damaging effects on young adults**: See Terada, "The Psychological Toll of High Stakes Testing."

175 **prediction of college success**: Galla, Shulman, Plummer, Gardner, Hutt, Goyer, D'Mello, Finn, Duckworth; and Westrick, Le, Robbins, Radunzel, and Schmidt.

178 **eliminating standardized test scores**: Nietzel.

179 **"working at a prestigious firm"**: Leonhardt, "The Misguided War on the SAT."

179 **"just a part of adolescence"**: Kaminer, "Where Yale Has Gone, Other Universities Will Follow."

180 **59 percent of IPSE graduates**: See https://thinkcollege.net/resources /resources-by-topic/job-development.

PARADIGM SHIFT

188 **medical contingency plans**: Silverman.

190 **stoked anxieties about student test scores**: Sarah Mervosh. "The Pandemic Erased Two Decades of Progress in Math and Reading," *New York Times*, September 1, 2022; "Test Scores Dropped to Lowest Levels in Decades During Pandemic," Associated Press, October 24, 2022.

190 **one-third of a year of learning loss**: Betthäuser, et al.

194 **"whereas the actual explanation is purely statistical"**: Kovacs and Conway, 190.

195 **IQ tests are pretty fallible predictors of individual academic ability**: McGrew, Evans.

197 **working memory and cognitive flexibility**: Schworer, Soltani, Altaye, Fidler, Esbensen; Schworer, Esbensen, Fidler, Beebe, Carle, Wiley.

201 **extended scoring below 40**: Sansone, Schneider, Bickel, Berry-Kravis, Prescott, Hessl; Thompson, Coleman, Riley, Snider, Howard, Sansone, Hessl.

203 **DSM-5 revisions**: The DSM-5-TR eliminated the phrase "To meet diagnostic criteria for intellectual disability, the deficits in adaptive functioning must be directly related to the intellectual impairments described in Criterion A," which appeared on page 38 of the DSM 5. As Schalock and his colleagues pointed out, the phrase inadvertently introduced a causal

relationship between intellectual impairment and adaptive functioning. The DSM-5-TR also changed "Intellectual Disability" to "Intellectual Developmental Disorder" to better match the language of the WHO ICD-11 classification system.

203 **DSM-5 and adaptive behavior:** Tassé, Luckasson, Schalock.

204 **paradigm of shared citizenship:** Schalock, Luckasson, Tassé, and Shogren.

NARRATIVES

209 **get married:** See Putka. The Charlotte Woodward Organ Transplant Discrimination Act (H.R. 2706/S. 1183) would prevent discrimination on disability in the organ transplant process. If two social security beneficiaries get married, the couple would receive 25 percent less benefits, including a lower asset limit for eligibility and a lower amount of monthly income allowed.

212 **memoirs written by people with Down syndrome:** The list includes Egan, *More Alike Than Different*, and Kingsley and Levitz, *Count Us In*.

Bibliography

Author's note: I consulted more texts than are represented here. I've limited this list to those I quoted or found essential to the development of my thinking on intelligence and the history of IQ tests.

Abraham, Willard. "Is There a Gifted Child in Your Family," *Los Angeles Times* (January 1, 1961): C12.

American Psychiatric Association. *Diagnostic and Statistical Manual for Mental Disorders.* First edition, 1952.

—————. *Diagnostic and Statistical Manual for Mental Disorders.* Second edition, 1968.

—————. *Diagnostic and Statistical Manual for Mental Disorders.* Third edition, 1980.

—————. *Diagnostic and Statistical Manual for Mental Disorders.* Fourth edition, 1994.

—————. *Diagnostic and Statistical Manual for Mental Disorders.* Fifth edition, 2013.

—————. *Diagnostic and Statistical Manual for Mental Disorders.* Fifth edition, text revision, 2022.

Arthur, Mary Grace. *A Point Scale of Performance Tests, Revised Form II.* 1947.

Baldwin, Bird T. "The Psychology of Mental Deficiency," *Popular Science Monthly* 79 (1911): 82–93.

Bard, Bernard, and Joseph Fletcher. "The Right to Die," *The Atlantic* (April 1968): 59–64.

Becker, Kirk A. "History of the Stanford-Binet Intelligence Scales: Content and Psychometrics," *Stanford-Binet Intelligence Scales, Fifth Edition, Assessment Service Bulletin Number 1* (Itasca, IL: Riverside Publishing, 2003).

Betthäuser, B.A., A.M. Bach-Mortensen, P. Engzell. "A Systematic Review and Meta-analysis of the Evidence on Learning During the COVID-19 Pandemic," *Nature Human Behavior* 7, no. 3 (March 2023): 375–385. doi: 10.1038/s41562-022-01506-4.

Bhatt, Rachana. "A Review of Gifted and Talented Education in the United States," *Education Finance and Policy* 6, no. 4 (Fall 2011): 557–582. https://nces.ed.gov /surveys/nels88/.

Binet, Alfred. "Nouvelles Recherches sur la Mésure du Niveau Intellectuel chez des Enfants d'École," *L'Année Psychologique* 17 (1911): 145–201.

————. *The Development of Intelligence in Children*. Translated by Elizabeth S. Kite. Vineland, NJ: Publications of the Training School, 1916.

Biss, Eula. "The Pain Scale," *Creative Nonfiction*, no. 32 (2007): 65–84.

Bliss, Rina. *Rethinking Intelligence: A Radical New Understanding of our Human Potential*. New York: Harper Wave, 2023.

Block, N. J., and Gerald Dworkin, eds. *The IQ Controversy: Critical Readings*. New York: Pantheon Books, 1976.

Boake, Corwin. "From the Binet-Simon to the Wechsler-Bellevue: Tracing the History of Intelligence Testing," *Journal of Clinical and Experimental Neuropsychology* 24, no. 3 (2002): 383–405. doi: 10.1076/jcen.24.3.383.981.

Boon, Richard, Debbie Voltz, Carl Lawson, Michael Baskette. "The Impact of High-Stakes Testing for Individuals with Disabilities: A Review Synthesis," *Journal of the American Academy of Special Education Professionals* (Fall 2007): 54–67.

Borges, Jorge Luis. *Ficciones* (1956), published in English translation as *Labyrinths*, (New York: New Directions Press, 1962).

Boring, Edwin G. "Intelligence as the Tests Test it," *New Republic* (June 6, 1923): 35–37.

Brim, Orville G., David C. Glass, John Neulinger, and Ira J. Firestone. *American Beliefs and Attitudes about Intelligence*. New York: Russell Sage Foundation, 1969.

Brown, JoAnne. *The Definition of a Profession: The Authority of Metaphor in the History of Intelligence Testing, 1890–1930*. Princeton, NJ: Princeton University Press, 1992.

Burt, Cyril. "Experimental Tests of Higher Mental Processes and Their Relation to General Intelligence," *Journal of Experimental Pedagogy and Training* 1 (1911): 93–112.

Butcher, L. M., O. S. P. Davis, I. W. Craig, and R. Plomin. "Genome-Wide Quantitative Trait Locus Association Scan of General Cognitive Ability Using Pooled DNA and

500K Single Nucleotide Polymorphism Microarrays," *Genes, Brain, and Behavior* 7 (2008): 435–446.

Byers, Joseph. *The Village of Happiness: The Story of the Training School*. Vineland, NJ : The Smith Printing House, 1934.

Calvan, Bobby Caina. "Schools Debate: Gifted and Talented, or Racist and Elitist?" Associated Press (October 28, 2021). https://apnews.com/article/new -york-education-new-york-city-united-states-race-and-ethnicity-f8cbdb50edba9802 fe9ad503cfe7d467.

Carson, John. *The Measure of Merit: Talents, Intelligence, and Inequality in the French and American Republics, 1750–1940*. Princeton, NJ: Princeton University Press, 2007.

Castles, Elaine. *Inventing Intelligence: How America Came to Worship IQ*. Santa Barbara, CA: Praeger, 2012.

Causton-Theoharis, Julie, George Theoharis, Fernanda Orsati, Meghan Cosier. "Does Self-Contained Special Education Deliver on Its Promises? A Critical Inquiry into Research and Practice," *Journal of Special Education Leadership* 24, no. 2 (September 2011): 61–78.

Chancellor, William Estabrook. "The Measurement of Human Ability," *Journal of Education* 77, no. 16 (April 17, 1913): 425–426.

Cianciolo, Anna T., and Robert J. Sternberg. *Intelligence: A Brief History*. Malden, MA: Blackwell Publishing, 2004.

Cohen, Adam. *Imbeciles: The Supreme Court, American Eugenics, and the Sterilization of Carrie Buck*. New York: Penguin Press, 2016.

Couzens, Donna, Monica Cuskelly, and Anne Jobling. "The Stanford Binet Fourth Edition and Its Use with Individuals with Down Syndrome: Cautions for Clinicians," *International Journal of Disability, Development and Education* 51, no. 1 (March 2004): 39–56.

Couzens, Donna, Monica Cuskelly, and Michele Haynes. "Cognitive Development and Down Syndrome: Age-Related Change on the Stanford-Binet Test (Fourth Edition)," *American Association on Intellectual and Developmental Disabilities* 116, no. 3 (May 2011): 181–204.

Cox, Catherine. *The Early Mental Traits of Three Hundred Geniuses*. Palo Alto, CA: Stanford University Press, 1926.

Cravens, H. Hamilton. "The Wandering IQ: American Culture and Mental Testing," *Human Development* 28 (1985): 113–130.

Cronbach, Lee. "Five Decades of Public Controversy Over Mental Testing," *American Psychology* (January 1975): 1–14.

Davis, Lennard J. "Introduction: Disability, Normality, and Power," In *The Disability Studies Reader*, edited by Lennard J. Davis, 1–14. New York: Routledge, 2017.

Deary, Ian J., *Intelligence: A Very Short Introduction*. Oxford: Oxford University Press, 2001.

Deary, Ian J., Frank M. Spinath, and Timothy C. Bates. "Genetics of Intelligence," *European Journal of Human Genetics* 14 (2006): 690–700.

Detterman, Douglas. "What Happened to Moron, Idiot, Imbecile, Feebleminded, and Retarded?" *Intelligence* 38 (2010): 540–541.

Diamond, Solomon. "Buckle, Wundt, and Psychology's Use of History," *Isis* 75, no. 1 (March 1984): 143–152.

—————. "Francis Galton and American Psychology," *Annals of the New York Academy of Sciences* 291 (1977): 47–55.

Doll, Edgar A. "A Genetic Scale of Social Maturity," *American Journal of Orthopsychiatry* 5, no. 2 (1935): 180–190.

——————. "Preliminary Standardization of the Vineland Social Maturity Scale," *American Journal of Orthopsychiatry* 6, no. 2 (April 1936): 283–293.

——————. "The Clinical Significance of Social Maturity," *Journal of Mental Science* 81 (1935): 766–782.

Doll, Eugene. "Before the Big Time: Early History of the Training School at Vineland, 1888 to 1949," *American Journal on Mental Retardation* 93, no. 1 (1988): 1–15.

Drescher, Jack. "Out of DSM: Depathologizing Homosexuality," *Behavioral Sciences* 5 (2015): 565–575.

Egan, David, and Kathleen Egan. *More Alike Than Different: My Life with Down Syndrome*. Buffalo: Prometheus, 2020.

Engler, David. *How to Raise Your Child's IQ*. New York: Criterion Books, 1958.

Esbensen, Anna J., et al. "Outcome Measures for Clinical Trails in Down Syndrome," *American Journal on Intellectual and Developmental Disabilities* 122, no. 3 (2017): 247–281.

Fancher, Raymond. *The Intelligence Men: Makers of the IQ Controversy*. New York: W. W. Norton, 1985.

Fass, Paula. "The IQ: A Cultural and Historical Framework," *American Journal of Education* 88, no. 4 (August 1980): 431–458.

Fine, Benjamin. "U.S. Treasure Hunt on for Talented Students," *Boston Globe* (June 14, 1959): A12.

Fish, Jefferson M., ed. *Race and Intelligence: Separating Science from Myth*. Mahwah, NJ: Lawrence Erblaum Associates, 2022.

Flanagan, Dawn P., Erin M. McDonough. *Contemporary Intellectual Assessment: Theories, Tests, and Issues, Fourth Edition*. New York: The Guilford Press, 2018.

Galla, B. M., E. P. Shulman, B. D. Plummer, M. Gardner, S. J. Hutt, J. P. Goyer, S. K. D'Mello, A. S. Finn, and A. L. Duckworth. "Why High School Grades Are Better Predictors of On-Time College Graduation Than Are Admissions Test Scores: The Roles of Self-Regulation and Cognitive Ability," *American Educational Research Journal* 56, no. 6 (December 2019): 2077–2115. https://doi.org/10.3102/0002831219843292.

Gallagher, James, and Patricia Weiss. *The Education of Gifted and Talented Students: A History and Prospectus*. Washington, DC: Council for Basic Education, 1979.

Galton, Francis. *Hereditary Genius: An Inquiry Into Its Laws and Consequences*. New York: D. Appleton and Company, 1900.

————. "On the Anthropometric Laboratory at the Late International Health Exhibition," *Journal of the Anthropological Institute of Great Britain and Ireland* 14 (1885): 205–221.

————. "The History of Twins, as a Criterion of the Relative Powers of Nature and Nurture," *Fraser's Magazine* (November 1875): 566–576.

Gentry, Marcia, et al. *System Failure: Access Denied, Gifted Education in the United States, Laws, Access, Equity, and Missingness Across the Country by Locale, Title 1 School Status, and Race* (West Lafayette, IN: Purdue University, 2019).

Ghaziuddin, Mohammad. "Brief Report: Should the DSM V Drop Asperger Syndrome?" *Journal of Autism and Developmental Disorders* 40 (2010): 1146–1148.

Glasser, Alan, and Irla Lee Zimmerman. *Clinical Interpretation of the Wechsler Intelligence Scale for Children*. New York: Grune & Stratton, 1967.

Glidden, Laraine Masters. *APA Handbook of Intellectual and Developmental Disabilities*, 2 volumes. Washington, DC: American Psychological Association, 2021.

Goddard, Henry Herbert. "A Measuring Scale for Intelligence," *Training School Bulletin* 6, no. 11 (January 1910): 146–155.

————. "A Suggested Definition of Intelligence," *American Journal of Mental Deficiency* 50 (1945): 245–250.

————. *Feeble-Mindedness: Its Causes and Consequences*. New York: The Macmillan Company, 1920.

—————. "Four Hundred Feeble-Minded Children Classified by the Binet Method," *Journal of Psycho-Asthenics* 15, no. 1 and 2 (September and December 1910).

—————. *Human Efficiency and Levels of Intelligence.* Princeton, NJ: Princeton University Press, 1920.

—————. "Mental Tests and the Immigrant," *Journal of Delinquency* 2, no. 5 (September 1917): 243–277.

—————. "The Binet Tests in Relation to Immigration," *Journal of Psycho-Asthenics* 18 (1913): 105–110.

—————. *The Kallikak Family.* New York: MacMillan, 1912.

—————. "The Story of Abbie," *Training School* 7 no. 1 (March 1910): 182–185.

—————. "Two Thousand Normal Children Measured by the Binet Measuring Scale of Intelligence," *Pedagogical Seminary* 18 (June 1911): 232–259.

—————. "What Can the Public School Do for Subnormal Children?" *Journal of Education* 72, no. 2 (July 14, 1910): 36–37.

—————. "Who Is a Moron?" *Scientific Monthly* 27 (1927): 24, 41–46.

Goodey, C. F. "Behavioural Phenotypes in Disability Research: Historical Perspectives," *Journal of Intellectual Disability Research* 50, no. 6 (June 2006): 397–403.

Gottfredson, Linda. "Mainstream Science on Intelligence," *Wall Street Journal* (December 13, 1994); Republished in *Intelligence* 24, no. 1: 13–23.

Gould, Stephen Jay. *The Mismeasure of Man.* New York: W. W. Norton, 1981.

Government Accountability Office. *Discipline Disparities for Black Students, Boys, and Students with Disabilities*, March 2018. https://www.gao.gov/assets/gao-18-258.pdf.

Greenfield, Patricia. "The Cultural Evolution of IQ," in *The Rising Curve: Long-Term Gains in IQ Test Scores and What They Mean.* Edited by Ulric Neisser, 81–122. Washington, DC: American Psychological Association, 1998.

Grissom, J. A., et al. "Money Over Merit? Socioeconomic Gaps in Receipt of Gifted Services," *Harvard Educational Review* 89, no. 3: 337–369.

Grob, Gerald N. "Origins of DSM-I: A Study in Appearance and Reality," *American Journal of Psychiatry* 148, no. 4 (April 1991): 421–431.

Harden, Kathryn Paige. *The Genetic Lottery: Why DNA Matters for Social Equality.* Princeton, NJ: Princeton University Press, 2021.

Haskell, R. H. "Mental Deficiency Over a Hundred Years," *American Journal of Psychiatry* 100 (194): 107–118.

Hefling, Kimberly. "Do Students Take Too Many Tests? Congress to Weigh Questions," Associated Press (January 17, 2015). https://www.pbs.org/newshour/education/congress-decide-testing-schools.

Hettleman, Kalman. *Mislabeled as Disabled: The Educational Abuse of Struggling Learners and How We Can Fight It*. New York: Radius Book Group, 2019.

Hines, Harlan. *Measuring Intelligence*. New York: Houghton Mifflin, 1923.

Hithersay, Rosalyn, et al. "Cognitive Decline and Dementia in Down Syndrome," *Current Opinion in Psychiatry* 30, no. 2 (March 2017): 102–107.

Hollowood, Tia, et al. "Use of Instructional Time in Serving Students with and without Disabilities," *Exceptional Children* 61 (1995): 242–253.

Hurtes, Sarah. "Despite Bans, Disabled Woman Are Still Being Sterilized in Europe," *New York Times* (November 25, 2023). https://www.nytimes.com/2023/11/25/world/europe/europe-disabled-women-sterilization.html?unlocked_article_code=1.ME0.ttkI.FQNW0lW4ZCLw&smid=url-share.

Jastrow, Joseph. "Some Currents and Undercurrents in Psychology," *Psychological Review* 9 (1901): 1–26.

Jensen, Arthur. "How Much Can We Boost IQ and Scholastic Achievement?" *Harvard Educational Review* 39, no. 1 (Winter 1969): 1–124.

Joseph, Jay. "A Reevaluation of the 1990 'Minnesota Study of Twins Reared Apart' IQ Study," *Human Development* 66, no. 1 (2022): 48–65.

Kaminer, Ariel. "Where Yale Has Gone, Other Universities Will Follow," *New York Times,* February 22, 2024. https://www.nytimes.com/live/2024/02/20/opinion/thepoint#college-test-scores.

Kaufman, Alan S. *IQ Testing 101*. New York: Springer, 2009.

Kevles, Daniel. *In the Name of Eugenics: Genetics and the Uses of Human Hereditary*. New York: Alfred A. Knopf, 1985.

————. "Testing the Army's Intelligence: Psychologists and the Military in World War I," *Journal of American History* 55, no. 3 (December 1968): 565–581.

Kingsley, Jason, and Mitchell Levitz. *Count Us In: Growing Up with Down Syndrome*. New York: Harvest Books, 1994.

Koenig, Katherine A., Meredith C. Frey, and Douglas K. Detterman. "ACT and General Cognitive Ability," *Intelligence* 36, no. 2 (March–April 2008): 153–160.

Kohs, Samuel. *Intelligence Measurement: A Psychological and Statistical Study Based Upon the Block Design Tests*. New York: Macmillan, 1923.

Kovacs, Kristof, and Andrew Conway. "What Is IQ? Life Beyond 'General Intelligence,'" *Current Directions in Psychological Science* 28, no. 2 (2019): 189–194.

Kover, Sara T., and Leonard Abbeduto. "Toward Equity in Research on Intellectual and Developmental Disabilities," *American Journal on Intellectual and Developmental Disabilities* 128, no. 5 (2023): 350–370.

Lemann, Nicholas. *The Big Test: The Secret History of the American Meritocracy.* New York: Simon & Schuster, 1999.

Leonhardt, David. "The Misguided War on the SAT," *New York Times*, January 7, 2024. https://www.nytimes.com/2024/01/07/briefing/the-misguided-war-on-the-sat.html.

Lippmann, Walter. "A Defense of Education," *The Century* 106 (May 1923): 95–103.

—————-. "The Mental Age of Americans," *New Republic* 32, no. 412 (October 25, 1922): 213–215.

—————-. "The Mystery of the 'A' Men," *New Republic* 32 no. 413 (November 1922): 246–248.

—————-. "The Reliability of Intelligence Tests," *New Republic* 32, no. 414 (November 8, 1922): 275–277.

Liu, J., Y. Cui, L. Li, et al. "The Mediating Role of Sleep in the Fish Consumption— Cognitive Functioning Relationship: A Cohort Study," *Scientific Reports* 7 (2017). https://doi.org/10.1038/s41598-017-17520-w.

Luckasson, Ruth, Marc J. Tassé, and Robert Schalock. "Professional Responsibility in the Field of Intellectual and Developmental Disabilities: Its Definition, Application, and Impacts," *Intellectual and Developmental Disabilities* 60, no. 3 (2022): 183–198.

McGrew, K. S., and J. Evans, *Expectations for Students with Cognitive Disabilities: Is the Cup Half Empty or Half Full? Can the Cup Flow Over? (Synthesis Report 54).* Minneapolis: University of Minnesota, National Center on Educational Outcomes, 2004.

Mukherjee, Siddhartha. *The Gene: An Intimate History.* New York: Scribner, 2016.

Naglieri, Jack, and Sam Goldstein. *Assessing Intelligence and Achievement.* Hoboken, NJ: John Wiley & Sons, 2009.

National Council on Disabilities. "The Segregation of Students with Disabilities" (February 7, 2018). https://ncd.gov/sites/default/files/NCD_Segregation-SWD_508 .pdf.

Neisser, Ulric, et al. "Intelligence: Knowns and Unknowns," *American Psychologist* 51, no. 2 (February 1996): 77–101.

Nielsen, Kim E. *A Disability History of the United States.* Boston: Beacon Press, 2012.

Nietzel, Michael. "More Than 80% of Four-Year Colleges Won't Require Standardized Tests for Fall 2023 Admissions," *Forbes* (November 15, 2022).

Nisbett, Richard E. *Intelligence and How to Get It: Why Schools and Cultures Count.* New York: W. W. Norton, 2009.

Nisbett, R. E., J. Aronson, C. Blair, W. Dickens, J. Flynn, D. F. Halpern, and E. Turkheimer. "Intelligence: New Findings and Theoretical Developments," *American Psychology* 67, no. 2 (February–March 2012): 130–159. doi: 10.1037/a0026699.

Noll, Steven, and James W. Trent. *Mental Retardation in America: A Historical Reader.* New York: New York University Press, 2004.

O'Rourke, Meghan. *The Invisible Kingdom: Reimagining Chronic Illness.* New York: Riverhead Books, 2022.

Otis, Arthur S. "An Absolute Point Scale for the Group Measurement of Intelligence," *Journal of Educational Psychology* 9, no. 5 (May 1918): 239–261.

————. "Considerations Concerning the Making of a Scale for the Measurement of Reading," *Pedagogical Seminary* 23 (1916): 528–549.

Parsloe, Sarah M., Austin S. Babrow. "Removal of Asperger's Syndrome from the DSM V: Community Response to Uncertainty," *Health Communication* 31, no. 4 (2016): 485–494.

Plomin, Robert, and Sophie Von Stumm, "The New Genetics of Intelligence," *Nature Reviews Genetics* 19, no. 3 (2018): 148–159.

Pollock, Robert H,. and Margaret W. Brenner. *The Experimental Psychology of Alfred Binet.* New York: Springer Publishing Company, 1969.

Porter, Jim Wynter. "A 'Precious Minority': Constructing the 'Gifted' and 'Academically Talented' Student in the Era of *Brown v. Board of Education* and the National Defense Education Act," *Isis* 108, no. 3 (2017): 581–605.

"The Psychological Examination of Recruits," *Science* 46, no. 1189 (October 12, 1917): 355–356.

Putka, Sophie. "Kidney Transplant Less Likely in Adults with Developmental Disabilities," MedPage (February 15, 2023).

Quetelet, Lambert A. J. *A Treatise of Man and the Development of His Faculties* (1842). Gainesville, FL: Scholars' Facsimiles & Reprints, 1969.

Raposo, Vera Lucia. "The First Chinese Edited Babies: A Leap of Faith in Science," *JBRA Assisted Reproduction* 23, no. 3 (2019): 197–199.

Redding, Christopher, and Jason A. Grissom. "Do Students in Gifted Programs Perform Better? Linking Gifted Program Participation to Achievement and Nonachievement

Outcomes," *Education Evaluation and Policy Analysis* 43, no. 3 (September 2021): 520–544.

Ritchie, Stuart. *Intelligence: All That Matters.* London: Mc-Graw Hill, 2015.

Roberts, Michelle. "Is This Smart? IQ Tests for Sale on eBay," *Seattle Times* (December 18, 2007).

Sansone, S. M., A. Schneider, E. Bickel, E. Berry-Kravis, C. Prescott, and D. Hessl. "Improving IQ Measurement in Intellectual Disabilities Using True Deviation from Population Norms," *Journal of Neurodevelopmental Disorders* 6, no. 16 (2014).

Schalock, Robert. "The Evolving Understanding of the Construct of Intellectual Disability," *Journal of Intellectual and Developmental Disability* 36, no. 4 (December 2011): 223–233.

Schalock, Robert L., et al. *Intellectual Disability: Definition, Classification, and Systems of Supports* 11th edition. Silver Spring, MD: American Association of Intellectual and Developmental Disabilities, 2010.

Schalock, Robert L., Ruth Luckasson, and Marc J. Tassé. *Intellectual Disability: Definition, Diagnosis, Classification, and Systems of Supports,* 12th edition. Silver Spring, MD: AAIDD, 2021.

————. "Professional Responsibility in the Field of Intellectual and Developmental Disabilities: Its Definition, Application, and Impacts," *Intellectual and Developmental Disabilities* 60, no. 3 (2022): 183–198.

Schalock, Robert, Ruth Luckasson, Marc Tassé, and K. A. Shogren. "The IDD Paradigm of Shared Citizenship: Its Operationalization, Application, Evaluation, and Shaping for the Future," *Intellectual and Developmental Disabilities* 60, no. 55 (2022): 426–443.

Schanzenbach, Diane Whitmore, and Lauren Bauer. "The Long-Term Impact of the Head Start Program," Brookings Institute (August 19, 2016). https://www.brookings.edu /articles/the-long-term-impact-of-the-head-start-program/.

Scheer, Jessica. "Impairment as a Human Constant: Cross-Cultural and Historical Perspectives on Variation," *Journal of Social Issues* 44, no. 1 (1998): 23–37.

Schworer, E. K., A. J. Esbensen, D. J. Fidler, D. W. Beebe, A. Carle, and S. Wiley. "Evaluating Working Memory Outcome Measures for Children with Down Syndrome," *Journal of Intellectual Disability Research* 66, no. 1–2 (2022): 195–211.

Schworer, E. K., Amanallah Soltani, Mekibib Altaye, Deborah J. Fidler, and Anna J. Esbensen. "Cognitive Flexibility Assessment in Youth with Down Syndrome; Reliability, Practice Effects, and Validity," *Research in Developmental Disabilities* 133 (2023): 1–11.

Seligman, Daniel. *A Question of Intelligence: The IQ Debate in America*. New York: Birch Lane Press, 1992.

Shapiro, Eliza. "Should a Single Test Determine a Four-Year-Old's Educational Future?" *New York Times* (September 4, 2019).

Silverman, Amy. "People with Intellectual Disabilities Might Be Denied Lifesaving Care Under These Plans as Coronavirus Spreads," *Arizona Daily Star* (*ProPublica*) (March 27, 2020).

Smith, J. David, and Michael L. Wehmeyer. *Good Blood, Bad Blood: Science, Nature, and the Myth of the Kallikaks*. Washington, DC: American Association on Intellectual and Developmental Disabilities, 2012.

————. "Who Was Deborah Kallikak?" *Intellectual and Developmental Disabilities* 50, no. 2 (2012): 169–178.

Smith, Phil. "Have We Made Any Progress? Including Students with Intellectual Disabilities in Regular Education Classrooms," *Intellectual and Developmental Disabilities* 45 no. 5 (October 2007): 297–309.

Sokal, Michael M., ed. *Psychological Testing and American Society, 1890–1930*. New Brunswick, NJ: Rutgers University Press, 1987.

Spearman, Charles. *The Abilities of Man: Their Nature and Measurement*. New York: The Macmillan Company, 1927.

————. *The Nature of "Intelligence" and the Principles of Cognition*. London: Macmillan, 1923.

Spencer, Herbert. *Principles of Psychology*, 1855.

Staub, Debbie, and Charles A. Peck. "What Are the Outcomes for Nondisabled Students?" *Educational Leadership* 52, no. 4 (1995): 36–40.

Sternberg, Robert J., and Elena Grigorenko, eds. *The General Factor of Intelligence: How General Is It?* Mahwah, NJ: Erlbaum Associates, 2002.

Stetler, Pepper. "Laboring Under Discrimination," *The Progressive* (January 30, 2023).

————. "My Daughter Expects to Work. Will She Make Only $3.35 an Hour?" *New York Times* (January 4, 2023).

Strand, Michael. "Where Do Classifications Come From? The DSM-III, the Transformation of American Psychiatry, and the Problem of Origins in the Sociology of Knowledge," *Theory and Society* 40 (2011): 273–313.

Tassé, Marc, Ruth Luckasson, and Robert Schalock. "The Relation between Intellectual Functioning and Adaptive Behavior in the Diagnosis of Intellectual Disability," *Intellectual and Developmental Disabilities* 54, no. 6 (2016): 381–390.

Terada, Youki. "The Psychological Toll of High-Stakes Testing," *Edutopia* (October 14, 2022) https://www.edutopia.org/article/psychological-toll-high-stakes-testing/.

Terman, Lewis M. "A New Approach to the Study of Genius," *Psychological Review* 29, no. 4 (1922): 310–318.

—————. "Genius and Stupidity: A Study of Some of the Intellectual Processes of Seven 'Bright' and Seven 'Dull' Boys," *Pedagogical Seminary* 13 (1906): 307–373.

—————. "The Discovery and Encouragement of Exceptional Talent," *American Psychologist* 9, no. 6 (June 1954): 221–230.

—————. *The Intelligence of School Children.* Boston: Houghton Mifflin Company, 1919.

—————. "The Intelligence Quotient of Francis Galton in Childhood," *American Journal of Psychology* 28 (1917): 209–215.

—————. *The Measurement of Intelligence.* Boston: Houghton Mifflin Company, 1916.

—————. "Were We Born This Way?" *World's Work* 44 (1922): 655–660.

Terman, Lewis, et al. *Intelligence Tests and School Reorganization* (World Book Company, 1922).

Thompson, Talia, Jeanine M. Coleman, Karen Riley, Laurel A. Snider, Londi J. Howard, Stephanie Sansone, and David Hessl. "Standardized Assessment Accommodations for Individuals with Intellectual Disability," *Contemporary School Psychology* 22, no. 4 (2018): 443–457. doi:10.1007/s40688-018-0171-4.

Tomaszewski, B., D. Fidler, D. Talapatra, and K. Riley. "Adaptive Behavior, Executive Function and Employment in Adults with Down Syndrome," *Journal of Intellectual Disability Research* 62, no. 1 (January 2018): 41–52.

Trent, James W. *Inventing the Feeble Mind: A History of Mental Retardation in the United States.* Berkeley: University of California, 1994.

Tsou, Jonathan Y. "Natural Kinds, Psychiatric Classification and the History of the DSM," *History of Psychiatry* 27, no. 4 (2016): 406–424.

US Commission on Civil Rights, *Minorities in Special Education,* 2009.

van der Maas, Han L. J., Kees-Jan Kan, and Denny Borsboom. "Intelligence Is What the Intelligence Test Measures. Seriously," *Journal of Intelligence* 2 (2014): 12–15.

Wagner, Mary, et al. "The Academic Achievement and Functional Performance of Youth with Disabilities," in *A Report of Findings of the National Longitudinal Study-2.* Menlo Park, CA: SRI International, 2006.

Wahlstrom, Dustin, et al. "The Weschler Preschool and Primary Scale of Intelligence—Fourth Edition, Wechsler Intelligence Scale for Children—Fifth Edition, and Wechsler Individual Achievement Test—Third Edition," *Contemporary Intellectual*

Assessment: Theories, Tests, and Issues, fourth edition, edited by Dawn Flanagan and Erin M. McDonough (New York: Guilford Press, 2018): 249–250.

Wallin, J. E. Wallace. "Intelligence Defined and Undefined: A Relativistic Appraisal," *American Psychologist* (February 1975): 135–139.

————-. "The Problem of the Feeble-Minded in Its Educational and Social Bearings," *School and Society* 2 (July 24, 1915): 115–121.

————-. "Who Is Feeble-Minded?" *Journal of Criminal Law and Criminology* 6, no. 5 (1916): 706–716.

Wechsler, David. "Measuring the IQ Test," *New York Times Magazine* (January 20, 1957): 197, 222.

————-. *The Measurement of Adult Intelligence*. Baltimore: Williams & Wilkins, 1939.

Wehmeyer, Michael L. ed. *The Story of Intellectual Disability: An Evolution of Meaning, Understanding, and Public Perception*. Baltimore: Paul H. Brookes, 2013.

Westrick, Paul A., Huy Le, Steven B. Robbins, Justine M. R. Radunzel, and Frank L. Schmidt. "College Performance and Retention: A Meta-Analysis of the Predictive Validities of ACT Scores, High School Grades, and SES." *Educational Assessment* 20, no. 1 (January 2015): 23–45. doi:10.1080/10627197.2015.997614.

Whitman, James. *Hitler's American Model: The United States and the Making of Nazi Race Law*. Princeton, NJ: Princeton University Press, 2017.

Williams, Valerie. "Discipline Discussions: Our Discipline Policies Reflect Our Priorities" (January 30, 2023). https://sites.ed.gov/osers/2023/01/discipline-discussions -our-discipline-policies-reflect-our-priorities/.

Wilson, Mitchell. "DSM-III and the Transformation of American Psychiatry: A History," *American Journal of Psychiatry* 150, no. 3 (March 1993): 399–410.

Winzer, Margaret A. *From Integration to Inclusion: A History of Special Education in the 20th Century*. Washington, DC: Gallaudet University Press, 2009.

Woodward, William, and Michael Ash, eds. *The Problematic Science: Psychology in Nineteenth-Century Thought*. New York: Praeger, 1982.

Yerkes, Robert M., ed. *Psychological Examining in the United States Army*. Washington, DC: National Academy of Sciences, 1921.

————-. "The Binet versus the Point Scale Method of Measuring Intelligence," *Journal of Applied Psychology* (1917): 111–122.

Yerkes, Robert, and J. W. Bridges, "The Point Scale: A New Method for Measuring Mental Ability," *Boston Medical and Surgical Journal* 171 (1914): 857–866.

Yerkes, Robert, James W. Bridges and Rose S. Hardwick. *A Point Scale for Measuring Mental Ability.* Baltimore: Warwick & York, 1915.

Young, Kimball. "The History of Mental Testing," *Pedagogical Seminary* 31, no. 1 (March 1923): 1–48.

Zabaneh, Delilah, Eva Krapohl, H. A. Gaspar, Charles Curtis, S. Hong Lee, Hamel Patel, Stephen Newhouse, et al. "A Genome-Wide Association Study for Extremely High Intelligence," *Molecular Psychiatry* 23, no 5 (2018): 1226–1232.

Zenderland, Leila. *Measuring Minds: Henry Herbert Goddard and the Origins of American Intelligence Testing.* Cambridge: Cambridge University Press, 1998.

Index